Cloud Application Architecture Patterns

Building secure observable applications with cloud architectures

Anubhav Kumar Gupta

www.bpbonline.com

First Edition 2025

ISBN: 978-93-65895-131

LIMITS OF LIABILITY AND DISCLAIMER OF WARRANTY

www.bpbonline.com

Dedicated to

My respected parents:

Sri G P Gupta, Smt Manjula Gupta

My beloved wife

Ruchika Jain Gupta

and

My lovely daughter Lavanya

About the Author

Anubhav Kumar Gupta has been working in the software industry for more than 20 years, playing central roles in numerous projects as a technical leader and software architect, delivering projects using open-source technologies for various big companies, including successful projects in South America, Europe, and the United States. Currently, he is a Director of Engineering at Pitney Bowes and a Certified Independent Director, specializing in building and scaling cloud-native SaaS platforms and microservices-driven solutions that power mission-critical applications, and has led cross-functional global teams to drive engineering excellence, product innovation, and multi-million-dollar revenue growth, transforming complex business challenges into scalable, resilient, and customer-centric solutions. He is also an accomplished graduate with a degree in Information Technology. In the meantime, he successfully got many certifications, including TOGAF 9.1 Enterprise Architect and SCJP 5.0. He is a member of the Enterprise Architecture Association of India community. Furthermore, he participates as a speaker in various IT conferences and writes technical articles on software development and related topics. He was also awarded as one of the Top 100 Great Managers in India by Great Manager Institute in 2022, and was listed on Forbes India magazine in the same year.

About the Reviewer

Wajid Abdul is a technology leader specializing in enterprise architecture, systems integration, cloud computing, AI/ML, and cybersecurity. He designs scalable, high-impact solutions that bridge legacy systems with modern, cloud-native platforms across complex enterprise environments. With hands-on expertise in platforms such as AWS, Azure, and Kubernetes, Wajid builds resilient architectures that emphasize modularity, scalability, and future readiness.

He is deeply involved in integrating enterprise systems—from ERPs and CRMs to data pipelines and APIs—ensuring seamless information flow and business continuity. In the AI/ML domain, he develops predictive models and automation pipelines that enhance decision-making, reduce inefficiencies, and unlock data-driven opportunities.

Security is foundational to his work. Wajid incorporates cybersecurity best practices such as Zero Trust Architecture, secure DevOps (DevSecOps), and automated threat detection to protect cloud and hybrid infrastructures from evolving risks.

He also serves as a technical reviewer for books and industry publications, contributing insights on cloud architecture, machine learning, and secure system design. Wajid is passionate about building intelligent, secure, and integrated systems that align with long-term enterprise goals.

Whether designing digital transformation strategies or deploying advanced analytics, he brings a systems-level mindset and deep technical expertise to every challenge.

Acknowledgement

I want to express my deepest gratitude to my family and friends for their unwavering support and encouragement throughout this book's writing, especially my parents, my wife **Ruchika**, and my daughter **Lavanya**.

I am also grateful to BPB Publications for their guidance and expertise in bringing this book to fruition. It was a long journey of revising this book, with valuable participation and collaboration of reviewers, technical experts, and editors.

I would also like to acknowledge the valuable guidance of my mentors, especially **Vivek Kumar, Gitika Jain** and **Anuj Kamra**, and all my co-workers of many years working in the tech industry, who have taught me so much and provided continued valuable feedback on my work.

Finally, I would like to thank all the readers who have taken an interest in my book and for their support in making it a reality. Your encouragement has been invaluable.

Preface

Cloud computing is not just a technology shift; it is a mindset revolution. It has fundamentally changed how we build, scale, secure, and think about software. As someone who has spent the better part of two decades working across the layers of cloud-native stacks – from stubborn monoliths reluctantly lifted into the cloud, to microservices dancing harmoniously on Kubernetes – I have seen the cloud's triumphs and its turbulence alike.

This book is a product of those real-world earthworks.

You would not find marketing fluff here, nor will you slog through dry academic theory. Instead, this is a practitioner's playbook. It is a structured tour through the landscape of Cloud Application Architecture Patterns, blending design principles with pragmatic advice. Whether you are leading architecture reviews, replatforming legacy systems, or building greenfield apps designed to scale to millions of users, this book is written with your journey in mind.

Over the years, I have worked with smaller enterprises trying to find product-market fit, as well as global enterprises grappling with decades of tech debt. The patterns you will read about here are from resilience and observability to scalability and security, all forged in experience. They come from the lessons learned launching products in production environments where downtime was not an option, budgets were not infinite, and user expectations were unforgiving.

If you are a software architect, engineering leader, cloud consultant, or even an ambitious developer ready to design cloud-native systems that last, you are in the right place. This book will help you avoid the common pitfalls, embrace proven strategies, and most importantly, develop an architectural way of thinking suited for the cloud era.

Each chapter is shaped to be digestible yet deep, and rich with patterns that solve real-world problems. From foundational concepts to advanced integration strategies, every section offers examples, comparisons, and practical context you can put to work immediately. Think of it as a field guide that does not just tell you what to do, but why it matters and how to do it well.

If you are looking for shortcuts, well, this book will not hand you any. But if you are looking for the wisdom to build systems that are robust, scalable, and future-proof, then let us dive in.

Welcome to the architecture you have always wanted to design.

Chapter 1: Introduction to Cloud Computing - This chapter sets the stage by explaining the why behind the book; what it covers, who it is for, and how it is structured. It introduces key cloud architecture concepts while sharing a personal lens from years of practical experience. You will learn what outcomes to expect, how to get the most out of each chapter, and why architectural thinking in the cloud is fundamentally different from traditional environments. It is your map before the journey begins.

Chapter 2: Evolution of Cloud Computing - Here, we zoom out and take a historical lens on how cloud computing came to redefine software delivery. From early virtualization to today's hybrid and multi-cloud ecosystems, this chapter highlights the evolution of cloud services, economic benefits, and architectural implications. You will also gain insights into the challenges companies face when adopting cloud and why there is no one-size-fits-all approach.

Chapter 3: Fundamental Concepts - Before you can architect anything meaningful in the cloud, you need to internalize its principles. This chapter dives briefly into concepts like on-demand self-service, scalability, elasticity, and resource pooling, but without the jargon overload. We break down the essence of what makes cloud-native different from just running things on someone else's server and how to think like a cloud-native architect.

Chapter 4: Services and Deployment Models - This chapter decodes the alphabet soup of IaaS, PaaS, SaaS, FaaS, and deployment models like public, private, and hybrid clouds. We explore where each shines and where it falls short, not in theory, but in real-world use cases. You will walk away with a tactical understanding of how to choose the right model, plan migrations, and modernize legacy systems smartly.

Chapter 5: Scalability Patterns - Scalability is not just about handling growth, it is about handling it gracefully. In this chapter, we explore in detail the time-tested patterns such as load balancing, partitioning, caching, and microservices, all through the lens of elasticity. You will see how these patterns play out in production and how to mix and match them to suit different business and technical constraints.

Chapter 6: Resiliency Patterns - Failure in the cloud is not a matter of if, but when. This chapter arms you with resilience strategies, from health checks and automated recovery to failover systems and graceful degradation. You will learn how to design for failure, create redundancy where it counts, and ensure your application stays reliable under pressure.

Chapter 7: Data Management Patterns - Managing data in the cloud is both a blessing and a balancing act. This chapter covers patterns for consistency, availability, and performance.

We will look at eventual consistency, partitioning, replication, and governance, all with a practical take on how to architect systems that respect both speed and safety when it comes to data.

Chapter 8: Security Patterns - Security is just not a feature; it is a responsibility. In this chapter, we unpack how identity management, encryption, API security, and threat modeling come together in a modern cloud stack. You will also learn how to build for compliance, not as a check-the-box activity but as a foundational pillar of your architecture.

Chapter 9: Messaging and Integration Patterns - In a world of microservices and distributed systems, communication is everything. This chapter explores how to stitch together services using queues, streams, pub/sub, and integration APIs. We also touch on choreography versus orchestration and how to architect for hybrid and cross-cloud integrations that do not end in disaster.

Chapter 10: Monitoring and Observability Patterns - You cannot fix what you cannot see. This chapter dives into observability, centralized logging, metrics, traces, and dashboards, not as buzzwords, but as tools to keep your systems healthy. We cover both black-box and white-box monitoring strategies, with real-world lessons on setting up observability pipelines that engineers actually use.

Chapter 11: Future Trends – At the end, we look forward. This chapter explores what is on the horizon; serverless, edge computing, AI-native infrastructure, sustainable architectures, and zero trust models. You will leave with a future-ready mindset, equipped not just to adapt, but to lead in an ever-evolving cloud landscape.

Code Bundle and Coloured Images

Please follow the link to download the
Code Bundle and the ***Coloured Images*** of the book:

https://rebrand.ly/l37csnb

The code bundle for the book is also hosted on GitHub at **https://github.com/bpbpublications/Cloud-Application-Architecture-Patterns**. In case there's an update to the code, it will be updated on the existing GitHub repository.

We have code bundles from our rich catalogue of books and videos available at https://github.com/bpbpublications. Check them out!

Errata

We take immense pride in our work at BPB Publications and follow best practices to ensure the accuracy of our content to provide with an indulging reading experience to our subscribers. Our readers are our mirrors, and we use their inputs to reflect and improve upon human errors, if any, that may have occurred during the publishing processes involved. To let us maintain the quality and help us reach out to any readers who might be having difficulties due to any unforeseen errors, please write to us at :

errata@bpbonline.com

Your support, suggestions and feedbacks are highly appreciated by the BPB Publications' Family.

Piracy

If you come across any illegal copies of our works in any form on the internet, we would be grateful if you would provide us with the location address or website name. Please contact us at business@bpbonline.com with a link to the material.

If you are interested in becoming an author

If there is a topic that you have expertise in, and you are interested in either writing or contributing to a book, please visit www.bpbonline.com. We have worked with thousands of developers and tech professionals, just like you, to help them share their insights with the global tech community. You can make a general application, apply for a specific hot topic that we are recruiting an author for, or submit your own idea.

Reviews

Please leave a review. Once you have read and used this book, why not leave a review on the site that you purchased it from? Potential readers can then see and use your unbiased opinion to make purchase decisions. We at BPB can understand what you think about our products, and our authors can see your feedback on their book. Thank you!

For more information about BPB, please visit www.bpbonline.com.

Join our Discord space

Join our Discord workspace for latest updates, offers, tech happenings around the world, new releases, and sessions with the authors:

https://discord.bpbonline.com

Table of Contents

CHAPTER 1

Introduction to Cloud Computing

Introduction

Have you ever thought that in the vast ocean of cloud computing, there are numerous options, and how to utilize them to take full advantage effectively? You are not alone. Cloud computing is indeed a major driver of innovation in the IT and software business. In the fast-paced evolution of the digital landscape we see today, it is one of the key factors in the modern technology environment because of radical changes it is introducing into to the operations of corporate world and how consumers interact with technology. However, for the most part, cloud architecture is becoming increasingly difficult to comprehend, cluttered by muddled technology jargon and ever-changing best practices.

Structure

In this chapter, we will go over the following topics:

- Introduction to Cloud Application Architecture Patterns
- Key concepts in cloud architecture
- Target audience and book objectives
- Personal experience and holistic viewpoints
- Book structure and content overview
- Practical examples and learning outcomes

Objectives

By the end of this book, you will have a broad eye on cloud architecture patterns and principles. You will gain the skills and knowledge needed to design, deploy, and operate scalable, highly available, and secure cloud solutions. Whatever your need, whether it is to migrate existing systems to the cloud, build new native applications on the cloud, or make more informed decisions about navigating your organization's cloud strategy, you can find the insights and guidance you need in these pages.

Introduction to Cloud Application Architecture Patterns

Enter **Cloud Application Architecture Patterns**. Having spent a significant amount of time and gained extensive experience in the cloud over the years, the author has participated in and contributed to numerous design sessions with customers and cloud architects worldwide. Through these experiences, he has come to understand how, when designed properly, cloud architectures fundamentally change the way we work toward achieving incredible results. At the same time, it is also seen how painful and costly the trials and tribulations are that come from ill-conceived, poorly executed solutions.

Cloud computing has evolved beyond its early days. What started out as a discussion topic for IT infrastructure, has since become the backbone for digital innovation. Organizations of all sizes, from small and mid-size start-ups to multinational corporations, are leveraging cloud computing to maximize efficiency, scalability, and innovation. However, with this broad application comes a new set of challenges. And then also, how do you build systems that scale exponentially? How do you ensure the security and integrity of your data in a multi-user environment? How do you navigate the sea of service and deployment models to find one that suits your specific needs?

These are the questions that IT professionals and business leaders are losing sleep over, and this book aims to answer them. But what is the difference between this book and many other books on this topic? It is not just a how-to or best practices guide. Instead, this book takes a more holistic and altruistic perspective, integrating technical analysis with practical applicability and proactive thoughts.

Key concepts in cloud architecture

As you read through this book, we will cover some key concepts that you should master with cloud architecture. The very top of that list is the scalability concept. As a cloud ages, your systems need to scale upward in areas where they are necessary, without significant changes. This book delves into the intricacies of vertical vs horizontal scaling and the magic of elasticity that enables cloud environments to scale up and down based on demand.

Another theme is resilience. In this age of massive over-optimism, when downtime could cost millions and a tarnished brand, it becomes essential to design systems that are fault-tolerant and actually work even when all odds are against them. We will cover concepts like redundancy and graceful degradation that can help you create systems that maintain functionality even in the face of failure.

Another important aspect is security, and it is a major area of focus. However, more sensitive data is being migrated to the cloud, and we need to enforce protection for that data. We will explore the security best practices that safeguard your applications and data, such as identity management, encryption techniques, and secure API development.

Data management is another crucial aspect. Data is exploding, both in terms of generation and consumption, and so efficient ways of storing, processing, and analysing that data become imperative. We will discuss data patterns to partition, replicate, and guarantee consistency, as well as trade-offs between different classes of storage solutions, including data lakes and data warehouses.

Lastly, we will look at the future of cloud computing. New paradigms, technologies enter the field all the time. Knowing the trends that will shape the future of cloud architecture enables you to make informed, long-lasting decisions.

Target audience and book objectives

If you are an IT professional looking to learn everything from scratch about cloud architecting, this book is for you. If you are a business leader seeking to wrap your brain around cloud strategy for your own company, this is a treasure trove of insight. If nothing else, you will find much to grasp within these pages, even if you are simply a student or an enthusiast trying to get your head around one of the most transformative technologies to come along in our lifetimes. Cloud computing has moved from being a nice-to-have in today's digital economy to being a must-have. Cloud architecture knowledge is paramount in today's era for success in every enterprise, regardless of whether an individual is an IT administrator, enterprise or cloud architect, or a business leader, as it enables them to make informed decisions. This book is a guide for you to get to know cloud landscape, practices, and fill the missing pieces in your knowledge.

So why should you bother reading this book? First and foremost, you will learn the fundamental principles and patterns that form the basis for successful cloud architectures. You will learn how to design systems that are not only functional but also scalable, reliable and secure. The book will also help you determine proper service and deployment models that may better suit your requirements, along with tips for optimal usage and cost-effectiveness of the cloud for your organization.

But again, it is not just the technical know-how that you will get; realistically, you will get a new perspective on cloud computing. You will also understand how cloud architecture intersects with the business strategy and the way it can catapult innovation and open new doors. You will begin to think like a cloud architect, where you consider not only the technical problems you are solving at any given time but also the long-term consequences of the design choices you are making.

Personal experience and holistic viewpoint

To illustrate the power of this knowledge, author's personal experience is shared. During the span of his career, being a part of a team developing a complex enterprise app and migrating it to the cloud, there was excitement about the benefits — better scalability, lower infrastructure costs, faster time to deploy. However, the complexity of the challenge was underestimated. Challenges with data consistency, unexpected performance bottlenecks, and security issues that were not anticipated were faced. It was a grueling experience, but one of the greatest moments. It also left a need to know cloud architecture principles and building blocks far more deeply. It taught that success in cloud computing is not just about the technical skills, but also the human element of how all the moving pieces fit together – technology, business needs, user experience. That is the kind of holistic viewpoint this book aims to communicate.

Book structure and content overview

We will begin mapping the evolution of cloud computing from its traditional IT infrastructure origins to modern-day configurations. You will develop a sense of historical context that will help you understand just how disruptive cloud computing is.

After that, we will also dive into the principles of cloud architecture. You will be introduced to concepts such as on-demand self-service, resource pooling, and measured service, foundational principles that make cloud computing so dynamic and powerful. Such principles result in tangible benefits for both businesses and users, and you will learn how they are realized on the ground.

Then we will look into the various service and deployment models used in the cloud. You will learn all key differentiators, **Infrastructure as a Service** (**IaaS**), **Platform as a Service** (**PaaS**), and **Software as a Service** (**SaaS**) and when to use them. The advantages and disadvantages and the risk–reward ratio of deploying public, private, and hybrid clouds, as well as case studies of organizations that have adopted such models.

With this in place, we can finally explore the architectural patterns that make cloud systems scalable and resilient. You will learn traffic balance strategies for splitting up traffic over multiple servers, and auto-scaling strategies for dynamically growing and limiting your systems based on demand. We shall explore data partitioning and caching strategy that can potentially save our users from milliseconds to hours of agony.

But scalability is not the whole story. We will also conduct pattern analysis to build resilient systems, which are resilient to failure and can continue functioning even when issues arise. You will learn about health monitoring and automated recovery mechanisms, redundancy schemes, and the circuit breaker pattern to block cascading failures in distributed systems.

Data management is another thing we will explore in detail. Learn data partitioning and replication best practices that become handy on using the cloud in an efficient way when working with this data. In addition, you will discover how to choose the appropriate storage solutions based on your use case, whether it is a data lake architecture or a data warehouse.

Moreover, if you are talking about cloud architecture, you are talking about security. You will explore patterns that help establish strong identity management and data encryption, as well as secure APIs. You will learn about the more relevant regulatory considerations and ultimate guidelines for limiting your cloud architectures to meet them.

We will cover messaging and integration patterns for inter-component communication in distributed applications as our topics move on to more advanced ones. You are introduced to message queues, publish-subscribe systems, and service meshes, enabling technologies that allow you to create flexible, loosely coupled architectures that can evolve and adapt over time.

We will also discuss monitoring and observability patterns, as keeping your cloud systems reliable and performant is a necessary concern. You will read about centralized logging, metrics collection, distributed tracing, and proactive alerting, tools and techniques that will equip you with a profound understanding of your systems and to diagnose and resolve problems quickly.

Finally, we look not to the past but forward into the future, to the emerging trends that will shape the generations of cloud architectures to come. In this book, you will learn about the technologies and paradigms that will shape cloud computing over the next few years, ranging from edge computing to serverless architectures, from AI and machine learning to blockchain and beyond.

Practical examples and learning outcomes

The book will also guide you through real-world examples and case studies that demonstrate these concepts throughout the book. You will discover that these cloud architecture patterns are embraced by organizations from all industries to realize innovation, improve efficiency, and provide new value for customers to deliver. Those stories will not just serve to showcase the real-life implementation of the concepts we talk about but will also inspire you to consider how those patterns could be applied in your work.

The book will discuss common challenges and bad practices in cloud architecture, drawing on the experiences of other experts in the field. Learn from the pitfalls to avoid, the trade-offs to consider, and the best practices that lead to success in your cloud initiatives.

Conclusion

This book will not only equip you with technical knowledge but also inspire you to rethink your approach to cloud computing. To view it not merely as a collection of technologies, but as a new paradigm that is radically changing our understanding of technology and our relationship to it. To realize the intense capability that the cloud has to fuel innovation, enable new business models, and address complex challenges at scale.

Begin this journey with your curiosity, creativity, and thought process. Always question assumptions, challenge conventional wisdom, and keep your eyes open for opportunities to leverage these ideas within your own unique environment. There were some facts that brought the golden era of cloud architects, but the cloud has no one-size-fits-all, and the cloud architects who can come up with similar new design patterns are going to win and be the most successful.

Are you ready to explore the cloud, then? To gain a thorough understanding of architectural patterns, you need to develop scalable, resilient, and innovative solutions. Acquire the skills and competencies that will give you the edge in a cloud-centric world. Let us begin our journey.

CHAPTER 2
Evolution of Cloud Computing

Introduction

Every technology has altered the way our world works, but few have made the impact as drastically as cloud computing. This radical shift has compelled organizations to relook the approaches on how to store their data, run applications, and use technology to achieve their strategic objectives. A comprehensive understanding of Cloud Application Architecture Patterns encompasses not only current technologies but also provides historical context to inform our current position. Join us as we embark on an investigative journey through the history of cloud computing, tracing the events that led to the establishment of the cloud as we know it today.

In this chapter, we will explore the foundations of cloud application architecture, setting the stage for the patterns and practices we will dive into, throughout the rest of the book. We will examine how cloud computing has revolutionized the IT landscape, discuss the key benefits and challenges it presents, and introduce the core concepts that underpin successful cloud architectures.

Structure

In this chapter, we will go over the following topics:

- Brief history of the cloud revolution
- Cloud application architecture
- Cloud service and deployment models
- Economic implications in business case for cloud
- Challenges and considerations

Objectives

At the end of the chapter, you will be adept and well aware of the history and advent of the cloud, its core concepts and design principles, and various services and deployment models to help you delve deeper and connect with complex mechanisms relevant to architecting your cloud solutions.

Brief history of the cloud revolution

Before we delve into the nuts and bolts of a cloud application architecture, let us take a moment to reflect on how we arrived here. The concept of cloud computing is far from new, with its roots dating back to utility computing as early as the 1960s. However, cloud computing, as we know it today, began to take shape in the early 2000s.

Imagine this real-life scenario, sometime around the 1960s, when the most significant crown jewels of technology were room-sized mainframe computers. Run by specially trained professionals, these machines were the wonders of the age, able to perform calculations and process figures at speeds unimaginable for mankind. But that was mostly restricted to corporate and government computing overlords, and for individuals, this was quite some way off.

In the 1970s and 80s, the **personal computer** (**PC**) was a computing revolution. It was a revelation, putting the power of computing within reach of every office and every home in an entirely new way. People were starting to realize how computers could significantly enhance productivity and creativity in numerous subtle ways, and a palpable buzz was building.

Software development has accelerated at a great pace during this time, ushering in the new generation of applications for users, anything from word processors to rudimentary database managers. But this new access did not come without its drawbacks; the architecture had limitations. The PC was powerful but could not share its resources well enough to kill off the next major paradigm in computing.

Do you remember when deploying a new application involved purchasing physical servers, having them shipped, waiting weeks for them to arrive, and then spending even more days setting them up, racking, and configuring them? It was a laborious and capital-heavy process, where one would often over-provision (just in case) or under-provision (because of budget constraints).

1st generation of distributed computing

Initially, desktop applications were the primary means of interaction. Whatever was needed to perform a task, was right there in the PC in the form of dlls and executables. When you installed the Imaging AutoCAD application into your computer, it extracted all the dlls and executables into a local folder and then it had everything it needed to create any magnificent design, that one wanted to create, be it 2D or 3D designs. However, the drawback of such desktop applications was that there was per CPU licensing costs and for larger enterprises, this was a significant deal and could put a deep hole in the pockets.

To address these needs, we came up with the client server architecture. As PCs became mainstream, the client-server model evolved to distribute workloads between powerful servers and more limited client machines. This architecture was a basic first step to distributed computing, so that users could access resources more effectively. In fact, if you ever used an early email system or queried a company database, you worked directly with client-server architecture.

In the client-server architecture, data processing was divided between clients (the machines followed by users) and servers (centralized computers). Clients would be user interfaces, while servers would process all the heavy functions behind the scenes, from their databases and applications. This enabled new forms of collaboration and information sharing, but not without significant downsides. This model often had to be maintained, making it very complicated to support, because each application needed its own server, which meant underutilization of hardware and complexity in the infrastructure management. In the late 1990s, there were ever-noisier server rooms, with machines that would fight the good fight, though often at the cost of HQ tranquility. Scaling infrastructure in these systems costs a lot of money in hardware and hours in expensive upgrades and endless troubleshooting. This was unsustainable, and this required the new architecture of a more flexible and efficient computing, and also was cheaper from a licensing cost perspective compared to desktop applications.

Things changed with advent of the internet

The internet turned the computing world upside-down. The way the **World Wide Web** could knit people, computers, and information together opened possibilities we could barely begin to imagine. Our devices were now more inter-connected than ever, and traditional computing thinking was beginning to shift. With the development of browsers that provided access to applications via the internet opened up new avenues.

These were web-based applications before this idea adopted the name **Software as a Service** (**SaaS**). The requirement to install and maintain software on individual machines disappeared overnight. This meant that web-based email, calendars, and even databases were accessible from any internet-connected device, making information more flexible and pervasive. One of the more memorable experiences from my early tech-related job in town was access to my very first web-based email account, being able to check messages was something from the future.

But at the same time as these consumer-facing, web-based applications were sweeping the world, another revolution was underway beneath the surface of the internet revolution, whose lessons would become the foundation of the cloud.

Virtualization enters the stage

While the internet drew public interest and enabled the shift to consuming software, virtualization went on to revolutionize data centers and set up the infrastructure of what we know as cloud computing. This technology enables you to execute many virtualized machines on one server; consider it as operating a bunch of separate computer systems within a single box. This innovation, for example, overcame a basic international problem (wasting underused hardware) that had shuffled consumers (client servers).

In the early 2000s, we were driving the implementation of virtualization technology in corporate data centers, and the impact was immediate and large. We consolidated dozens of antiquated servers into a few machines that deliver orders of magnitude less physical size and energy footprint. Operational efficiency increased significantly with the lower management overheads. More importantly, virtualization enabled the elastic, on-demand resource allocation that defines cloud computing today.

But virtualization also laid the groundwork for dynamic resource scaling, that is, the ability to provision more compute power or storage space on the fly as demand at a moment's notice provides the basis for dynamic resource scaling. As a result, IT departments were better positioned to respond to fluctuating workloads, scaling up to accommodate spikes in demand with much less lag than Moore's law could keep up with in ordering new hardware.

Birth of cloud computing

The cloud and virtualized computing are above anything else. It was the advent of virtualization technology, after the prime of the internet was already in full play, that introduced cloud computing in the mid-2000s. **Amazon Web Services** (**AWS**) was a pioneer in this space, launching its debut cloud services in 2006, which provided online virtualized computing resources. It was a paradigm shift that made computing resources, well, a utility, like electricity or water.

That upending concept of being able to *turn on* computing power whenever you needed it and *turn it off* when you did not, changed what enterprises even considered to be resources in the first place. Customers could now only pay for what they needed, and avoid extremely high operational costs, whether it be from maintaining physical data centers packed with proprietary hardware.

As a personal experience, when an initial proposal to migrate the company's applications to the cloud was made, it was met with reluctance from peers. A common reaction was, *Where should we store the data?* However, the advantages of cloud computing, such as, reduced costs, increased flexibility, and rapid scalability to meet evolving business needs, soon became undeniable. The shift in mindset was driven by early exposure to cloud services, which quickly transformed the organization's approach to technology.

As a result, the cloud offering landscape has exploded with the likes of Microsoft Azure, Google Cloud Platform, and countless more. In fact, cloud computing is no longer simply about virtual machines today; much more has been added to the picture, from serverless computing and containerization to machine learning and edge computing.

Cloud application architecture

Let us now understand some of the core concepts in cloud application architecture, starting with what cloud application architecture is, its key benefits, and so on.

Defining cloud application architecture

You might be wondering what exactly we mean by *cloud application architecture*. At its core, cloud application architecture refers to the way we design, structure, and organize applications that run in cloud environments. It is about leveraging the unique capabilities of cloud platforms to build scalable, resilient, and cost-effective applications.

Cloud application architecture is not just about lifting and shifting existing applications to the cloud (although that can be a starting point). It is about rethinking our approach to application design to take full advantage of cloud-native capabilities.

When one starts working with cloud architectures, a lot has to be unlearned, and many of the practices developed over years of working with on-premises systems have to be let go. For example, instead of planning for peak capacity and purchasing hardware accordingly, learn to design for elasticity to allow the application to scale automatically based on demand.

Key benefits of cloud application architecture

Now that we have a basic understanding of what cloud application architecture is, let us explore some of the key benefits it offers:

- **Scalability:** One of the most significant advantages of cloud architecture is the ability to scale resources up or down based on demand. This elasticity allows you to handle traffic spikes without overprovisioning for peak loads.
- **Cost-effectiveness:** With cloud computing, you typically pay only for the resources you use. This model can lead to significant cost savings, especially for applications with variable workloads.
- **Agility and speed:** Cloud platforms provide a wealth of services and tools that can accelerate development and deployment. You can quickly prototype new ideas and bring products to market faster.
- **Global reach:** Major cloud providers have data centers around the world, making it easier to deploy applications closer to your users for better performance.
- **Managed services:** Cloud providers offer a wide range of managed services, from databases to machine learning APIs, allowing you to focus on your application logic rather than infrastructure management.
- **Reliability and availability:** Cloud platforms are designed with redundancy and fault tolerance in mind, often providing better uptime than many on-premises solutions.
- **Security:** While security in the cloud requires a shared responsibility model, cloud providers often offer advanced security features and compliance certifications that would be challenging for individual organizations to implement.

These benefits are not just theoretical. People have experienced first-hand how adopting cloud architecture can transform organizations. A start-up was able to scale from a few hundred users to millions in a matter of months, thanks to the elasticity of their cloud infrastructure. Another enterprise client reduced their IT costs by 40% by migrating to a cloud-native architecture and optimizing their resource usage.

Core concepts in cloud application architecture

To effectively design cloud applications, it is crucial to understand some core concepts that underpin cloud architecture. Let us explore these fundamental ideas.

Distributed systems

Cloud applications are inherently distributed systems. Unlike traditional monolithic applications that run on a single server, cloud applications typically consist of multiple components running on different machines, often in different geographical locations.

This distributed nature brings benefits like improved scalability and fault tolerance, but it also introduces challenges in areas like data consistency and network communication. As you design cloud applications, you will need to consider how to handle these distributed system challenges.

Microservices

Microservices architecture is a popular approach in cloud application design. Instead of building a single, monolithic application, you break it down into smaller, loosely coupled services that can be developed, deployed, and scaled independently.

There was a project where the team refactored a monolithic e-commerce platform into microservices. It was a complex process, but the resulting architecture was much more flexible and easier to maintain. Each team could work on their service independently, and they could scale individual components based on their specific needs.

Stateless design

In cloud environments, it is generally beneficial to design stateless applications where possible. Stateless applications do not store client session information between requests, making them easier to scale horizontally.

This does not mean your entire application has to be stateless; you can use distributed caching or database services to store state when necessary. The key is to design your application components to be as stateless as possible.

Event-driven architecture

Event-driven architecture is another common pattern in cloud applications. In this model, components communicate through events, which can help decouple services and improve scalability.

People have used event-driven architectures to build real-time analytics systems that could process millions of events per second. The decoupled nature of the components allowed for easy scaling of different parts of the system independently based on load.

Infrastructure as Code

In the cloud world, infrastructure can be defined and managed through code. This approach, known as **Infrastructure as Code** (**IaC**), allows you to version control your infrastructure definitions, automate deployments, and ensure consistency across environments.

Tools like AWS CloudFormation, Azure Resource Manager templates, or third-party solutions like Terraform have revolutionized the way we manage cloud infrastructure.

CI/CD

Continuous Integration and Continuous Deployment (**CI/CD**) practices are crucial in cloud environments. They allow you to automate the testing and deployment of your applications, enabling faster iterations and more reliable releases.

Setting up robust CI/CD pipelines takes effort, but the payoff is enormous. Teams transition from monthly releases with frequent issues to daily or even hourly releases, thanks to well-implemented CI/CD practices, resulting in improved stability.

Observability

With distributed cloud applications, traditional monitoring approaches often fall short. Observability, that is, the ability to understand the internal state of a system by examining its outputs, becomes crucial.

This involves not just monitoring metrics, but also centralizing logs and implementing distributed tracing to understand how requests flow through your system.

Shared responsibility model

The **shared responsibility model** is like a well-coordinated responsibility between you and your cloud provider. It defines who handles what, making sure that no one steps on each other's toes when it comes to securing and managing systems. Simply put, the cloud provider (such as AWS, Azure, or GCP) is responsible for securing the underlying infrastructure, the physical servers, networking, and foundational services that run the cloud. On the other hand, the customer is responsible for what you put in the cloud: your applications, your data, your access policies, and how you configure services. Think of it like renting an apartment; the landlord ensures the building is structurally sound, but it is up to you to lock your doors and install a safe if you store valuables. Understanding this division of responsibilities is crucial because many security breaches happen not from cloud provider failures, but from customers misconfiguring their environments. In the end, it is a partnership where success relies on both parties playing their role well.

Key principles for designing for the cloud

Now that we have covered the core concepts, let us discuss some key principles to keep in mind when designing cloud applications.

Design for failure

In cloud environments, you need to assume that failures will happen and design your applications accordingly. This means implementing proper error handling, retries, and fallback mechanisms.

Imagine a system where we did not adequately plan for the failure of a critical service. When that service went down, it took the entire application with it. After that painful lesson, we redesigned the system with multiple layers of redundancy and fallback options.

Decouple components

Loosely coupled components are easier to scale and maintain. Use messaging queues, pub/sub systems, or API gateways to decouple different parts of your application.

Design for elasticity

Take advantage of the cloud's ability to scale resources dynamically. Design your application to scale out (adding more instances aka horizontal scaling) rather than up (increasing the size of existing instances aka vertical scaling) where possible.

Leverage managed services

Use managed services provided by your cloud provider where appropriate. This can significantly reduce your operational overhead and allow you to focus on your core application logic.

Implement security at every layer

Security should be a consideration at every level of your architecture, from the network layer to the application layer. Implement the principle of least privilege, encrypt data in transit and at rest, and regularly audit your security posture.

Optimize for cost

While the cloud can be cost-effective, it is easy to overspend if you are not careful. Implement cost monitoring and optimization practices from the start.

Design for data gravity

Consider where your data lives, and try to keep processing close to the data to minimize latency and data transfer costs. For example, if you have accumulated petabytes of transactional data as part of your hosted application stored on AWS S3 in the US-East region, and now you want to provide analytics on the same, it is advisable to run the compute clusters in the US-East region, instead of US-West. Otherwise, this will attract significant data transfer costs and latency.

Plan for disaster recovery

Implement robust backup and disaster recovery strategies. The cloud offers many tools to help with this, but you need to plan and implement them intentionally.

Measured service

Another key foundational principle of cloud architecture is measured service. Cloud services are designed to monitor and auto-control resource consumption, which allows providers and consumers to track the utilization level. This will enable organizations to not only manage their resources more effectively, but also budget for IT expenses altogether differently.

Cloud service and deployment models

One important thing that cloud computing has, is its service models.

As time went on, cloud computing kept gaining traction, and three primary types emerged: **Infrastructure as a Service** (**IaaS**), **Platform as a Service** (**PaaS**), and SaaS. These models come with their pros and cons and are best suited to different organizations. Let us go over them now:

- **IaaS:** This is the most basic model of cloud computing. IaaS provides the delivery of popular compute resources through the internet, permitting organizations to rent virtual machines, storage, customers, and networking abilities. In other words, it is like having a data center, without the pain of physical hardware. It enables for dynamic adjustment of infrastructure which results in very high level of operational flexibility.
- **PaaS:** These services offer customers with efficient platform to develop, run and manage the applications without building and maintaining the performance stack. It is good for applications to host and develop tools in a package, that takes the onus of server management away from the hands of developers. PaaS is one of the key enablers of rapid application development and deployment.
- **SaaS:** It is the most comprehensive cloud service model; it provides entire software solutions wrought up in the cloud and that you gain admittance to online on a pay-more only as costs arise premise. Salesforce, Google Workspace, Microsoft 365 and other commonly used applications are all SaaS examples, which allow you to make use of a complete and functioning software stack without having to download or install anything, configure updates, security patches or infrastructure.

Together, these service models have redefined IT strategies for every type of organization, as they are coming to rely on the cloud to promote innovation, enhance collaboration, and lower capital expenditures.

While cloud computing has a myriad of benefits, organizations face several cloud challenges during the transition to cloud solutions. The biggest concern is data security, compliance, and integration with existing systems. As organizations take sensitive information into the cloud, strong security standards and regulatory compliance are critical to safeguarding their data.

Organizations must also be cautious with a single vendor (vendor lock-in) and/or a sole cloud service provider. Considering that such risks are currently at hand, it rightly calls for a plan to be deployed right now in the wake of a cloud strategy, in tandem with vendor management practices, so that all facets of the entire process remain advantageous.

Internal culture shifts are also necessary to engender greater organizational buy-in. Due to the adoption of cloud technology, teams have to move from rigid ways of working to agile methodologies, so as to work collectively towards a successful project. It is as much a story of cultural evolution as it is of technological shift itself.

Cloud deployment models

In addition to service models, it is important to understand the different deployment models for cloud applications. Let us go over them now:

- **Public cloud:** In this model, cloud services are provided by third-party providers and made available to the general public over the internet. This is what most people think of when they hear *cloud computing*.
- **Private cloud:** A private cloud is dedicated to a single organization. It can be hosted on-premises or by a third-party provider, but the services and infrastructure are maintained on a private network.
- **Hybrid cloud:** A hybrid cloud is a combination of public and private clouds, allowing data and applications to be shared between them. This model can offer the best of both worlds, providing the scalability of public cloud with the security and control of private cloud.
- **Multi-cloud:** A multi-cloud strategy involves using multiple cloud providers. This can help avoid vendor lock-in and allow you to leverage the best services from each provider.

When it comes to choosing the models as a part of an organization, the choice often depends on factors like security requirements, existing infrastructure investments, and specific application needs. Refer to the following figure:

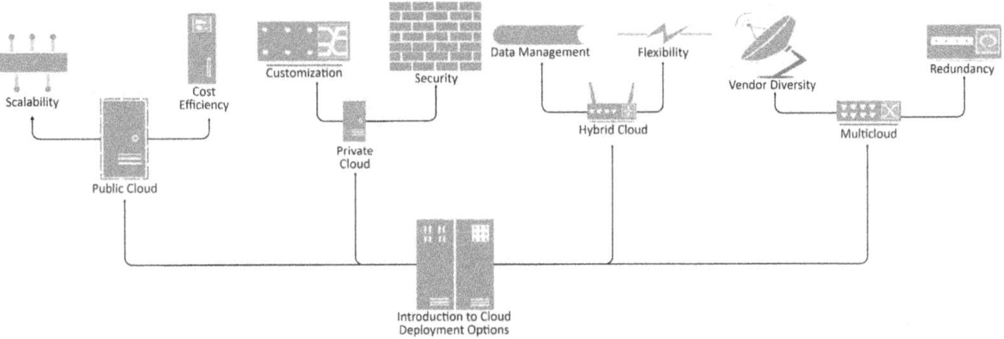

Figure 2.1: Different types of cloud, with their attributes

Economic implications in business case for cloud

Cloud computing represents not just an evolutionary step in IT, but a tectonic shift in how companies access and leverage their IT resources. For the deep economic consequences, let us consider the following:

- **CapEx to OpEx:** Imagine a world where you no longer need to make large up-front investments on costly hardware. Cloud computing basically rationalizes this scenario, allowing businesses to only pay for the services they use. This helps in moving the organization from CapEx to OpEx allows the organization to invest the capital into business innovation and expand.
- **Scalability and elasticity:** Dynamic playground that expands and contracts in response to user demand cloud services provide this kind of flexibility, enabling organizations to scale operations up and down rapidly to meet live-time demands. This allows companies to stop the bleeding that can be caused by procurement of people infrastructure that is not yet deployed, and from systems which companies may need to pivot away from in the case of spikes in demand.
- **Reduced maintenance costs:** Think about a world where the constant demand of system maintenance and software updates are taken care of by pros whose only goal is to empower you. Leveraging on cloud services reduces the need for IT guys, allowing them to focus on right initiatives by transferring these responsibilities to the cloud provider.
- **Accelerated time to market:** Maximize development agility cloud services can help speed up the process of developing and delivering new solutions for businesses, as getting a new solution out there in the fast-moving competitive space can help make or break a business.
- **Beyond the borders:** Visualize your company as a global enterprise, with an office in every corner of the world. We humanize a brand where the cloud providers' global network of data centers make access to a worldwide audience seamless and vastly less expensive, resulting in being able to reach customers of all shapes and sizes.

Startups and small companies take advantage of the cloud to compete against large enterprise companies, and large enterprises use their transition to the cloud as a catalyst to create efficiencies and increased agility. Cloud computing offers significant economic benefits, and yet, this needs to be properly evaluated in the context of your environment.

Getting started with cloud application architecture

Here are some bonus points to keep in mind while thinking about designing the cloud architecture, which go a long way for a robust implementation:

- **Learn the basics:** Start by understanding the fundamental concepts we have covered in this chapter. Familiarize yourself with the services offered by major cloud providers.
- **Start small:** Begin with a simple application or component. Maybe migrate a non-critical application to the cloud or build a small project using cloud services.
- **Experiment:** Take advantage of free tiers offered by cloud providers to experiment with different services and architectures.
- **Learn from others:** Study case studies and reference architectures provided by cloud providers and the community. Attend cloud-focused conferences and meetups.
- **Stay updated:** Cloud technologies evolve rapidly. Make a habit of staying updated with the latest developments and best practices.
- **Practice:** There is no substitute for hands-on experience. The more you work with cloud technologies, the more comfortable and proficient you will become.

For your help, here is a table depicting various services offered by different cloud providers for various needs like storage, compute and many others:

Category	AWS	GCP	Azure
Compute	EC2	Compute Engine	Virtual Machines
Storage	S3	Cloud Storage	Blob Storage
Databases	RDS, Aurora	Cloud SQL	Azure SQL
Networking	VPC	VPC	Virtual Network
AI/ML	SageMaker	Vertex AI	Azure ML
Analytics	Redshift	BigQuery	Azure ML
CI/CD	CodePipeline	Cloud Build	Azure DevOps
Security & IAM	IAM	Cloud IAM	Azure AD

Table 2.1: *Services comparison among various cloud providers*

The following figure shows a comparison of more services among various other cloud providers:

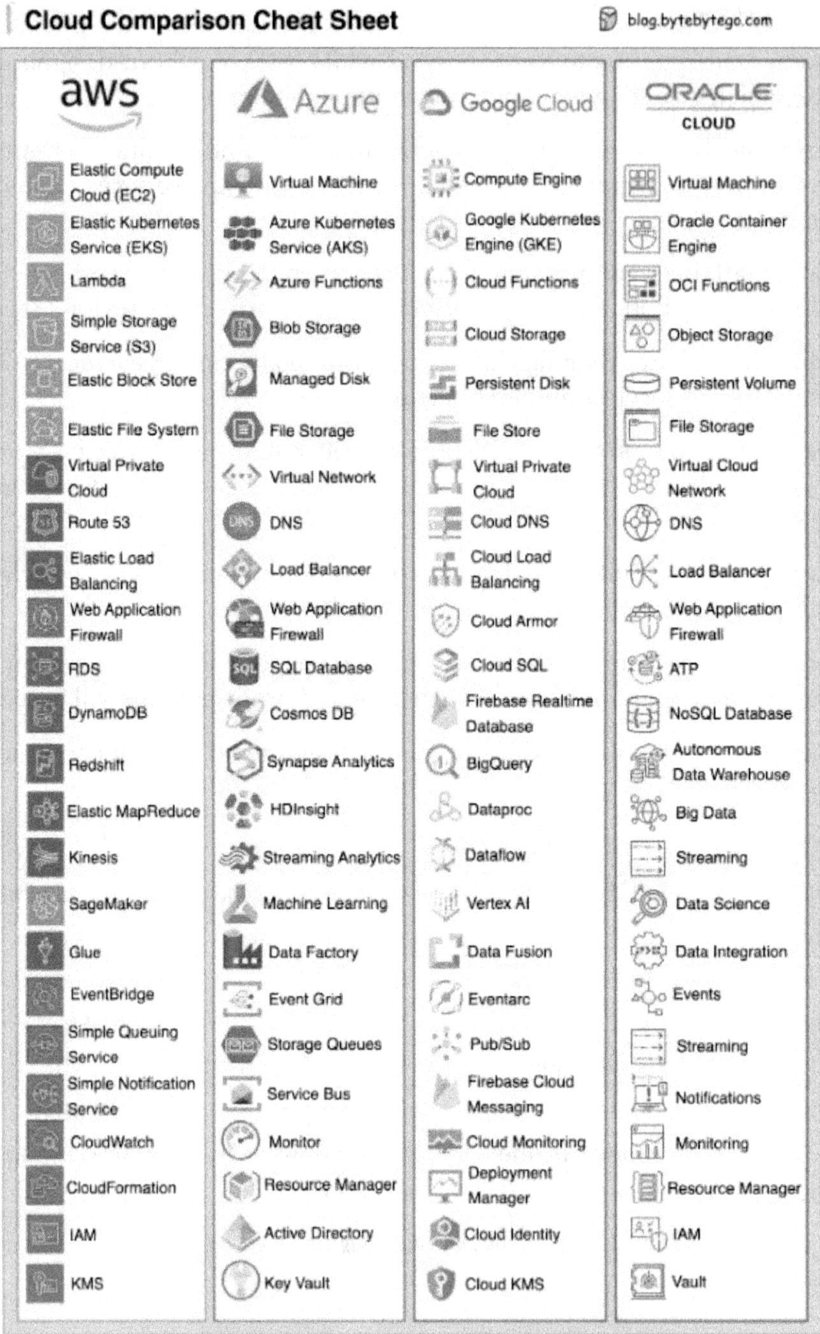

Cloud Comparison Cheat Sheet blog.bytebytego.com

aws	Azure	Google Cloud	ORACLE CLOUD
Elastic Compute Cloud (EC2)	Virtual Machine	Compute Engine	Virtual Machine
Elastic Kubernetes Service (EKS)	Azure Kubernetes Service (AKS)	Google Kubernetes Engine (GKE)	Oracle Container Engine
Lambda	Azure Functions	Cloud Functions	OCI Functions
Simple Storage Service (S3)	Blob Storage	Cloud Storage	Object Storage
Elastic Block Store	Managed Disk	Persistent Disk	Persistent Volume
Elastic File System	File Storage	File Store	File Storage
Virtual Private Cloud	Virtual Network	Virtual Private Cloud	Virtual Cloud Network
Route 53	DNS	Cloud DNS	DNS
Elastic Load Balancing	Load Balancer	Cloud Load Balancing	Load Balancer
Web Application Firewall	Web Application Firewall	Cloud Armor	Web Application Firewall
RDS	SQL Database	Cloud SQL	ATP
DynamoDB	Cosmos DB	Firebase Realtime Database	NoSQL Database
Redshift	Synapse Analytics	BigQuery	Autonomous Data Warehouse
Elastic MapReduce	HDInsight	Dataproc	Big Data
Kinesis	Streaming Analytics	Dataflow	Streaming
SageMaker	Machine Learning	Vertex AI	Data Science
Glue	Data Factory	Data Fusion	Data Integration
EventBridge	Event Grid	Eventarc	Events
Simple Queuing Service	Storage Queues	Pub/Sub	Streaming
Simple Notification Service	Service Bus	Firebase Cloud Messaging	Notifications
CloudWatch	Monitor	Cloud Monitoring	Monitoring
CloudFormation	Resource Manager	Deployment Manager	Resource Manager
IAM	Active Directory	Cloud Identity	IAM
KMS	Key Vault	Cloud KMS	Vault

Figure 2.2: *Services comparison among various cloud providers*

Source: *https://blog.bytebytego.com/p/ep70-cloud-services-cheat-sheet?utm_source=publication-search*

Remember, becoming proficient in cloud application architecture is a journey. It takes years of dedication, study, and practice to feel truly comfortable designing complex cloud systems, and it is an ever-evolving journey with learning new things every day.

Challenges and considerations

However, there are challenges inherent to cloud computing, in spite of the tempting rewards. Let us go over them now:

- **Security and privacy:** Large-scale platforms handle massive storage and processing workloads, with data stored in secure, protected layers. While security threats like data theft remain a concern, the continuous, dedicated efforts of cloud providers ensure investments in security far beyond what any single organization could justify. This creates an interesting paradox: trusting external providers can ultimately lead to a stronger protection.
- **Compliance:** The initial slip into the cloud for the industry can be damaged as there is a minefield of regulatory requirements, especially when it comes to industries where the data governance laws like GDPR, CCPA, HIPPA, and others are strict, as in the case of healthcare and finance. The touchpoints of compliance to policy and cloud integration is very fine.
- **Vendor lock-in:** Utilizing just one cloud provider can lock organizations into a tangle of obstacles when it is time to change providers; this type of lock-in will need a strategic approach, considering implications, and so an approach towards cloud agnostic design development and configurations is a must to hold the advantage.
- **Network dependency:** Get that third-party cloud application signed up and now you have a network dependency. A disruption in the service would immediately deny access to critical data and applications; that is why reliable connectivity is a major requirement.
- **Cost control:** Cloud computing can specifically help in lower operational costs. But it can also set free costs which are hard to predict if developers fail to carefully track their resources. Provisioning resources at a speed greater than you can manage them, results in ever-growing bills that can spiral out of control.

With foresight and vigilance, the pains of cloud adoption are controllable. The secret to that is being completely aware of the lay of the cloud land before you get there and, more importantly, with its nifty upper registers as well as its possible lower registers.

Conclusion

The evolution of the cloud has been marked by significant innovations, paradigm shifts, and visionaries whose imagination rendered the potential of interconnectivity. From the constraints of mainframe computing to the limitless potential of the cloud, we have witnessed a dramatic transformation in the way we generate technology, how we deliver it, and how we consume it.

And so, in this digital age, the cloud is an opportunity for transformation, from the way businesses collaborate to the way they find efficiency in their processes. By understanding the past and future of cloud computing, organizations can navigate their cloud journey, discover the full capabilities of the cloud, and define and implement a strategy for success, ultimately making their enterprise future-proof. The decision is only a portion of the whole procedure; however, it will be essential in subsequent steps, as we are using the cloud. Cloud services can continue to evolve, but we have reached the limit of what information can be shared through applications and among individuals.

Hopefully, the reader will now have a clearer understanding of how cloud computing is evolving and its increasing importance to the current IT landscape. We evolved from a monolithic mainframe to client-server architectures, but in many respects, we are still running only on the ground. The cloud revolution still has a way to go.

Subsequent chapters will address the architectural patterns that make cloud applications so successful. In other words, scalable, resilient, and efficient. We will cover design principles you can leverage to truly realize your cloud potential while practically managing its challenges.

This is the stage of cloud computing where you are trained to understand that the cloud is not just about technology adoption, but about a shift in mindset regarding how you think about your IT resources and capabilities.

Chapter 3
Fundamental Concepts

Introduction

Welcome to the core of cloud computing! If you have ever wondered what makes the cloud tick, you are in the right place. In this chapter, we are going to dive deep into the fundamental concepts that form the backbone of cloud architecture. Think of these as the Lego blocks that, when put together, create the magnificent structures we call cloud systems.

As we embark on this journey together, let us imagine you are an architect. Not the kind that designs buildings, but a cloud architect. Your canvas is virtual, your tools are code and concepts, and your creations can span the globe. Exciting, is it not? Let us start by breaking down these core principles. They might sound a bit technical at first, but do not worry; as we progress ahead, we will back these concepts with real-world examples and analogies that will make them stick.

Structure

In this chapter, we will go over the following topics:

- Achieving seamless growth in cloud computing via scalability
- On-demand self-service
- Resource pooling

- Measured service
- Cloud and cloud-native applications
- Cloud architecture mentality

Objectives

After finishing this chapter, you will be well versed with fundamental building blocks and concepts for cloud application architecture that should always be on top of your mind when you take up the challenge and sail smoothly in on these choppy waves of cloud computing and architecture.

Achieving seamless growth in cloud computing via scalability

Let us kick things off with scalability. If you have ever worried about your application crumbling under the weight of its own success, you are in the right place. This chapter is going to guide you through the fascinating world of scalability in cloud architecture. Remember when Instagram crashed on New Year's Eve 2012 due to the sheer volume of photo uploads? That is exactly because it did not scale up to the expected load it was supposed to handle.

In simple terms, scalability is your system's ability to handle growth. Imagine you are running a lemonade stand. On a hot day, demand skyrockets. How do you handle it?

One approach is vertical scaling, or *scaling up*. This is like getting a bigger lemonade jug. You are increasing the capacity of your existing setup. In cloud terms, this means beefing up your server; more CPU, more RAM, more storage.

The second approach is horizontal scaling, or *scaling out*. Instead of relying on one big jug, you set up multiple smaller jugs. In the cloud, this means adding more servers rather than scaling up existing ones.

Here is a real-world example: **Netflix**. They do not rely on a few super-powerful servers. Instead, they utilize thousands of smaller instances that can be spun up or down as needed. This architecture allows them to handle those Friday night binge-watching spikes without breaking a sweat, demonstrating the power of horizontal scaling in a live environment.

The concept of scalability is not just applicable to servers and instances; it extends to database architectures, network configurations, and application designs. The choice between vertical and horizontal scaling often depends on the application requirements, budget constraints, and long-term growth projections.

Let us now dig deeper into vertical and horizontal scaling.

Horizontal versus vertical scaling

As touched upon previously, when it comes to scaling in the cloud, we have two main approaches: horizontal scaling and vertical scaling. Let us break these down.

Vertical scaling or scaling up

Vertical scaling, or scaling up, is like supercharging your existing machine. You are essentially adding more power to your current setup. This could mean upgrading the CPU, adding more RAM, or increasing storage on a single server.

In projects where the team initially relies heavily on vertical scaling, as the user base grows, the team must continually upgrade the server to more powerful machines. It does work well for a while, but it soon hit a ceiling; there is only so much one can upgrade a single machine before it becomes prohibitively expensive or technically unfeasible.

The advantages of vertical scaling are as follows:

- **Simplicity:** It is straightforward to implement. Instead of re-architecting your application or setting up clusters of machines, you just add more CPU, memory, or storage to your existing server. It is like upgrading your car's engine instead of buying a fleet of cars.
- **Consistency:** All your resources are in one place. Having everything centralized on a single beefy machine means there is no need to coordinate data synchronization or consistency across multiple servers. This reduces complexity and eliminates some of the classic challenges of distributed systems, such as eventual consistency, network partitioning, or race conditions.
- **Suitable for applications with state:** Great for applications that maintain session state. Applications that maintain user sessions, in-memory caches, or long-lived transactions often perform better when everything stays in one place. State management across distributed nodes can be messy and error-prone, while a vertically scaled system keeps everything nicely contained and predictable.

The disadvantages of vertical scaling are as follows:

- **Limited scalability:** There is a limit to how much you can scale up. No matter how much money you throw at it, there is always a ceiling. Hardware can only get so big and after a point, you physically cannot add more CPUs or memory. This creates a natural upper bound to how much your application can handle.
- **Potential for single point of failure:** If your souped-up server goes down, everything goes down. When you place all your eggs in one (admittedly very shiny) basket, you run the risk of losing everything if that server fails.
- **Costly:** High-end hardware can be expensive. Not only are the upfront costs significant, but ongoing maintenance, warranties, and even physical space requirements (like better cooling and power) can drive up operational costs.

Horizontal scaling or scaling out

Horizontal scaling, or scaling out, is like calling in reinforcements. Instead of making one server more powerful, you add more servers to share the load. This is where cloud computing really shines.

While working on a project for a shipping platform that experienced rapid growth, we implemented horizontal scaling, and it was like watching a well-choreographed dance. As user numbers spiked, new server instances were automatically spun up to handle the load, and when traffic died down, unnecessary instances were terminated to save costs.

The advantages of horizontal scaling are as follows:

- **Theoretically unlimited scalability:** You can keep adding servers as needed. Instead of being trapped by the limits of a single machine, you can keep adding resources indefinitely. This elasticity makes horizontal scaling ideal for modern cloud-native architectures.
- **Cost-effective:** You can use commodity hardware. In cloud environments like AWS, Azure, or GCP, it is even more economical because you can pay for just what you need, when you need it. This *pay-as-you-go* model has democratized access to serious computing power without draining budgets.
- **High availability:** If one server fails, others can pick up the slack. If one server crashes or misbehaves, others are standing by to take over. Load balancers, auto-healing mechanisms, and redundancy setups ensure that a hiccup in one server does not translate to downtime for your users.
- **Flexibility:** Easy to scale up or down based on demand. You can add instances automatically through auto-scaling policies. Scale down to save money, when traffic dips. This level of operational agility is crucial in today's world, where unpredictable workloads have become the norm.

The disadvantages of horizontal scaling are as follows:

- **Complexity:** Requires more complex architecture and load balancing. Scaling out means your architecture needs to evolve, you will need load balancers, service discovery, distributed databases, orchestration layers and sophisticated monitoring. Managing all these moving pieces adds significant complexity compared to simply scaling up a single machine.
- **Data consistency challenges:** Ensuring data consistency across multiple servers can be tricky. When data is spread across multiple nodes, keeping it consistent becomes tricky. Issues like eventual consistency, replication lag, or conflicting writes need to be tackled carefully.
- **Not all applications are suitable:** Some applications are hard to distribute across multiple servers. Apps that rely heavily on shared state, sticky sessions, or complex interdependencies can become very difficult to scale horizontally.

Therefore, these basics on scalability should always be considered, and an informed decision should be taken as to where to apply vertical or horizontal scaling, as this strictly depends on need and situation, and there is never a one-size-fits-all paradigm while architecting a cloud application. *Figure 3.1* gives a comparison of horizontal versus vertical scaling:

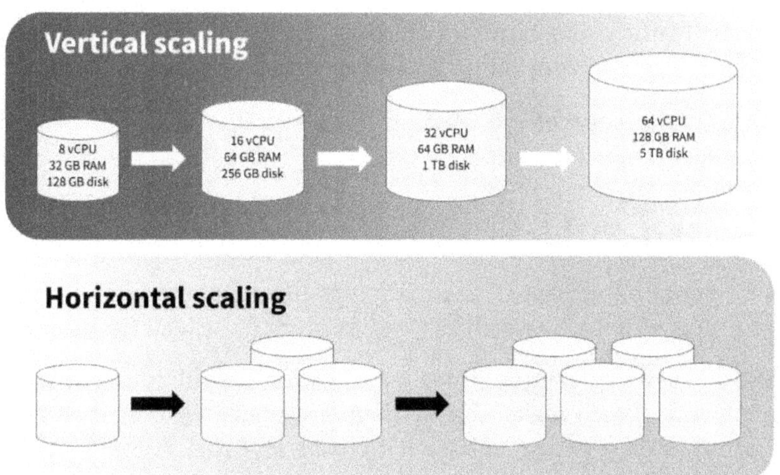

Figure 3.1: *Comparison of horizontal vs vertical scaling*

Source: *https://images.ctfassets.net/00voh0j35590/6wtOJjoIPbeqctg7dzjGS4/ca386d6416546a8ba6957e7b6407c5e4/vertical-versus-horizontal-scaling-compared-diagram.jfif*

Magic of elasticity

Now, let us discuss elasticity. If scalability is about handling growth, elasticity is about handling fluctuations. It is the ability to scale both up and down smoothly according to demand.

Think of elasticity like a rubber band. It can stretch to accommodate an increased load, but it also contracts when the load decreases. This flexibility is crucial in cloud environments because it allows you to match your resources and, ultimately, your costs to your actual needs.

The same shipping platform discussed previously also experienced massive traffic spikes during holiday sales. To manage these peaks effectively, the team set up auto-scaling groups that would automatically add servers when traffic increased and then remove them when the demand subsided. The result? The platform handled Black Friday traffic with ease and did not waste resources or money during slower periods.

The importance of elasticity is particularly notable in **Software as a Service** (**SaaS**) models, where usage can vary significantly among users. Companies like Spotify or Dropbox rely heavily on elasticity to ensure that they can provide seamless experiences for millions of users, regardless of fluctuations in demand.

Elasticity, however, is not just about scaling resources on-the-fly. It also encompasses the ability to manage and maintain infrastructure efficiently during scaling operations, which brings us to another critical aspect of cloud architecture: the management of resources and costs in a dynamic environment.

Example: Auto-scaling groups in AWS automatically adjust the number of running instances based on traffic loads. Similarly, Kubernetes enables containerized workloads to scale in real-time using **Horizontal Pod Autoscaler** (**HPA**).

Elasticity ensures that resources are used efficiently, preventing over-provisioning while maintaining application performance.

On-demand self-service

Next up is on-demand self-service. This principle is all about empowerment. It means users can provision resources without needing to go through IT or wait for human intervention.

Remember the days when setting up a new server meant filling out forms, getting approvals, and waiting for weeks? Those days are gone. With on-demand self-service, you can spin up a new server or database with just a few clicks or API calls.

This principle revolutionizes the way businesses operate, including their development and deployment cycles. Imagine a developer wanting to test a new feature. Instead of waiting for a week to get a server provisioned, they can instantly create a development environment tailored to their needs. It is like having a magic wand that can conjure up infrastructure at will. Need a test environment? It is there. Want to try out a new database technology? You have got one to play with.

However, with great power comes great responsibility. Teams can get carried away with this newfound freedom, spinning up resources left and right without considering costs or security implications. This is why it is crucial to have governance policies in place. Think of it like giving your teenager a credit card; you want to empower them, but you also need to set some ground rules.

The challenge lies in finding the balance between autonomy and governance. Implementing proper management tools, cost tracking, and security audits can help avoid common pitfalls associated with on-demand self-service. Cloud providers often offer native tools to monitor resource usage, costs, and security so that companies can maintain control while empowering their teams.

Example: AWS EC2 instance provisioning

With just a few clicks or API calls, users can launch virtual machines with predefined configurations, avoiding long procurement cycles.

Additionally, **Infrastructure as Code** (**IaC**), tools like Terraform and AWS CloudFormation allow users to automate infrastructure provisioning, making deployments repeatable and scalable.

Role of APIs in self-service

At the heart of on-demand self-service is the **application programming interface** (**API**). APIs allow different software components to interact, facilitating the automation of infrastructure provisioning. Cloud service providers offer robust APIs that enable users to create, manage, and monitor resources programmatically.

For instance, if a developer needs additional storage for a new application, they can use the relevant API endpoint to request that storage, without needing to manually navigate a dashboard or submit a ticket. This ability to code interactions with cloud resources streamlines workflows and enhances productivity, enabling developers to focus on writing code rather than managing infrastructure.

Moreover, the extensive libraries and **Software Development Kits** (**SDKs**) available for various programming languages have made it easier than ever to integrate cloud services into applications. This trend is accelerating the pace of innovation across industries, as companies leverage cloud capabilities to build and deploy applications faster than ever.

Resource pooling

Resource pooling is one fundamental principle of cloud architecture. This theory enables a group of consumers to share a resource store, thereby optimizing efficiency and lowering expenses. Cloud computing is possible by virtue of resource pooling, which allows for scalability and elasticity through the sharing of resources across client bases.

Imagine a neighborhood where instead of every person buying their own car (and dealing with the cost, parking hassle, and maintenance), a group of people share a few vehicles. Each person books a car when needed, and returns it when they are done. This way, the same set of cars is efficiently used throughout the day by different people at different times.

Now, translate that idea into the cloud. Cloud providers invest heavily in massive computing infrastructure servers, storage, and networking, and instead of each customer building their own data center, they allow thousands of customers to share this pooled infrastructure. Customers tap into the resources only when needed, and the provider keeps overall utilization high and efficient. It is smart, sustainable, and way more cost-effective, just like carpooling is better for your wallet (and the environment) than everyone driving solo.

Resource pooling is done at the compute, storage, and network levels. For instance, when you use online services, your requests get directed to several servers within a resource pool instead of a single service server. By decentralizing this load, more redundancy and reliability is achieved between these servers, as the workload can be easily distributed amongst all the servers.

Hypervisors are used by cloud providers to control this resource pooling, offering virtualized instances that can be assigned to users on demand. This abstraction layer helps them distribute applications efficiently while launching, meaning they will also not be limited by physical hardware constraints.

Resource pooling yields practical benefits for both cloud service providers and their customers. For providers, pooling resources enables them to support a diverse range of clients with varying needs without over-provisioning infrastructure. It results in increased efficiency and scalability, as providers can more rapidly respond to spikes in demand or changes in usage patterns, often utilizing automation and/or intelligent orchestration tools, such as Kubernetes, to distribute the load over their clusters. This also means better performance and reliability for customers, as their apps run on a highly available infrastructure that can allocate additional resources during periods of peak usage and reduce capacity when demand decreases, all while optimizing costs.

Particularly in multi-tenancy environments where several users work on a single physical infrastructure, resource pooling is important. In these environments, virtualization and containerization technologies help keep tenant data isolated and safe from each other, while leveraging the same underlying hardware. For instance, with a **Software-as-a-Service** (**SaaS**) model, resource pooling enables providers to deploy multiple client applications on the same aggregated servers, yielding very high operational savings by optimizing performance tuning based on consolidated demand patterns. Not only does this shared model increase efficiency, but it also drives innovation as providers can deploy updates and enhancements system-wide without any client-side configuration.

In conclusion, resource pooling in cloud computing plays a crucial role in promoting efficiency, scalability, and cost-effectiveness. It enables businesses to concentrate on building and enhancing their applications without the need to consider limiting hardware options and allows cloud providers to offer robust, responsive services that can satisfy diverse and changing requirements. This provider-customer symbiotic relationship is the foundation of the modern cloud, proving that resource pooling is at the heart of effective cloud application architecture.

Multi-tenancy

A crucial aspect of resource pooling is the concept of multi-tenancy. This design paradigm allows multiple users (or *tenants*) to access the same instance of a software application while keeping their data isolated. This isolation is paramount, particularly in industries where data security and compliance are non-negotiable.

Multi-tenancy can be compared to residential apartments in a building. While each apartment is distinct and tenants have private spaces, they all share the same infrastructure, that is, things like the building's roof, plumbing, and elevators. In cloud computing, numerous clients may use the same software application while their data remains secure and separate.

Another significant benefit of multi-tenancy is cost-effectiveness. When a vendor can offer a single instance of software to multiple clients, the overall operational costs decrease. This reduction is typically passed down to users in the form of lower subscription fees, making advanced technology accessible to even the smallest businesses.

However, designing software for multi-tenancy requires careful consideration to ensure that performance is consistent for all tenants and that one client's usage does not negatively impact another's experience. This aspect emphasizes the importance of robust cloud architecture and resource management.

Broad network access

Often, discussions of cloud architecture focus on the technical aspects, but we must also consider the connectivity and accessibility that the cloud provides. Broad network access ensures that cloud resources are available across the network and accessible through various devices, including smartphones, tablets, laptops, and even **Internet of Things** (**IoT**) devices.

This principle allows teams to work remotely, access applications anytime, and collaborate seamlessly across different regions. Whether you are a developer updating code from a coffee shop or a project manager reviewing documents from an airport lounge, the cloud enables that flexibility.

Importance of connectivity

The success of broad network access relies heavily on reliable internet connectivity. Cloud providers invest in global networks, establishing data centers in various locations to ensure low-latency access to resources. This global reach enables users from diverse geographical locations to connect with cloud services seamlessly, regardless of their physical location.

Companies like **Amazon Web Services** (**AWS**) and **Microsoft Azure** have extensive networks of data centers and edge locations. Edge computing, a recent trend, further enhances this capability by processing data closer to the point of origin, reducing latency and improving response times. For instance, streaming services can provide high-quality content to users regardless of their location because the content is cached at edge locations close to them.

However, security remains a critical concern when it comes to broad network access. With the increase in remote access points comes the risk of unauthorized entry. Organizations must employ robust security measures, including VPNs, encryption, and intrusion detection systems to safeguard sensitive data against threats.

Measured service

Another key foundational principle of cloud architecture is measured service. Cloud services are designed to monitor and auto control resource consumption, which allows providers and consumers to track the utilization level. This will enable organizations to not only manage their resources more effectively, but also budget for IT expenses altogether differently.

Do you know the monthly costs to keep the lights on, such as your electricity bill? You pay only for what you use with cloud services, which is a virtue of how much electricity the resources consume. Companies can better align their IT spending with their actual usage, thereby mitigating the risk of incurring large upfront costs on hardware that remains idle for the majority of its lifecycle.

Billing models

Multiple billing models, such as pay-per-use, reserved instances, or spot pricing are in line with this principle of measured service. Let us go over these models now:

- The simplest model is **pay-per-use**. You only pay for what you actually consume, billed on a pay-as-you-go basis. So, for example, if a company uses a virtual machine for 5 hours on one day and 15 hours the next, they are charged to the hour for that usage.
- **Reserved instances:** A billing model that provides capacity in advance for a specified duration for a lower cost compared to on-demand or pay-per-use. This is a cost-effective approach for businesses that can accurately forecast their future resource needs.
- **Spot pricing:** Spot pricing is a more flexible pricing model that enables users to purchase unused cloud capacity for a fraction of the cost. This model, however, has its risks, since the provider can terminate the instances depending on the market demand.

Figure 3.2 gives a brief comparison among the billing options:

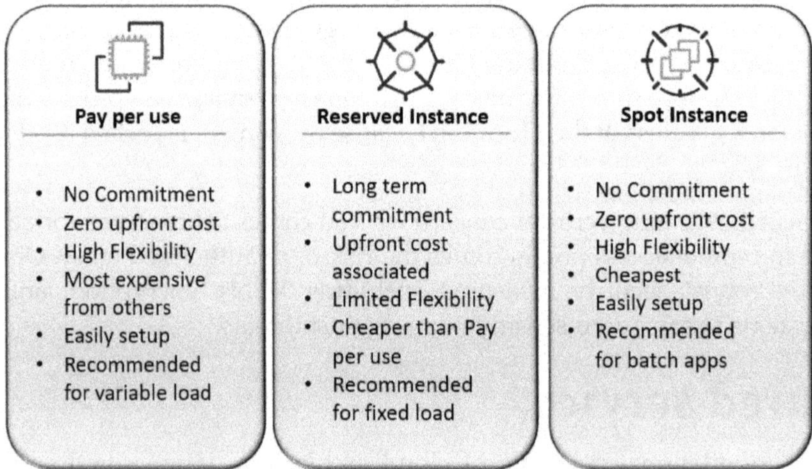

Figure 3.2: *Comparison among billing options*

Offering several billing models gives customers more choice over the plan that best fits their needs, improving financial flexibility and enabling effective resource utilization.

Cloud and cloud-native applications

Now that we have covered the core principles, let us talk about how they come together in cloud and cloud-native applications.

Cloud applications are those that run in the cloud, taking advantage of cloud services. But cloud-native applications go a step further. They are designed from the ground up to exploit the unique characteristics of the cloud.

Cloud-native applications embrace principles like micro services architecture, containerization, and declarative APIs. They are built to be resilient, manageable, and observable. Most importantly, they are designed to take full advantage of the cloud's elasticity and automation.

While transitioning a monolithic application to a cloud-native architecture, the difference in results is like night and day. The monolith was like a big, lumbering giant, powerful but slow to change and difficult to scale. The cloud-native version was like a swarm of agile, coordinated drones. We could update individual services without taking down the entire application, scale components independently, and recover from failures much more quickly.

Understanding cloud and cloud-native applications

Let us now understand more about cloud and cloud-native applications.

Cloud application

A cloud application is a software program that runs in a cloud environment, leveraging cloud infrastructure to provide scalability, reliability, and cost-effectiveness. These applications may be designed using virtual machines, storage, and networking resources provided by cloud service providers like AWS, Azure, and Google Cloud.

The key characteristics of cloud applications are as follows:

- Hosted on cloud infrastructure (IaaS, PaaS, or SaaS).
- Can be accessed via the internet.
- Scalable on demand.
- May follow a monolithic or microservices architecture.

Cloud-native application

A cloud-native application is designed and optimized specifically for cloud environments. Unlike traditional cloud applications, cloud-native applications leverage containerization, microservices, server-less computing, and DevOps practices to maximize efficiency.

The key characteristics of cloud-native applications are as follows:

- Built using microservices architecture.
- Designed for scalability, resilience, and flexibility.
- Uses containerization (Docker, Kubernetes).
- Implement DevOps and CI/CD automation.
- Serverless computing for efficient resource management.

Importance of cloud-native applications

The shift towards cloud-native applications is driven by the need for faster deployments, better scalability, and cost optimization. Organizations that adopt cloud-native architectures can innovate faster, respond to market demands more effectively, and enhance operational efficiency.

The key reasons why cloud-native applications matter are as follows:

- **Scalability:** Automatically scale applications based on demand.
- **Resilience:** Improve fault tolerance and self-healing capabilities.
- **Cost efficiency:** Pay only for the resources used.
- **Faster development and deployment:** Automate release cycles with DevOps practices.
- **Global accessibility:** Deploy applications across multiple regions with minimal latency.

Key components of cloud-native applications

Cloud-native applications incorporate several architectural components that differentiate them from traditional cloud applications. These include:

- **Microservices architecture:** Cloud-native applications use microservices, which break down applications into small, loosely coupled services that can be developed, deployed, and scaled independently.
- **Containerization:** Containers (for example, Docker) package applications and dependencies together, ensuring consistency across different environments.

- **Orchestration and management:** Kubernetes and other container orchestration tools automate the deployment, scaling, and management of containerized applications.
- **Server-less computing:** Server-less platforms like AWS Lambda and Google Cloud Functions allow developers to execute functions without managing infrastructure.
- **DevOps and Continuous Integration/Continuous Deployment (CI/CD):** CI/CD pipelines enable automated testing and deployment, reducing manual intervention and increasing reliability.
- **API-first approach:** APIs enable seamless communication between microservices and integration with third-party services.
- **Observability and monitoring:** Tools like Prometheus, Sumologic, and Dynatrace provide real-time monitoring and analytics to ensure application health.

Advantages and disadvantages of cloud and cloud-native applications

The advantages are as follows:

- **Scalability:** Automatically adjust resources based on traffic loads.
- **Resilience:** Self-healing capabilities ensure application uptime.
- **Faster time-to-market:** Accelerated development cycles with CI/CD pipelines.
- **Cost-effective:** Pay-as-you-go pricing reduces unnecessary expenditures.
- **Improved security:** Cloud providers offer robust security mechanisms.
- **High availability:** Redundancy and distributed architectures ensure uptime.

The disadvantages are as follows:

- **Complexity:** Managing microservices and containers requires skilled expertise.
- **Security challenges:** Requires strong governance to ensure compliance and security.
- **Migration complexity:** Refactoring traditional applications into cloud-native architecture is resource-intensive.
- **Monitoring overhead:** Requires advanced observability tools for tracking distributed services.

Use cases of cloud and cloud-native applications

Organizations across industries are leveraging cloud-native applications to enhance their digital capabilities. Here are some real-world use cases:

- **E-commerce platforms:** Cloud-native applications enable e-commerce giants like Amazon and Shopify to scale during peak shopping seasons while maintaining high availability.
- **Streaming services:** Netflix, Spotify, and YouTube rely on microservices and containerization to ensure smooth content delivery to millions of users.
- **Financial services:** Banks and fin-tech companies use cloud-native applications to provide secure and scalable online banking, fraud detection, and payment processing services.
- **Healthcare applications:** Cloud-native solutions help healthcare providers manage patient records, facilitate telemedicine, and ensure compliance with healthcare regulations like HIPAA.
- **AI and ML:** AI-driven applications leverage cloud-native technologies for large-scale data processing and predictive analytics.
- **IoT and smart devices:** Cloud-native architectures enable IoT applications to process and analyze vast amounts of sensor data in real-time.

Here is the quick comparison for Cloud and Cloud Native applications:

Feature	Traditional cloud app	Cloud native app
Architecture	Monolithic	Microservices
Scaling	Manual	Automated (Auto-scaling)
Deployment	Virtual machines	Containers/Kubernetes
Resilience	Limited	High (Self-healing, distributed)

***Table 3.1:** Comparison among cloud/cloud native apps*

Cloud-native architectures enable agility, faster deployments, and improved resilience, making them the preferred choice for modern applications.

Cloud architecture mentality

Now that we have reached the end of this chapter, it is essential to highlight that these principles are not merely academic theories. They are the backbone of how we think about and design cloud systems.

Here are some principles that need to be followed when you are architecting for the cloud:

- Build from day zero for scalability and elasticity.
- Focus on automation and self-service to offer agility.
- There are shared resources, and there is multi-tenancy.
- Always measure and optimize based on actual usage.
- Think about how your applications can be native to the clouds.

Keep in mind that cloud architecture is much more than just lifting and shifting your current applications to the cloud. It is about a new way to design and run applications to embrace the capabilities of the cloud. These principles will help guide you on your cloud journey going forward. They give you guidance for decisions about everything from services to use to how to architect your application.

Conclusion

In our exploration of the foundational elements of cloud architecture, we have unlocked some principles that empower organizations to take advantage of cloud computing. Scalability, elasticity, on-demand self-service, resource pooling, broad network access, and measured service combine to provide a robust foundation for building and managing cloud systems.

Every principle has a place in how organizations deploy, manage and optimize their clouds. These foundational concepts are more than just technical guidelines; they are strategic considerations that can revolutionize the way your organization approaches cloud adoption, and they can be a defining factor in realizing your vision for your cloud-native future as you journey into cloud architecture.

With this knowledge in hand, these principles enable you to become a capable cloud architect, designing systems that can meet the challenges of scaling and adapting to changing requirements in a dynamic technology environment. Spend some time at this fundamental level, as it will be the foundation for building your cloud knowledge and your company's cloud.

This is one such field where learning and adaptation will be ongoing. New technologies and best practices are continually shaping the cloud landscape. Moreover, by staying informed and adaptable, you can help ensure that your cloud architecture is well-positioned to remain resilient, efficient, and prepared to further your organization's objectives today and here.

In the next chapter, we will use these concepts as we explore service and deployment models within a cloud context.

Join our Discord space

CHAPTER 4
Services and Deployment Models

Introduction

Now that we are well-versed in the fundamental concepts and building blocks of cloud computing architecture, it is time to delve deeper into the world of cloud computing and explore the various types of services involved and supported deployment models, which are the backbone of this engaging technology. In this chapter, we will dive into the nuances of **Infrastructure as a Service** (**IaaS**), **Platform as a Service** (**PaaS**), and **Software as a Service** (**SaaS**), as well as the different deployment strategies available to organizations. By the end of this chapter, the reader will have a comprehensive understanding of these models and be better equipped to choose the right solutions for their specific needs.

Structure

In this chapter, we will go over the following topics:

- Detailed comparisons, advantages, and use-case scenarios
- Deployment strategies
- Application migration and modernization
- Case studies and real-world examples
- Future of cloud service and deployment models

Objectives

After finishing this chapter, the reader will possess a foundational and comprehensive understanding of the types of cloud services and deployment models, as well as a detailed understanding of practical scenarios where they can make informed decisions about the appropriate usage and applications of these strategies.

Detailed comparisons, advantages, and use-case scenarios

Let us now go over some detailed comparisons, advantages, and use-case scenarios among IaaS, PaaS, and SaaS.

Cloud services models

Let us take one step back and talk about the three main service models in cloud computing. Think of these as a layered cake of abstraction and control.

Infrastructure as a Service or IaaS

Let us say you are moving into a new apartment. The landlord gives you the basic structure, walls, floors, and a roof, but it is up to you to furnish it and make it livable. That is broadly what IaaS is in the cloud world.

With IaaS, you are provided with low-level computing resources, including virtual machines, storage, and networking, but you are responsible for administering the operating systems, middleware, and applications. It is like having your own data center but without all the physical hardware headaches.

The key features of IaaS are:

- Most flexible and powerful control.
- Pay-as-you-go pricing model.
- Scalability on demand.
- Lower capital expenditure on hardware.

You should choose IaaS if you are a start-up that wants to avoid costly initial hardware investments or an enterprise that wants to control your infrastructure while leaving it all to the cloud provider.

Real-world example

For instance, you start a small e-commerce business. With IaaS, you can quickly provision more instances of servers in peak shopping seasons (such as Black Friday) without spending on permanent hardware. After the rush is over, you can scale back down, paying for only what you used.

Platform as a Service or PaaS

Now, let us move up a layer. If IaaS is like renting an empty apartment, PaaS is like moving into all the amenities of a fully furnished one. You do not have to worry about the underlying infrastructure or even the operating system; that is all done for you.

What PaaS means is that it provides a platform for developers to build, run, and manage applications without the intricacy of underlying development (maintaining the underlying infrastructure). You basically get a pre-fabricated developer setup at your fingertips.

The key features of PaaS are:

- A focus on simplifying the development process.
- Integrated testing and deployment tools and services.
- Automatic scaling and load balancing.
- Decreased application time-to-market.

When to choose PaaS

If you are a developer or a company with a focus on developing applications at a fast pace, PaaS is best suited for your deployment. It lets you focus on writing code and creating features without getting lost in server management and configuration.

Real-world example

Imagine that you are a member of a team working on a new mobile app. With PaaS, you need to focus on coding the app's unique features and business logic, while the platform manages server configurations, database management, scaling, and other operating processes. That means you move faster and get your app in the market sooner than managing all the plumbing yourself and wasting time in boilerplate code.

Software as a Service or SaaS

SaaS sits on top of our cloud layer cake. This is sort of like renting a furnished apartment with a hotel concierge service that does it all for you. Just move in and enjoy; there is nothing to do.

- SaaS provides software applications over the Internet, eliminating the need for users to install and run the application locally, thereby enabling them to access and use the application on their computers. It is the most hands-off way to cloud computing.

The key features of SaaS are:

- Any device that connects to the internet.
- Automatic update and patch management.

- Pricing is based on consumption or use (per use or with a subscription).
- No local installation or maintenance required.

When to choose SaaS

Without installation efforts required, SaaS is the best fit for businesses seeking out instant application maintenance or upgrades. It is also good for apps that need web or mobile access, such as collaboration tools or **Customer Relationship Management** (CRM) systems.

Real-world example

Consider a small marketing agency using Google Workspace (formerly G Suite). Instead of maintaining their own email servers, document storage, and collaboration tools, they simply log in through their web browsers. Google handles all the backend infrastructure, security, and updates, allowing the agency to focus on its core business activities.

Comparing IaaS, PaaS, and SaaS

To help you visualize the differences between these service models, let us use an analogy of transportation options:

- **IaaS** is like leasing a car. You have control over where you go and how you get there, but you are not responsible for manufacturing or maintaining the vehicle.
- **PaaS** is akin to taking a taxi. You are still in charge of the destination, but you don't have to worry about driving or maintaining the vehicle.
- **SaaS** is comparable to using public transportation. The route is predetermined, and all you need to do is hop on and enjoy the ride. Each model offers a different balance of control and convenience. The choice depends on your specific needs, technical expertise, and business goals.

Refer to the following figure:

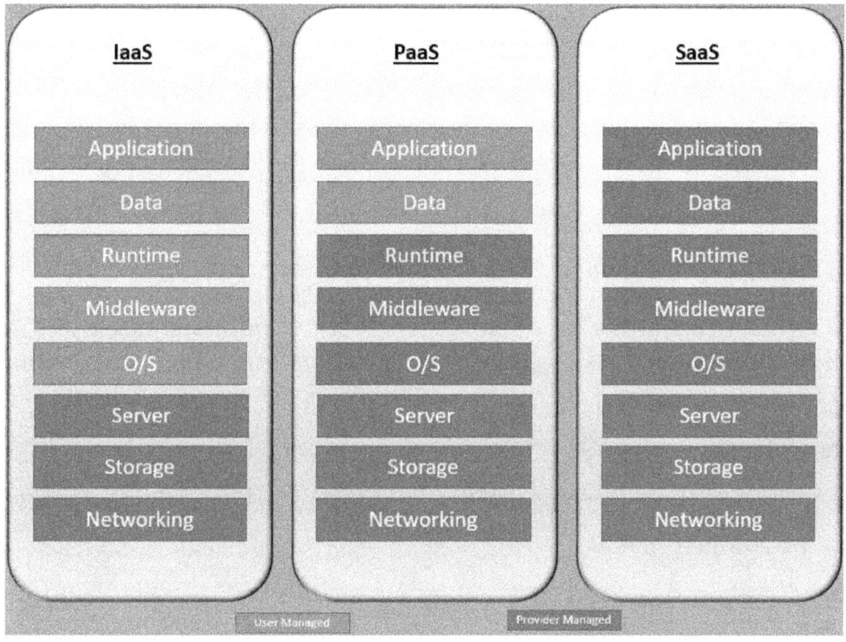

Figure 4.1: *Comparison among IaaS, PaaS, SaaS*

Let us also look into the detailed comparison of IaaS, PaaS, and SaaS on various parameters to identify key differences:

Aspect	IaaS	PaaS	SaaS
Definition	Provides raw infrastructure (compute, storage, networking)	Offers a platform to build, test, and deploy applications.	Delivers complete software applications over the internet.
Control level	Full control over OS, middleware, and runtime.	Control over application and data, not infrastructure.	Minimal control—just configure and use the app.
Use case	Custom hosting environments, lift-and-shift migration.	Rapid app development without managing servers.	Email, CRM, file storage—end-user applications.
User responsibility	Manage OS, runtime, apps, data, and middleware.	Focus on app and data; provider handles rest.	Only manage user access and data.
Best for	Enterprises needing control & custom setups	Developers building and deploying apps quickly	Businesses needing ready-to-use solutions

Table 4.1: *Comparison details on IaaS, PaaS, SaaS*

Deployment strategies

With the service models covered, let us now look into the different methods available for deploying these cloud services. Just as there is a wide variety of building types, from single-family dwellings to massive skyscrapers, so is cloud computing, as per taxonomy and cloud services.

Busy metropolis

Envision a city center that is rich yet accessible, with resources and services available at the fingertips of anyone who needs them. And that is exactly what a public cloud is in the digital world.

The key characteristics are:

- Multi-tenant, shared infrastructure.
- Pay-as-you-go pricing.
- Cloud, managed by third-party providers such as AWS, Google Cloud, or Microsoft Azure.
- Highly scalable and flexible.

The benefits are as follows:

- Economies of scale make them cost-effective.
- No need to pay upfront for hardware.
- Rapid deployment and scaling.

The challenges are as follows:

- Give up some control over underlying infrastructure.
- Risks of security issues arising from multi-tenancy.
- Regulatory challenges for specific industries.

When to choose public cloud

Public cloud is best for organizations that have high flexibility and scalability needs and is suitable for the following:

- Startups and small businesses with little to no IT resources.
- Companies with variable workloads.
- Applications with variable traffic patterns.

Real-world example

Imagine a media streaming service that has spikes of viewership during peak prime time hours or when new content is released. They can quickly scale up during those peak times by using a public cloud and downsize in quieter moments, providing a seamless user experience without overspending on permanent infrastructure.

Private cloud

If the public cloud is a crowded city, the private cloud is your gated community. It is a single-tenant cloud environment for your organization's exclusive use with an added layer of control and security.

The key characteristics are:

- Dedicated infrastructure for a single organization.
- It can either be hosted on premises or by a third-party provider.
- More control on security and compliance.
- Can be tailored to address unique organizational use cases.

The benefits are:

- Enhanced security and privacy.
- Performance with dedicated resources.
- Less cumbersome process in complying with industry regulations.

The challenges are:

- Higher upfront costs.
- Requires internal knowledge to set up and govern.
- Not as scalable as public cloud alternatives.

When to choose private cloud

Private cloud is a great option for organizations dealing with sensitive data, consistent workloads, or specific regulatory needs. It is especially great for:

- Financial institutions dealing with sensitive customer information.
- Organizations that are sensitive towards compliance like GDPR, HIPPA, CCPA and so on.
- Large enterprises that have the resources to set up their cloud infrastructure.

Real-world example

For example, a multi-country bank may choose a private cloud because it wants complete, end-to-end control over its customers' financial data. This enables them to implement compliance with financial regulations and tailor the infrastructure to their specific needs.

Hybrid cloud

A hybrid cloud is like having a vacation home next to your primary address. A hybrid cloud solution incorporates the advantages of both a public and private cloud, with data and applications shared between them.

The key characteristics are as follows:

- Consolidates public and private cloud resources.
- Enables workloads to migrate between clouds as appropriate.
- Provides flexibility in data storage and computing power.

The benefits are:

- Maintains a balance of security and scale.
- Efficient utilization of resources.
- Facilitates a gradual move to cloud computing.

The challenges are:

- Managing multiple environments can be cumbersome.
- Latency problems between clouds.
- Need to plan the data integration well.

When to choose hybrid cloud

Hybrid cloud is best suited for organizations that wish to utilize the scalability of public clouds while still controlling sensitive data. It is especially good for:

- Organizations running both critical and non-critical workloads.
- Organizations that have seasonal traffic spikes.
- Businesses wanting to gradually transition from on-premise infrastructure to cloud.

Real-world example

For example, a retail company might maintain its customer database and enterprise resource planning or payment processing systems on a private cloud for security purposes while hosting its e-commerce website with a public cloud provider. During the holiday shopping season, they can quickly add more public cloud resources to deal with more traffic and still maintain secure access to sensitive data in the private cloud.

Multi cloud

Hybrid cloud is like having a primary home and a vacation home, while multi-cloud is like owning properties in several different cities. It is about using multiple cloud providers to address different requirements.

The key characteristics are:

- Uses services from two or more cloud providers.
- Enables selection of best-of-breed services from multiple providers.
- Decreased reliance on a single vendor.

The benefits are:

- Avoids vendor lock-in.
- Optimize performance and cost across multiple providers.
- Improves disaster recovery operations.

The challenges are:

- More complicated management.
- Potential issues with data consistency across platforms.
- Requires expertise in multiple cloud environments.

When to choose multi-cloud

Multi-cloud strategies enable organizations to avoid vendor lock-in, extracting better value from cloud infrastructure tailored to individual requirements. It is ideal for:

- Enterprise deployments with large, heterogeneous IT requirements.
- Businesses seeking to reduce the chance of service outages.
- Organizations requiring specific services from different providers.

Real-world example

Perhaps a global technology company is using AWS for its core infrastructure, Google Cloud for its machine learning capabilities, and Microsoft Azure for its productivity tools. This enables them to benefit from the strengths of each provider while also preventing over-reliance on any one vendor.

Application migration and modernization

While we analyze those various service and deployment models, it is also vital to cover a common challenge for many organizations: running existing applications in the cloud. This process, known as application migration and modernization, is like remodeling your house to meet modern standards.

Six Rs of cloud migration

From a cloud migration perspective, there are typically six kinds of strategies (known as the 6 Rs) for how to move your applications into the cloud. They are:

- **Re-host (Lift and Shift):** This involves moving all your data and applications from one environment to another without modifying their configuration. You move the app as-is to the cloud. Often used for applications that are not cloud native.
- **Re-platforming (Lift, Tinker, and Shift):** This approach involves making several cloud optimizations to achieve a measurable benefit without altering the core architecture of the application.
- **Repurchase (Drop and Shop):** This implies migrating to an alternative product, most of the time, migrating to a SaaS platform.
- **Refactor/Re-architect:** This involves reimagining how the application is designed and built, typically leveraging cloud-native capabilities.
- **Retire:** This means eliminating unneeded applications.
- **Retain:** This implies maintaining certain apps on the site (if they are not prepared to be migrated or they do not have a business reason to migrate), usually due to compliance needs, data residency requirements or other such business needs.

Choosing a migration strategy

Your strategy will vary depending on many factors like your application complexity, your business goals, and your timeline. Let us consider a few scenarios.

Scenario 1: Legacy monoliths

Let us say you have this old monolithic CRM system that is critical for your business, but it is becoming more and more difficult to maintain and scale. In this scenario:

- **Option A- Re-host:** You could re-host this application to IaaS. This would be the fastest option, but it would fail to leverage cloud-native capabilities.
- **Option B- Refactor:** You may consider re-architecting the application into micro services and deploy it on a PaaS solution. It would be more time and resource intensive, but would produce a more scalable, cloud-native application.
- **Option C- Repurchase:** The third option brings us to full circle. You can purchase a new SaaS CRM solution to replace the entire system (Salesforce would be a prime candidate). This would be faster than refactoring and transfer maintenance tasks to the SaaS provider.

Which option is best for you depends on in-house development capabilities, budget, long-term strategy, and other factors.

Scenario 2: Data-intensive analytics application

Say you have a data analytics app that processes a large amount of data but only runs periodically. In that case:

- **Option A- Re-platform:** Move the application to a cloud platform and migrate to managed services for the database. This would lower the amount of overhead you would have for managing the database, but still give you control over the application.
- **Option B- Refactor:** You might change the application's configuration so that it separates the data processing tasks from the application code by using serverless computing. This would ensure that it is cost-optimised since you would only pay for compute resources when the application is running.

The decision here may depend on how frequently the application runs and how predictable its resource usage is.

Modernization best practices

The strategy you choose may differ, but here are some best practices to remember:

- **Assessment:** Start with a thorough assessment of your application, their dependencies, and your business needs prior to determining a migration strategy.
- **Prioritize applications:** Not all applications should be synchronized in one shot. Implement less critical applications to build experience and confidence.
- **Think about security from day one:** Security should be an integral part of your migration plan, not an afterthought.
- **Data migration planning:** The next step is data migration. The transfer. particularly of large datasets, has to be well planned.
- **Automate:** Employ infrastructure-as-code and automated deployment pipelines to enable a more scalable and reproducible migration.
- **Plan migration:** Assess your current environment and plan a migration strategy that takes advantage of cloud-native features.

Note: **Migration is not a one-time event, but a continuous process of optimizations and improvements.**

Case studies and real-world examples

To illustrate all of these ideas, let us explore some real-world examples of companies successfully deploying different cloud services and deployment models.

Netflix and going all-in on the public cloud

Netflix is one of the extreme examples of a company that has gone all in on the public cloud. In 2008, Netflix experienced a significant database corruption and came to understand that the limitations of their data centers would not be sufficient for them moving forward. This incident was the catalyst for their decision to move to the cloud.

The challenge: Netflix required a scalable and dependable infrastructure that could accommodate the enormous volatility of user demand, which the soon–to be streaming service underwent, as it rapidly grew.

The solution: Netflix decided to move all its streaming operations to **Amazon Web Services** (**AWS**), a public cloud provider. They implemented a microservices architecture and used several AWS services, such as:

- Amazon EC2 compute resources
- Amazon S3 for content storage
- **Database service:** Amazon DynamoDB
- AWS Lambda for serverless compute

The result: Migration to the public cloud allowed Netflix to provide:

- Significantly better scalability for millions of concurrent streams.
- Building redundancy for increased reliability.
- Quicker time-to-market for new features.
- Massive cost savings versus running their own global data centers.

This case study illustrates how a public cloud solution can deliver the necessary scalability and flexibility to a rapidly growing global service.

Capital One with a hybrid cloud journey

Citing the need for innovation, as well as security and regulatory compliance, a major U.S. bank, Capital One, opted for the hybrid cloud over the public cloud.

The challenge: Capital One faced the challenge of modernizing its IT infrastructure in order to increase agility and customer service, all while still adhering to the strict security and compliance standards of the financial industry.

The solution: Take a hybrid cloud approach at Capital One:

- They also had a private cloud for sensitive customer data and core banking functions.
- They used public cloud services (mostly AWS) for customer-facing applications and data analytics.
- They adopted a cloud-first approach for new applications, building them to be natively cloud-based from the ground up.

The outcome: Thanks to this hybrid approach, Capital One accomplished:

- Faster development and deployment of new features.
- Enhanced data analytics capabilities.

- Advance cloud security tools enhances the security.
- Ensured adherence to financial regulations.

This case study illustrates how one organization leveraged a hybrid cloud strategy to strike a balance between the scalability and cost-savings of public cloud with security and compliance requirements of sensitive industries.

Spotify and multi-cloud for resilience

Adding cloud computing to the model overhead, Spotify, the popular music streaming service, chose a multi-cloud strategy to provide its service uptime and performance.

The challenge: Spotify had to ensure high availability and performance for its global audience without over-relying on a single cloud provider.

The solution: Spotify adopted a multi-cloud strategy:

- They adopted GCP as their main cloud provider for most of their services.
- They have a dedicated presence on AWS for certain use cases as well as a backup.
- They have created tools to make their infrastructure cloud-agnostic, meaning that they can run workloads on any one cloud provider.

The outcome: Some results of Spotify's multi-cloud strategy include:

- Better service reliability and disaster recovery capabilities.
- Take advantage of the different strengths of the providers to optimize performance.
- Decreased risk of vendor lock-in.
- Greater negotiating strength with cloud providers.

This demonstrates how a multi-path strategy can add extra resilience and flexibility for global-scale services.

Decision framework for choosing the right model

So, with so many options available, how do you pick the appropriate service and deployment model for your organization? This is a framework to help you decide:

- **Assess your current state:**
  - o Which apps do you have running right now?
  - o How much do you currently pay for your infrastructure?
  - o What are your frustrations with your current setup?

- **Define your goals:**
  - Are you trying to cut down on expenditures?
  - Are you lacking in scalability?
  - Is quicker time-to-market a goal?
  - What are your specific security or compliance requirements?
- **Evaluate your resources:**
  - How much cloud experience do you possess internally?
  - Can you afford the initial investments upfront?
  - How much control do you need on your infrastructure?
- **Consider your workloads:**
  - Do your workloads have constant or variable nature?
  - Do you have any legacy applications that need special treatment?
  - Are there restrictions on where your applications' data can reside?
- **Assess security and compliance requirements:**
  - What is the nature of the data that you are dealing with?
  - Do you need to comply with industry-specific regulations?
  - How sensitive is your IP?
- **Think long-term:**
  - How do you anticipate your needs growing over the years?
  - Are you making any drastic changes to your business model or application architecture?

Based on your answers to these questions, you can start to narrow down your options. For example:

- If you need maximum control and have strict security requirements, a private cloud or hybrid solution might be best.
- If you are a small company looking for cost-effectiveness and quick deployment, public cloud services might be ideal.
- If you have a mix of sensitive and non-sensitive workloads, a hybrid approach could offer the best balance.
- If you are a large enterprise with diverse needs and want to avoid vendor lock-in, a multi-cloud strategy might be worth considering.

Here is a cloud service and deployment model decision matrix for easy reference:

Decision area	Key questions	Implications	Recommended directions
Assess current state	• What apps are running now? • How much are your spending on infra?	• Understand dependencies, budget, and operational gaps	• Use as baseline-for fitmen; legacy heavy = Hybrid or IaaS, cost concerns = SaaS or PaaS
Define goals	• Cut down expenses? • Need scalability? • Faster time-to-market? • Security requirements?	• Goals define constraints and trade-offs	• Use as baseline for tit-ment: legacy heavi/yrr id or IaaS: cost concerns = SaaS or Hybrid
Evaluate internal resources	• Cloud skills in-house? • Budget for upfront investment? • Required infra control?	• Skill level influences support models, cost and control trade-offs	• Low cloud skills = SaaS • Strong infra team = IaaS • Limited budget = Public Cloud
Consider workloads	• Variable or static workloads? • Any legacy apps? • Data residency requirements?	• Impacts elasticity and data governance	• High sensitivity/ compliance = Private Cloud • Moderate = Hybrid • Low = Public
Think long-term	• Projected growth? • Business/app-model shifts?	• Helps future-proof investments and avoid lock-in	• Dynamic roadmap = Multi-cloud • Stable = PaaS/ SaaS • High customization: IaaS

Table 4.2: *Decision matrix for cloud service deployment*

Remember, cloud adoption is not an all-or-nothing proposition. Many organizations start with a hybrid approach, gradually moving more workloads to the cloud as they become more comfortable with the technology and processes.

Future of cloud service and deployment models

As we complete our exploration of cloud service and deployment models, it is going to be worth looking ahead to some emerging trends that may shape the future of cloud computing:

- **Edge computing:** As IoT devices become widespread, we have a growing trend to process data where it is produced. This may result in new mixed models of cloud and edge computing.
- **Serverless:** Although not new, serverless is gaining momentum and may change the face of the business.
- **The phenomenon of AI and ML as a service:** All cloud providers are now offering advanced AI and ML services, making it more accessible to all organizations.
- **Industry-specific cloud:** Clouds specific to industries, like healthcare or financial services, are starting to take off, as they potentially offer more specific solutions for industry-specific use cases and regulations.
- **Green cloud computing:** With a rising emphasis on environmental sustainability, green cloud design aims to make cloud computing energy-efficient and sustainable.

Trends that indicate that the cloud landscape will just keep changing, offering a broader selection to enterprises of all sizes.

Conclusion

We have traversed quite a distance in this chapter, from understanding IaaS, PaaS, and SaaS as broad categories of service models, to the different types of deployment strategies such as public, private, hybrid, and multi-cloud. We have observed how different organizations relied on these models to reach their business goals; we have kept a framework for your own decisions regarding cloud.

Remember, there is no one-size-fits-all in cloud computing. The ideal solution for your company will hinge on the needs, budget, resources, and objectives of your organization. Whether you are just getting started in the cloud or optimizing an existing cloud strategy, keeping up with available options and staying agile as your needs and technology landscape evolve is key.

As we look forward to the next chapter on architectural patterns for scalability and resiliency, remember that these service and deployment models lay the groundwork for the robust, scalable cloud applications we will build upon them. How you choose at this ground level will drive the architectural decisions we will discuss in the following chapters.

CHAPTER 5
Scalability Patterns

Introduction

To discuss the scalability patterns, let us picture a house being constructed. It is not just any house, but a house that seems to miraculously adjust its size depending on how many humans need to reside within its walls at any moment. Sounds impossible, right? Well, in the case of cloud computing, this is just what the goal of our applications is.

In this chapter, we are going to check the architecture patterns that help make your cloud application scalable, in order to match the dwellers of your imaginary growing house. By successfully handling a sudden burst of users or a steady increase in data size, these patterns will be your proven way to go.

Recall the terms of service controversy on New Year's Eve 2012, when Instagram users expressed significant concern and backlash over the number of photos they uploaded. That is precisely the kind of situation we are trying to avoid here. So, without further ado, let us now learn patterns to keep your applications up and running, no matter how popular they become.

Structure

In this chapter, we will go over the following topics:

- Importance of scalability in cloud architecture
- Load balancing

- Auto scaling
- Partitioning
- Caching
- Microservices architecture
- Bringing it all together

Objectives

After finishing this chapter, the reader will be well versed in the key points and concepts of scalability, and what constitutes creating a scalable application that can sustain the load on demand during high peaks. The reader will also learn about architecting a cloud application that is robust enough to respond to dynamic needs, load, and traffic reaching the application.

Importance of scalability in cloud architecture

Before we jump into the specific patterns, we should discuss why scalability is so important when using a cloud. Think of a situation where a small e-commerce startup successfully delivered a visually appealing and feature-rich application, but with insufficient emphasis on scalability. When their product became a viral craze during the holiday season, their entire system collapsed under the load. It was a painful lesson to learn, but it instilled the critical lesson of incorporating scalability into the architecture from the first day.

In the cloud, scalability is not just nice to have; it is a core necessity. A well-designed cloud application can handle increased load without a significant performance degradation. It is about being ready for success so that when your moment comes, your infrastructure can handle the demand.

Now, let us familiarize ourselves with the scalability patterns that are going to get us there.

Load balancing

Load balancing is like hosting a busy restaurant. When new customers (user requests, in cloud paradigm) come in, you want to make sure you do not overwhelm any single waiter (or server). Rather, you have all guests spread evenly throughout all the available staff so that service can go as planned.

Load balancing is distributing incoming network traffic across multiple servers, in technical terms. This prevents any one server from being overwhelmed, leading to a crash, bad performance, or loss of service.

Working of load balancers

The following steps explain the working of load balancers:

1. All incoming client requests go through a single entry point.
2. These requests hit the load balancer.
3. The load balancer distributes requests among available servers based on pre-defined algorithms.
4. Servers handle those requests and return responses through the load balancer to the client.

Types of load balancers

Let us now understand the different types of load balancers:

- **Hardware load balancers:** These are a specific type of hardware/physical load balancers. They are powerful and fast, but can be costly and less flexible than software solutions.
- **Software load balancers:** They are applications running on commodity hardware or in the cloud. They provide more flexibility and ease of cost in most cases.
- **DNS load balancing:** This technique distributes loads between several devices over the **Domain Name System** (**DNS**). It is easy but not as accurate as other approaches. It relies on DNS caching and lacks real-time awareness of server health or load, often leading to uneven traffic distribution or requests hitting offline nodes.

Here are load balancers from a different lens of categorization:

- **Layer 4 load balancer (Transport layer):** Operates at the TCP/UDP level of the OSI model.
    - **Characteristics:**
        - Distributes traffic based on IP address, TCP port, and protocol.
        - Quick and efficient, as it does not look at the contents of the packets.
        - Good for raw data throughput (VoIP, gaming, streaming, and so on).
    - **Use cases:**
        - High-performance apps that have simple routing needs.
        - Backend traffic or internal microservices communication.

- **Layer 7 load balancer (Application layer):** Operates at the HTTP/HTTPS level of the OSI model.
  - **Characteristics:**
    - **Content-based routes:** URL path, host headers, cookies, and so on.
    - This will support SSL termination, caching, compression, sticky sessions.
    - Can perform advanced routing like path-based or host-based routing.
  - **Use cases:**
    - Web applications, REST APIs.
    - Multi-tenant SaaS applications that require tenant-aware routing.
    - A/B testing, blue-green deployments.
- **Geo load balancer (Global load balancer):** Load balances geo-based traffic between regions or continents.
  - **Characteristics:**
    - Manages to send traffic based on the geographic location, latency or health of the user.
    - Uses DNS-based load balancing or Anycast routing.
    - Provides high availability and disaster recovery globally.
  - **Use cases:**
    - Applications that have users all over the world.
    - Active–active deployments across multiple regions.
- **Private load balancer (Internal load balancer):** Used for internal traffic only, typically within a VPC or subnet.
  - **Characteristics:**
    - Not exposed to the internet.
    - Useful for service-to-service communications in microservices/ backend.
  - **Use cases:**
    - Internal microservices and/or backend.
    - Supporting multi-tier app architectures (e.g. web → API → DB)

Putting all categorization together

Refer to *Table 5.1:*

Type	Layer	Use case	Examples
Hardware-based	L4/L7	On-prem enterprise, legacy systems	F5, Citrix ADC
Software-based	L4/L7	Cloud-native apps, Kubernetes, SaaS	NGINX, Envoy, HAProxy, AWS ALB/NLB
DNS-based	DNS	Geo-routing, failover, multi-region	Route 53, Azure Traffic Manager, NS1

Table 5.1: *Load balancers categorization*

The following figure illustrates the load balancer categorizations:

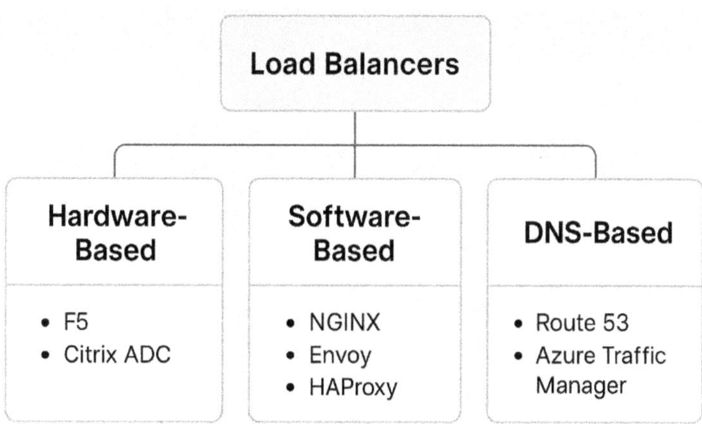

Figure 5.1: *Load balancers categorizations*

Using the different load balancers

Table 5.2 gives instances of when to use which load balancer:

Scenario	LB recommendation
Global user base with multi-region app	DNS-Based (with health checks)
Modern SaaS app on Kubernetes	Software-Based (e.g., Ingress + Envoy)
High throughput, low latency backend	L4 Load Balancer (NLB, HAProxy)
Web app with tenant-aware routing	L7 Load Balancer (ALB, Envoy)
Legacy app in datacenter	Hardware-Based LB

Table 5.2: *Load balancers usage scenarios*

Load balancing algorithms

One of the most important aspects of your load balancer is the algorithm that it uses to distribute traffic. Here are some common algorithms:

- **Round robin:** In the simplest methods, the requests are sent to each server one by one. It is like dealing cards around a table; everyone gets their fair share.
- **Least connections:** This algorithm forwards new requests to the server with the fewest open connections. This is especially useful in case you have servers with different capacities.
- **IP hash:** This algorithm determines which server will receive the request based on the IP address of the client. This is helpful to guarantee that a client always connects to the same server, which may matter for maintaining session data.
- **Weighted round robin:** Simply like round robin, but some servers have a high weight, and so they receive more requests. This comes in handy when you have servers of different capacities.

Some implementations that are specific to the cloud are:

- AWS elastic load balancing
- Azure load balancer
- Google cloud load balancing

Note: **Load balancing is widely the first line of defense to use when designing a scalable architecture. This is like the foundation to a house nail this step, and you are all set up for success.**

Implementing load balancing in the cloud

Most major cloud providers offer load balancing as a service. For example, **Amazon Web Services** (**AWS**) provides elastic load balancing, which automatically distributes incoming application traffic across multiple targets, such as EC2 instances, containers, and IP addresses.

Here is a simple example of how you might set up a load balancer in AWS using the AWS CLI:

```
"aws elbv2 create-load-balancer --name my-load-
balancer --subnets subnet-12345678 subnet-87654321 --security-groups sg-
12345678"
```

This command creates a new application load balancer named "`my-load-balancer`" in the specified subnets and security group. Remember, while load balancers are powerful tools for improving scalability, they are not a silver bullet. They need to be combined with other scalability patterns and best practices for optimal results.

Auto scaling

Auto scaling is like having a team of builders all working with the magic of expanding your house to instantly add more rooms, for increasing guests, and then, when they leave, remove those rooms from the house. In the cloud, auto-scaling would dynamically change the number of compute resources in your application depending on the current load.

Consider the news website that gets massive traffic spikes whenever major events happen. Auto-scaling here will be a revolution! When things are slow, it can operate on a bare minimum number of servers, thus saving on cost. But when breaking news strikes and traffic swells, more servers would automatically spin up to handle the load. It is like watching a clockwork mechanism.

Types of auto-scaling

The different types of auto-scaling are:

- **Horizontal scaling (Scaling out):** Adding more instances of a resource. Adding more web servers to process more traffic, for example.
- **Vertical scaling (Scaling up):** Increase capability within an existing resource such as upgrading a server from 2 CPU to 4 CPU.
- **Predictive scaling:** Using historical data to determine and anticipate the scaling needs and configure accordingly.
- **Scheduled scaling:** Scale the resources based on a fixed schedule for anticipated events like Black Friday and Cyber Monday.
- **Dynamic scaling:** Configure the scaling rules based on usage metrics for CPU, RAM, and other such parameters.

When we work with the cloud, we tend to apply horizontal scaling first since we gain more flexibility and resilience from that approach.

Auto-scaling triggers

Auto-scaling can be configured to respond to a variety of metrics, such as:

- **CPU utilization:** New instances are created when the average CPU usage across your instances reaches a defined threshold.
- **Network in/out:** Based on the volume of network traffic that your application is processing.
- **Custom metrics:** You can add your own metrics, such as how many active user sessions, or how deep a message queue is.
- **Time-based:** Scaling according to expected peak times. For example, an e-commerce website might scale every weekend.

Categorisation of auto scaling

We can categorize auto scaling based on **trigger mechanisms**, **resource types**, and **goals**.

Table 5.3 explains the trigger-based categorization:

Type	Characteristics	Use cases
Reactive	Based on thresholds	E-commerce during flash sales
Scheduled	Fixed intervals (daily, weekly)	Backup jobs or predictable daily load
Predictive	AI/ML-based scaling prediction	Banking systems with steady user peaks

Table 5.3: *Trigger based auto scaling*

Table 5.4 explains the resource-based categorization:

Resource type	AWS examples	Use cases
Compute	EC2, Lambda, Fargate scaling	Web servers, background workers
Container	EKS (Kubernetes), ECS, AKS	Microservices, CI/CD agents
Database	Aurora Auto Scaling, DynamoDB	Data-heavy APIs, real-time analytics
Serverless	Auto scaling built-in	Event-driven apps, cron jobs, chatbots

Table 5.4: *Resource based auto scaling*

Implementation considerations

Here are some considerations for implementations:

- Choose appropriate metrics that truly reflect your application's load.
- Set reasonable thresholds to avoid unnecessary scaling events.
- Implement proper monitoring and alerting to keep track of scaling activities.

Table 5.5 explains the recommended scaling strategy for various situations:

Situation	Recommended scaling strategy
Burst traffic with unpredictable timing	Dynamic/Reactive auto scaling
Predictable usage patterns (for example, 9-to-5 workers)	Scheduled or predictive auto scaling
Stateless microservices (containerized)	Horizontal scaling with HPA (K8s) or ECS/Fargate
Multi-tenant SaaS architecture	Combine predictive + dynamic for balance

Table 5.5: *When to use what*

Note: Always combine auto scaling with observability (Prometheus, CloudWatch, and so on) and use circuit breakers to prevent crashing under load.

Implementing auto scaling

Let us go through an example of implementing or setting up on AWS using EC2 auto scaling groups. Follow the given steps:

1. **Launch configuration:**

```
aws ec2 create-launch-template \
  --launch-template-name my-web-app-template \
  --version-description "v1" \
  --launch-template-data '{
    "ImageId": "ami-0abcdef1234567890",
    "InstanceType": "t3.micro",
    "SecurityGroupIds": ["sg-0abcd1234efgh5678"],
    "KeyName": "my-keypair"
  }'
```

   This will ensure the following:

   a. **create-launch-template**: Creates a reusable blueprint for launching EC2 instances.

   b. **--launch-template-name**: Gives it a human-readable name.

   c. **--version-description**: Versioning helps when you later want to modify your instance settings.

   d. **--launch-template-data**: Contains the actual instance configuration like:

      i. **AMI ID (ImageId)**: Replace with your region-specific Linux/Windows AMI.

      ii. **Instance type**: t3.micro is free tier eligible and good for demo/testing.

      iii. **Security group**: Needed for networking rules (SSH, HTTP, and so on).

      iv. **Key pair**: Used for SSH access to the EC2 instances (must already exist in your AWS account).

2. **Create autoscaling group:**

```
aws autoscaling create-auto-scaling-group \
  --auto-scaling-group-name my-asg \
  --launch-template LaunchTemplateName=my-web-app-
template,Version=1 \
  --min-size 2 \
```

```
  --max-size 10 \
  --desired-capacity 2 \
  --vpc-zone-identifier «subnet-abc123, subnet-def456»
```

This will ensure the following:

a. **create-auto-scaling-group**: Tells AWS how many EC2s to launch and where.
b. **--launch-template**: Links to the template we just created.
c. **--min-size/--max-size**: Boundaries for scaling.
d. **--desired-capacity**: Initial number of instances to launch immediately.
e. **--vpc-zone-identifier**: Comma-separated list of subnet IDs where EC2s will be launched.

3. **Attach scaling policies:**

```
aws autoscaling put-scaling-policy \
  --auto-scaling-group-name my-asg \
  --policy-name cpu-scale-out \
  --scaling-adjustment 1 \
  --adjustment-type ChangeInCapacity
```

   This will ensure the following:

   a. **put-scaling-policy:** Adds a rule to increase capacity.
   b. **scaling-adjustment: Adds** 1 instance when triggered.
   c. **adjustment-type: `ChangeInCapacity`** means relative increase (vs. exact or percentage).

4. **Link policy to a CloudWatch alarm:**

```
aws cloudwatch put-metric-alarm \
  --alarm-name HighCPU \
  --metric-name CPUUtilization \
  --namespace AWS/EC2 \
  --statistic Average \
  --period 300 \
  --threshold 70 \
  --comparison-operator GreaterThanThreshold \
  --dimensions Name=AutoScalingGroupName,Value=my-asg \
  --evaluation-periods 2 \
  --alarm-actions arn:aws:autoscaling:region:account-
id:scalingPolicy:policy-id:autoScalingGroupName/my-asg:policyName/
cpu-scale-out
```

Here, we have:

a. **Alarm name:** Human-readable name.
b. **Metric:** CPU utilization from EC2.
c. **Period:** Every 5 minutes (300s).
d. **Threshold:** 70% CPU.
e. **Evaluation periods**: Trigger if condition met for 2 consecutive periods.
f. **Alarm action:** ARN of the scaling policy (you get this ARN when running the previous put-scaling-policy command).

To test the preceding code, one can use AWS cloud shell, as it offers a hassle free way to execute the code. Here are the other features:

- No need to install AWS CLI locally.
- Authenticated with your logged-in IAM user.
- Has access to your account's AWS resources immediately.

To use AWS cloud shell, follow these steps:

1. Go to AWS Console.
2. Click **CloudShell** (top right).
3. Type your CLI code step-by-step.
4. Observe the results directly in the terminal.

Once you are done testing make sure to clean up the resources, so that you are not charged.

For clean up, use the following code:

```
aws autoscaling delete-auto-scaling-group --auto-scaling-group-name my-
asg --force-delete
aws ec2 delete-launch-template --launch-template-name my-web-app-template
```

Partitioning

In the world of cloud applications, scale is not just a nice-to-have; it is survival. Whether you are building a nimble SaaS product or a monolithic enterprise beast that serves millions, one architectural concept silently powers your ability to grow fast without falling apart: **partitioning**.

Let us take a deep dive into what partitioning means, its different flavours, how it plays out in real-world environments, and why it is the silent hero behind high-performance systems.

At its core, partitioning is the act of breaking data (and sometimes the workload itself) into smaller, more manageable pieces. Think of it like splitting a giant pizza into slices. Each slice is easier to handle, and everyone can eat at once. In computing terms, partitioning allows systems to:

- Scale horizontally
- Improve performance
- Reduce contention and bottlenecks
- Isolate failures and recovery scopes

It is not just a backend optimization; it is a fundamental building block for designing cloud-native applications.

Types of partitioning

Let us now explore the different types of partitioning:

- **Horizontal partitioning (Sharding):** When data is broken up between servers with a partition key. User data, for instance, may be split by the first letter of the username. The features are as follows:
    - Data is split by rows.
    - Each shard holds a subset of the data (for example, users A-M in one shard, N-Z in another).
    - Best for scale-out strategies.
    - Common in SaaS apps, multi-tenant systems, or social media platforms.
- **Vertical partitioning:** This is where different data types are stored on different servers. One common approach is to design database to separate tables. The features are as follows:
    - Data is split by columns.
    - Different tables or services handle different sets of attributes.
    - **Example:** Separating user profile info from authentication data.
    - Useful for isolating high-traffic columns or data with different performance/storage needs.
- **Functional partitioning:** Here, your application is divided into isolated services on the basis of functionality. It is the core principle behind microservices architecture. The features are as follows:
    - Systems are split based on domain or functionality.
    - Microservices are a classic example (e.g., orders, payments, inventory).
    - Great for aligning teams and independently scaling subsystems.

Table 5.6 features the different partitioning types and their use cases:

Partitioning type	Characteristics	Common use cases
Horizontal	Even distribution, scalable, fault-isolated	Multi-region user bases, high read / write systems
Vertical	Independent optimization, tighter control	Data privacy (**Personal Identifiable Information** or **PII**), mixed storage needs
Functional	Modular, team-aligned, scalable independently	Microservices, large enterprise systems

***Table 5.6**: Partitioning characteristics and use cases*

Partitioning is not just technical; it is very strategic also. Think partitioning from the perspective from ownership and access, such as:

- **Explicit partitioning:** This is by design defined by the developer, wherein developer chooses how the data is split.
- **Implicit partitioning:** This by design is off loaded to cloud or database services. For example, Cosmos DB's automatic partitioning on a defined partition key.
- **Hybrid partitioning:** Combination of the preceding approaches, wherein some are defined in the app and other scheme is off-loaded to services.

Let us take a look at how partitioning technique differs in SQL v NoSQL databases:

Feature	RDBMS (Relational)	NoSQL
Schema	Fixed schema	Flexible schema
Partitioning support	Manual or via features like table partitioning	Built-in in many systems (for example, MongoDB shards, Cassandra rings)
Partitioning goal	Performance tuning, archival, indexing	Scalability, availability
Example use	Azure SQL Database with table partitioning	Azure Cosmos DB with partition keys

***Table 5.7**: Partitioning techniques*

Partitioning is trickier in traditional RDBMS because of rigid schema enforcement and joins. NoSQL systems are naturally built for scale and typically require partitioning to function.

Implementing partitioning

Let us look at how we can create a partition using a SQL database (Azure SQL DB, Amazon RDS).

Suppose we have a millions of records (let us say e-commerce orders) stored in a table, and we want to partition the table based on **Order Date** for efficient queries and maintenance. Follow the given steps:

1. **Create a partition function:**

```
CREATE PARTITION FUNCTION pfOrderRange (DATE)
AS RANGE LEFT FOR VALUES (
    '2023-01-01', '2023-04-01', '2023-07-01', '2023-10-01'
);
```

2. **Create a partition scheme:**

```
CREATE PARTITION SCHEME psOrderRange
AS PARTITION pfOrderRange
ALL TO ([PRIMARY]);
```

3. **Create a partition table:**

```
CREATE TABLE Orders
(
    OrderID INT PRIMARY KEY,
    OrderDate DATE,
    CustomerID INT,
    Amount DECIMAL(10, 2)
)
ON psOrderRange (OrderDate);
```

The benefits are as follows:

- Efficient range scans on date filters.
- Easy archival of older partitions.
- Lower index fragmentation.

Key points to remember for partitioning

Partitioning warrants proper due diligence as it is not all sunshine and scale. Poor design can lead to:

- **Hot partitions:** Where one partition receives disproportionate traffic (for example, timestamp-based keys in IoT data).

- **Skewed data:** Some partitions grow faster than others, leading to storage or performance imbalance.
- **Cross-partition joins:** These can destroy performance especially in RDBMS. Design your access patterns carefully.
- **Too many partitions:** Causes overhead in metadata and query planning.

Challenges of partitioning

While partitioning can greatly improve scalability, it also introduces some challenges:

- **Data consistency:** Ensuring data is consistent across partitions can be complex.
- **Repartitioning:** As your data grows, you may need to repartition, which can be a complex operation.
- **Query complexity:** Queries that span multiple partitions can become more complex.

Always test partitioning schemes under realistic workloads and continuously monitor distribution.

Partitioning is not just about faster queries. It is about architecting for growth, resilience, and autonomy. Whether you are managing gigabytes of customer data or petabytes of telemetry logs, partitioning will show up, either because you planned for it or because your system eventually demanded for it.

Caching

If you have ever complained at a loading spinner or stared blankly at a *Loading...* message, you have felt the pain that caching aims to solve. In cloud-native applications, where performance, scalability, and user experience are paramount, caching is not just an optimization. It is life saver.

This section breaks down caching in cloud architecture: the what, the why, the how, and even the gotchas. Whether you are building a microservices-based SaaS platform or an API for millions, let us demystify caching.

Caching in cloud architecture

At its core, caching is the practice of storing copies of data in a faster, temporary storage layer, so that future requests can be served faster without hitting the original (often slower) data source.

In cloud architecture, this concept is supercharged. With distributed systems, stateless services, and global scale, caching is not just about speed it is about paramount user experience.

Types of caching in the cloud

Cloud-based caching strategies fall into several buckets based on what you are caching and where:

- **In-memory caching:**
  - **Description**: Stores frequently accessed data in memory (RAM).
  - **Example**: Redis, Memcached.
  - **Use Case**: Low-latency reads, like product catalogs or user sessions.
- **CDN caching (Edge caching)**
  - **Description**: Caches static assets (images, scripts, videos) at the network edge.
  - **Example**: Cloudflare, AWS CloudFront.
  - **Use case**: Websites, media delivery, SaaS dashboards.
- **Application-level caching**
  - **Description**: Embedded within app logic; often per-request or per-session.
  - **Example**: Spring @Cacheable, Flask-Caching.
  - **Use case**: Caching DB queries or expensive computations.
- **Database caching**
  - **Description**: Caches query results or even entire tables/views.
  - **Example**: Amazon RDS Proxy, Query result cache in Snowflake.
  - **Use case**: Reducing DB load for repetitive queries.
- **Distributed caching**
  - **Description**: Shared cache across nodes in a microservices environment.
  - **Example**: Hazelcast, Redis Cluster.
  - **Use Case**: Shared auth tokens, config settings, tenant preferences.

Table 5.8 gives us the different cashing characteristics and use cases:

Type	Speed	Persistence	Scalability	Ideal for
In-Memory	Fast	Volatile	Scalable	Real-time data
CDN (Edge)	Ultra-fast	No write-back	Global	Static content
App-Level	Quick	Custom	Local only	API-level speed boosts
DB Caching	Moderate	Semi-persistent	DB-bound	Reducing expensive queries
Distributed Caching	Fast	Durable	Horizontal	Shared config/state

Table 5.8: *Caching characteristics and use cases*

Categorization of caching

Let us categorize caching through a few lenses:

- **By scope**
  - **Local cache**: Lives within a single instance. Fast but not shareable.
  - **Global cache**: Shared across instances/services.
- **By layer**
  - **Client-side**: Browser cache, service workers.
  - **Server-side**: App-level, in-memory.
  - **Edge-level**: CDNs or edge gateways.
- **By update strategy**
  - **Write-through**: Writes go to cache and DB simultaneously.
  - **Write-behind**: Write to cache, async update to DB.
  - **Cache-aside**: App controls what/when to cache.
  - **Read-through**: Cache fetches from DB on miss.

Table 5.9 features the technologies and tools for caching:

Purpose	Tool or service	Cloud providers
In-memory	Redis, Memcached	AWS ElastiCache, Azure Cache
CDN caching	Cloudflare, Fastly	AWS CloudFront, Azure CDN
App-level caching	Guava, Caffeine, Flask-Caching	N/A
DB caching	RDS Proxy, Aurora Read Replicas	AWS, GCP
Distributed caching	Hazelcast, Redis Cluster	Self-managed, AWS, Azure

Table 5.9: *Technologies and tools for caching*

Challenges with each caching strategy

Caching is not magic. It is more like a deal with the devil if you do not handle it right. Let us now go over the different challenge scenarios and their solutions that we can come across:

- **In-Memory**
  - **Challenge**: Volatile. Data is lost once the system is restarted.
  - **Workaround**: Use replication and persistence.

- **CDN caching**
  - o **Challenge**: Cache invalidation. "Hardest problem in computer science".
  - o **Workaround**: Use versioned URLs or cache-busting headers.
- **App-level**
  - o **Challenge**: Hard to scale in stateless services.
  - o **Workaround**: Limit to short-lived or localized data.
- **Database caching**
  - o **Challenge**: Stale data. When DB updates, cache does not always know.
  - o **Workaround**: TTLs, event-based invalidation.
- **Distributed caching**
  - o **Challenge**: Network latency and consistency.
  - o **Workaround**: Partitioning (sharding) + failover strategies.

With these theories in mind, let us take a stab at implementing a cache in a GoLang microservice.

Let us say we are building a shipping rate calculator for a SaaS logistics platform. Rates are expensive to compute but rarely change. So, we cache them.

The pre-requisites to run this code (assuming you have the latest GoLang version installed and set up) are:

1. Install Redis on your machine or run via Docker:

   ```
   docker run --name redis -p 6379:6379 -d redis
   ```

2. Install the Redis Go library:

   ```
   go get github.com/go-redis/redis/v8
   ```

   Run this code:

   ```
   import (
       "context"
       “github.com/go-redis/redis/v8”
       "time"
   )

   var ctx = context.Background()
   var rdb = redis.NewClient(&redis.Options{
       Addr: "localhost:6379",
   })
   ```

```

func getShippingRate(zipCode string) (string, error) {
    cacheKey := "rate:" + zipCode
    cached, err := rdb.Get(ctx, cacheKey).Result()
    if err == nil {
        return cached, nil
    }

    // Simulate DB call or API
    computedRate := computeRateFromDB(zipCode)

    // Store in cache for 1 hour
    err = rdb.Set(ctx, cacheKey, computedRate, time.Hour).Err()
    if err != nil {
        return "", err
    }

    return computedRate, nil
```

Caching in cloud-native apps is not about blindly stuffing Redis with everything. It is about strategy. You need to ask the following important questions:

- What is expensive to compute?
- What is safe to cache?
- What could go stale and cause havoc?

If used right, caching can scale your system like a pro athlete on energy drinks. If you use it wrong, you are in for a debugging session that makes you question your life choices.

Therefore, start small, measure impact, and evolve your strategy. Because in cloud architecture, caching is not optional—it is essential.

Microservices architecture

The world of software development has undergone a seismic shift in the past decade. From monolithic, all-in-one applications to distributed, independently deployable services, the move to microservices has been transformative. But you may wonder what exactly microservices are.

At its core, a microservices architecture is a collection of loosely coupled services, each responsible for a distinct feature or function of a larger application. These services communicate with one another over lightweight protocols such as HTTP/REST or messaging queues, and they can be developed, deployed, and scaled independently. The result is a system that is agile, resilient, and built for scale.

Microservices are not just about splitting an app into smaller pieces; they are about designing systems that align more closely with business capabilities and organizational agility.

Comparison with monolithic patterns

In a **monolithic architecture**, all components of an application are interconnected and interdependent. The entire application is packaged as a single deployable unit. While simple to develop and deploy initially, monoliths quickly become cumbersome as they grow. A small change in one module often requires redeploying the entire application.

Table 5.10 provides a comparison between microservices and monolithic services:

Feature	Monolith	Microservices
Deployment	Single unit	Independent units
Scalability	Entire app	Service-specific
Technology Stack	Uniform	Polyglot
Fault Isolation	Low	High
Development Speed	Slows down over time	Enables parallel development
Testing	Complex end-to-end testing	Easier unit/service testing

Table 5.10: *Comparison of microservice vs monolithic service*

Real-world analogy: Think of a monolith like a giant truck that carries all packages at once, powerful but inflexible. Microservices are like a fleet of delivery bikes: nimble, efficient, and able to navigate tight turns independently.

Key principles of microservices

The success of microservices lies in adhering to a few fundamental principles. Let us go over them now.

Single responsibility principle

Each microservice should focus on one business capability. By narrowing its scope, the service becomes easier to understand, test, and maintain. This principle promotes high cohesion within the service and minimizes the complexity of the overall system.

For example, in an e-commerce platform, the order management service should only handle order-related logic, while the inventory service is responsible solely for tracking stock levels. This clarity improves development velocity and reduces bugs due to fewer overlapping responsibilities.

Autonomous and independently deployable

Microservices should be designed to operate independently. This means each service has its own codebase, deployment pipeline, and release schedule. Teams can push updates to one service without affecting others, reducing coordination overhead and accelerating delivery.

Autonomy also allows services to fail or degrade gracefully without cascading failures. For instance, if a recommendation service is down, the core shopping experience can continue unaffected.

Decentralized data management

In a microservices architecture, each service should manage its own data, rather than sharing a single database. This reduces coupling and enhances scalability. Each service becomes a master of its own data model and persistence.

This also enables services to evolve their schema independently and select the most appropriate database technology, whether it is a relational database, NoSQL, or a time-series DB depending on the service needs.

API-first communication

Services interact with each other via well-defined APIs. An API-first approach ensures contracts are explicit, versioned, and discoverable. RESTful APIs, gRPC, or GraphQL can be used, depending on the use case.

This principle supports backward compatibility and paves the way for external integrations, mobile apps, and even third-party consumption.

Failure isolation

No matter how well services are designed, failures are inevitable. Microservices should be resilient enough to handle such failures gracefully without affecting the rest of the system.

Patterns like circuit breakers, bulkheads, retries with exponential backoff, and graceful degradation help build fault-tolerant systems. For instance, Netflix uses Hystrix (now deprecated) and has evolved to use Resilience4j for these purposes.

Decentralized governance and polyglot programming

Microservices encourage freedom of choice in technologies. Teams can select the best tool for the job, whether it is Golang for high-performance services, Python for machine learning, or Java for enterprise-grade components.

However, this flexibility comes with a need for standardized governance around observability, security, and deployment practices to ensure consistent performance and maintainability.

Product thinking over project thinking

Each microservice should be treated like a product, with dedicated ownership and a long-term lifecycle in mind. This mindset ensures better support, maintainability, and customer-centric evolution of services.

Teams are empowered to iterate based on usage data, feedback, and changing business requirements, rather than considering the service as a one-time deliverable.

Microservices communication

Communication is the lifeline of microservices. But too much of it, or the wrong kind, can lead to performance bottlenecks. Let us go over synchronous and asynchronous communications now:

- **Synchronous (Request-response)**
    - REST over HTTP.
    - gRPC (efficient for internal services).
    - Easy to implement but can cause cascading failures.
- **Asynchronous (Event-driven)**
    - Message brokers like Kafka, RabbitMQ, AWS SNS/SQS.
    - Decouples services and enhances scalability.

Tip: **Use async for non-critical flows (for example, sending emails, batch submission), and sync for critical paths (for example, payment confirmation).**

Challenges of microservices architecture

While microservices promise flexibility, scalability, and faster innovation cycles, they come with their own set of complexities, both technical and organizational. These are not just academic challenges; they are the realistic, day-to-day challenges that engineering teams face when moving from monolithic comfort to distributed dynamism.

Operational complexity

With a monolith, deploying is usually a one-click operation. With microservices, it is more like conducting an orchestra of services, each one with its lifecycle, scaling policy, and failure mode. Orchestrating these deployments, especially in production, requires tools like Kubernetes, CI/CD pipelines, service meshes, and an iron-clad rollback strategy (this is a must).

As the number of services grows, managing them at scale becomes exponentially complex. You are no longer thinking about a release, but rather hundreds of independent deployable, each potentially introducing risk.

Distributed system problems

Microservices are, by design, distributed systems and that means all the distributed computing headaches come for free. Network latency, retries, partial failures, and timeouts become frequent nightmares to deal with on a regular basis.

Services talk to each other over the network, which introduces:

- **Latency:** Every network hop adds delay.
- **Message loss:** Communication is not guaranteed.
- **Out-of-order messages:** Especially in asynchronous systems like event queues.
- **Split-brain scenarios:** What if one part of the system thinks another is down, but it is not?

Building resilience with retries, fallbacks, circuit breakers, and idempotent APIs becomes essential.

Data consistency and transactions

In monolithic systems, ACID transactions are straightforward. You update multiple records in a single transaction and sleep peacefully. Microservices are a challenge to that peace. Each service typically owns its own database, which is great for decoupling but tough for maintaining consistency across services.

You cannot just wrap a sblock across multiple microservices. Instead, teams have to rely on eventual consistency patterns such as:

- Saga pattern
- Compensating transactions
- Outbox pattern
- Eventual reconciliation jobs

Each comes with its own trade-offs and learning curve.

Observability and debugging

When something breaks in a monolith, logs and stack traces usually point you to the issue quickly. In microservices, you might need to trace a user's action across 12 services, 5 logs, 3 monitoring tools, and one existential crisis.

Effective observability in microservices requires:

- **Centralized logging** (for example, ELK, Fluentd, Sumologic)
- **Distributed tracing** (for example, OpenTelemetry, Jaeger)

- **Real-time alerting** (for example, Prometheus + Alertmanager)
- **Dashboards per service, and holistic system views**

Getting this right is not just about tooling; it is a cultural investment.

Versioning and backward compatibility

Microservices evolve independently. That is their superpower and a recipe for chaos if not managed well.

You have to ensure:

- APIs are **backward-compatible**.
- Database schemas do not break consumers.
- Services can run in **multiple versions side by side**.
- Contracts are clearly documented (for example, using OpenAPI specs).

Testing for all of this requires contract testing, integration tests, and strict API governance.

Team collaboration and ownership

Microservices impact not just architecture, but organization structure. Conway's Law suggests that systems mirror the structure of the teams that build them. In practice, this means service ownership must be clear.

However, challenges include:

- Cross-team communication overhead.
- Ambiguity in SLAs between services.
- Teams inadvertently coupling through shared libraries or data schemas.
- The *who owns this service?* mystery.

Setting up strong DevOps culture, internal documentation, and service catalogs (like Backstage) helps mitigate this.

Security at scale

With more services, there are more attack surfaces:

- APIs exposed across boundaries
- Token management (OAuth, JWT) for service-to-service auth
- Secrets management across environments
- Ensuring encryption in transit and at rest
- Enforcing zero-trust networking policies

Security in microservices must be *baked in,* and not bolted on. This includes tools like service meshes (for example, Istio) and identity providers (such as, OIDC, SPIFFE).

With the given ideas in mind, let us take a look at hands on example of writing a sample microservice in GoLang. This service will expose an API to return product information.

Folder structure

The folder structure is:

```
product-service/
├── main.go
├── handlers/
│   └── product.go
├── models/
│   └── product.go
├── go.mod
```

Refer to the following code blocks:

main.go

```
package main

import (
  «log»
  «net/http»
  «product-service/handlers»

  «github.com/gorilla/mux"
)

func main() {
  r := mux.NewRouter()
  r.HandleFunc("/products/{id}", handlers.GetProduct).Methods("GET")

  log.Println("Starting server on :8080")
  http.ListenAndServe(":8080", r)
}
```

handlers/product.go

```
package handlers

import (
```

```
    "encoding/json"
    "net/http"
    "product-service/models"
    "github.com/gorilla/mux"
    "strconv"
)

func GetProduct(w http.ResponseWriter, r *http.Request) {
    vars := mux.Vars(r)
    id, err := strconv.Atoi(vars["id"])
    if err != nil {
        http.Error(w, "Invalid product ID", http.StatusBadRequest)
        return
    }

    product := models.GetProductByID(id)
    if product == nil {
        http.NotFound(w, r)
        return
    }

    json.NewEncoder(w).Encode(product)
}
```

models/product.go

```
package models

type Product struct {
    ID    int     `json:"id"`
    Name  string  `json:"name"`
    Price float64 `json:"price"`
}

var products = []Product{
    {ID: 1, Name: "Book", Price: 9.99},
    {ID: 2, Name: "Pen", Price: 1.50},
}

func GetProductByID(id int) *Product {
```

```
for _, p := range products {
  if p.ID == id {
    return &p
  }
}
return nil
}
```

Running it

Follow the given steps:

1. Install dependencies: **`go mod init product-service`**
2. Run with: **`go run main.go`**
3. Test with: **`curl http://localhost:8080/products/1`**

Microservices offer a flexible, scalable alternative to monoliths but come with their own complexities. This section covered core concepts, challenges, and even included a simple Golang microservice to get your hands dirty.

Bringing it all together

Now that we have explored these scalability patterns individually, let us discuss how they can work together to create a highly scalable cloud architecture.

Imagine you are building a social media platform. Here is how you might apply these patterns:

- **Load balancing:** You use a load balancer to distribute incoming traffic across multiple web servers.
- **Auto-scaling:** You set up auto-scaling groups for your microservices, database read replicas, and any other services that might experience variable load.
- **Partitioning:** You should shard your database based on user ID, allowing you to horizontally scale your data layer.
- **Caching:** You implement a distributed cache (like Redis) to store frequently accessed data such as user profiles and popular posts.
- **Microservices:** You break down your application into microservices (user service, payment service, notification service, etc.), allowing you to scale and deploy them independently.

Figure 5.2 features a sample architecture:

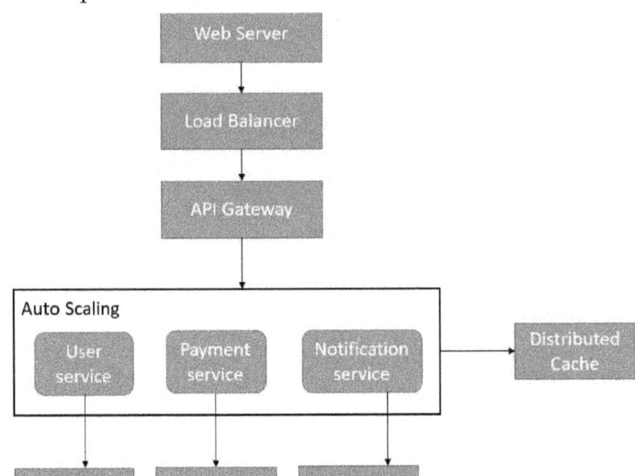

***Figure 5.2:** Sample architecture*

This architecture allows you to:

- Handle varying loads by automatically scaling your services.
- Distribute your data across multiple shards for better performance.
- Cache frequently accessed data to reduce database load.
- Independently scale and deploy different parts of your application.

Remember, this is just one possible architecture. The specific patterns and how you implement them will depend on your unique requirements and constraints.

Conclusion

Scalability is more than just being able to support lots of users or numerous amounts of data, it must be done efficiently, reliably, and cost-effectively. The patterns we have looked at in this chapter like load balancing, auto-scaling, partitioning, caching, and microservices, are essential weapons in your cloud architect arsenal.

However, with great power comes great responsibility. Each one of these patterns brings in its own complexities and trade-offs. The important thing is to find out how your specific application will require it and use these patterns judiciously.

So, as we transition into the next chapter on resiliency patterns, remember that scalability and resiliency tend to go hand in hand. A scalable system that collapses under load is not desirable. In the next chapter, we will discover how to create systems that scale up, but also do not crumble under their own weight, in the wake of failures and surprises.

With these scalability patterns at your disposal, you are almost there. Just keep in mind, the cloud is your playfield, so make mistakes and learn, to explore what you can do.

CHAPTER 6
Resiliency Patterns

Introduction

By now, you are well aware that creating scalable systems is just half the war. The other half? Making sure these systems are robust enough to ride out the inevitable hiccups, failures, and disasters that go hand in hand with the running of an application in the cloud.

Back in the days when building cloud systems by first-timers, there was so much intense focus on fast-forwarding all of it and making it scalable that the need for resiliency was completely missed, until a particularly nasty incident made it impossible to ignore.

Such incidents are the eye openers and realization of building a production environment using the latest and most updated tech stacks, but not accounting for robustness can make our entire environment go down with just a single outage.

In this chapter, we will explore to a deeper extent the patterns and strategies on how to create systems that not only scale well but also can sustain when things go wrong. We will explore how to perform health checks, inject redundancy, account for graceful degradation, and prevent cascading failures. By the end of this chapter, you will have what it takes to build cloud applications capable of standing up to whatever challenges come along.

So, let us get down to making your cloud applications virtually unbreakable.

Structure

In this chapter, we will go over the following topics:

- Importance of resiliency in cloud architecture
- Enhancing system resilience through early health monitoring
- Automated recovery mechanism
- Redundancy
- Failover capabilities
- Graceful degradation
- Resilient cloud architecture as a sample blueprint

Objectives

After finishing this chapter, you will be well versed with key points and concepts of resiliency, what constitutes to create a resilient application, which can be robust enough to survive the unexpected load on demand during high peaks and will help framing the mindset to design systems surviving real-world chaos, recover gracefully and even heal themselves.

Importance of resiliency in cloud architecture

The world is now digital first, and resiliency in cloud architecture has turned into mission-critical requirement and not a nice-to-have. Outages, latency spikes, or service degradation can impact user trust, business operations, and revenue instantaneously. That is why modern cloud systems must be architected assuming failure will occur at some point, somewhere. Resilient architectures are built to absorb shocks, whether that is a failed service, a data center outage, or a sudden spike in traffic, without collapsing under tension. This means designing for redundancy, graceful degradation, automatic failovers, and observability as part of the application. Disaster recovery is not just about bouncing back from failures; it is about ensuring continuity with minimal impact. For businesses, this means better availability, improved customer experience, and enhanced brand reputation. When a service is scaled to serve millions across the world, resiliency is the skeletal structure that strengthens the architecture against the whims of real-world conditions. Simply put, resilient cloud architecture resembles a finely-tuned orchestra; everything performs its part, and in the event of a misstep, the concert continues undeterred into the symphony.

Enhancing system resilience through early health monitoring

As modern software systems scale across distributed environments, spanning microservices, containers, and multi-region cloud infrastructure, the traditional approach of reactive monitoring is no longer sufficient. In such complex ecosystems, failure is not a possibility; it's an inevitability. The question is not *if* a component will fail, but *when*, and more importantly, *how early can you know about it?*

This is where **proactive health monitoring** and **early warning systems** step in, not as afterthoughts, but as foundational pillars of system resilience and reliability. These mechanisms are designed to identify subtle indicators of system degradation long before they appear as customer-visible incidents. They are the digital equivalent of preventive medicine, identifying risk factors early and intervening before they become crises.

System health is a multi-dimensional construct. It extends beyond uptime and CPU usage to include latency thresholds, memory leaks, disk I/O patterns, request queue depths, error rate anomalies, and even user behavior deviations. True health monitoring involves aggregating these signals across multiple layers of the stack, application, infrastructure, network, and correlating them contextually.

In distributed architectures, where services are loosely coupled but failure-prone, **early signs of systemic strain are often buried in noise**. A single microservice experiencing degraded throughput may not raise alarms on its own, but when that degradation cascades into increased retry storms or slower response times downstream, it can impact the entire customer experience.

Proactive health monitoring is not just a technical challenge; it is a cultural one. Organizations must evolve from the mindset of *we will fix it when it breaks* to *we will act before it impacts*. This requires cross-functional buy-in from engineering, SRE, QA, and product teams. Health indicators should be treated as first-class citizens, visible, tracked, and regularly reviewed. Service owners should be incentivized to define and refine **Service Level Indicators** (**SLIs**) and **Service Level Objectives (SLOs)** that reflect not just uptime, but performance quality and reliability trends.

In mature teams, **operational reviews** include deep dives into near-misses—situations where early warnings allowed for preventive action. Over time, these reviews cultivate operational intuition, empowering teams to not just **respond to** issues, but to **preempt** them.

As platforms grow increasingly complex, resilience will no longer be defined by the speed of response, but by the **depth of foresight**. The future of system health lies in **autonomous observability**—systems that can monitor themselves, detect symptoms, predict failures, and trigger self-healing workflows with minimal human intervention.

Ultimately, proactive health monitoring and early warning systems serve a greater purpose: they buy teams time. Time to investigate. Time to adapt. And time to protect the trust that users place in the product. In a world of ephemeral containers and persistent user expectations, **time** is the most valuable currency.

Importance of health checks

Consider, for instance, health monitoring in a cloud application is much like a heartbeat monitor in a hospital. You do not wait for the patient to flatline and step in before you see anomalies at an early stage and act fast. This is crucial for uptime and customer trust in a distributed system where failing fast and recovering automatically is mandatory.

Cloud-native systems today are not built for perfection. They are engineered to sense flaws and self-heal before a user can complain about it.

Let us picture a scenario: you have a complex cloud application with dozens of microservices, databases, and third-party integrations running. How do you make sure everything is working as intended? Here is where health monitoring plays a role, your primary line of defense to building resilient systems.

Health checks are the regular doctor's visits for your application components. They enable you to catch challenges before they become real issues. Pretty much when you implement some good health monitoring, your system can now convey: *Hey, there is something wrong here!*

So let us cover and understand in detail some key characteristics of health monitoring.

Liveness and readiness probes

Liveness checks whether your app is still running. Readiness checks whether your app is ready to serve live traffic.

Think of liveness as *Am I alive* and readiness as *Can I serve your order*. The following table indicates the comparison of external vs embedded health checks, in terms of their usability aspects:

Approach	Example	Use case
Embedded probes	`/health`, `/ready` endpoints	Auto-restart failed pods in Kubernetes
External monitoring	Azure Monitor, Dynatrace, Datadog	SLA dashboards, alerting, long-term trends

Table 6.1: *External vs Embedded health checks*

Implementing health checks

When it comes to implementing health checks, there are a few key points and concepts to keep in mind:

- **Keep it simple:** A good health check should be lightweight and fast. The health check in itself should not become a burden and overwhelm the system.
- **Make it meaningful:** Do not just verify it the service is up and running, check that it is functioning correctly too. For example, check if the database service is up and running, but also run a lightweight query on it to check if the correct results are being returned.
- **Set appropriate thresholds:** Thoroughly investigate and decide what exactly constitutes "healthy" for each component. It can be response time, error rate, or any other corresponding relevant metrics.
- **Automate the process:** Use tools and services provided either by a cloud provider or by third-party libraries to automate the health check and alerts.

Real-world example

Scenario: An e-commerce platform handling millions of API calls per day. One node experiences memory leaks and begins timing out.

Without a health check: Node remains in the load balancer pool, causing degraded performance, failed transactions, and customer complaints.

With health checks:

- Liveness probe detects timeouts.
- Kubernetes restarts the pod automatically.
- Traffic is routed to healthy instances.
- No one notices. Not even the ops team. Awesome!

The sample implementation (Kubernetes YAML) is as follows:

```
livenessProbe:
  httpGet:
    path: /health
    port: 8080
  initialDelaySeconds: 10
  periodSeconds: 5
  failureThreshold: 3

readinessProbe:
  httpGet:
    path: /ready
    port: 8080
  initialDelaySeconds: 5
  periodSeconds: 3
  successThreshold: 1
```

Make sure **/health** does not check external dependencies, otherwise, their failure becomes your restart reason. The following figure shows how a liveness and health probing gets in action in a microservices environment:

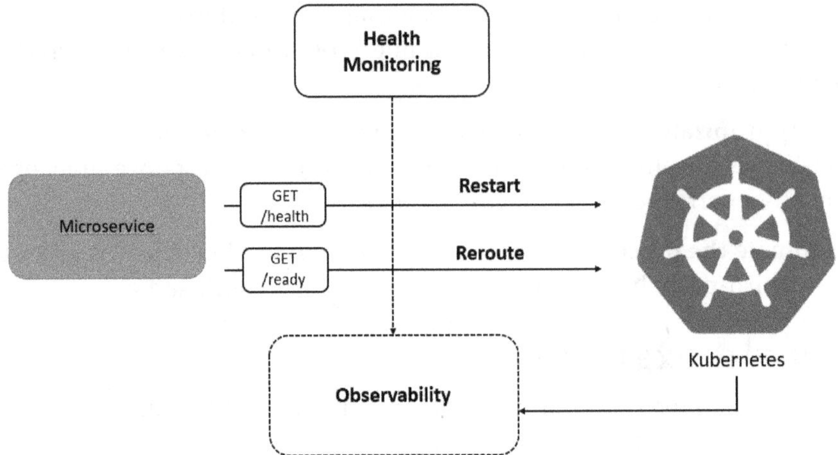

***Figure 6.1:** Health monitoring of a microservice on kubernetes pod*

Figure 6.1 illustrates how health monitoring (**liveness and readiness probes**) interacts with containerized service in a **kuberneKubernetes-nvironment**. Let us understand the flow and components of the above architecture:

- **Microservice pod:** At the core, we have a containerized microservice, which exposes **/health** and **/or** ready endpoints, which verify that the service is not hung or crashed and the service is ready to receive traffic, respectively.
- **Kubernetes node agent:** Periodically pings the liveness probe (If it fails x times, as defined in yaml, the container is terminated and restarted automatically) and pings for the readiness probe, and if not ready, no traffic is routed.
- **Observability:** Health checks metrics and results are fed to tools like Prometheus, Grafana, and Sumologic, enabling SRE and TechOps teams to monitor and configure alerts.

This architecture ensures that:

- Sick pods do not bring the system down.
- Failures are detected early.
- Services recover automatically, maintaining uptime without human intervention.

Automated recovery mechanism

Now that we have understood health checks in place, what do you do when the system detects a problem? This is where automated recovery mechanisms come into play.

These are predefined actions that your system can take to resolve issues without human intervention. However, before we plunge into the practical hands-on, let us understand the concepts behind automated recovery.

Imagine a cloud system managing millions of transactions per day. What happens when a key microservice goes down at midnight? Do you really want to wait for a human to get notified, rub their eyes, and reboot something?

Automated recovery is not just a luxury anymore. It is a core design principle of resilient cloud systems. It ensures that failures are detected quickly and resolved without human intervention, minimizing downtime and preserving customer trust.

Methods of automated recovery in the cloud

In this section, we will look at methods of automated recovery in the cloud.

Self-healing containers with liveness and readiness probes

One of the simplest and most widely adopted recovery mechanisms in cloud architectures is the use of **liveness** and **readiness** probes (which we just explored in the previous section):

- **Liveness probe:** Checks if the application is still running and healthy. If the check fails, the orchestrator (like Kubernetes) restarts the container.
- **Readiness probe:** Checks if the application is ready to serve traffic. If it fails, the container is removed from the load balancer pool but not restarted.

This matters because a container may be *up* but still be in a bad state, say, it is deadlocked, or stuck waiting on an external dependency. Liveness probes catch that. Readiness probes ensure only functioning instances serve user traffic.

The YAML configuration code for liveness and readiness was mentioned in the above section.

Coding health check with auto-restart friendly service

The following code sample is a minimal, production-safe implementation in Golang that includes a liveness check endpoint and simulates failure recovery logic:

```
package main

import (
	"fmt"
	"log"
	"net/http"
```

```
    "sync/atomic"
    "time"
)

var isHealthy int32 = 1

func main() {
    // Simulated app handler
    http.HandleFunc("/process", func(w http.ResponseWriter, r *http.Request) {
        if atomic.LoadInt32(&isHealthy) == 0 {
            http.Error(w, "Service Unavailable", http.StatusServiceUnavailable)
            return
        }
        fmt.Fprintln(w, "Payment processed successfully!")
    })

    // Liveness probe
    http.HandleFunc("/health", func(w http.ResponseWriter, r *http.Request) {
        if atomic.LoadInt32(&isHealthy) == 0 {
            http.Error(w, "Not healthy", http.StatusInternalServerError)
        } else {
            fmt.Fprintln(w, "Healthy")
        }
    })

    // Simulate failure after 20 seconds
    go func() {
        time.Sleep(20 * time.Second)
        log.Println("Simulating service failure...")
        atomic.StoreInt32(&isHealthy, 0)
    }()

    log.Println("Service starting on :8080")
    log.Fatal(http.ListenAndServe(":8080", nil))
}
```

To test this, perform the following functions:

1. Run the app locally: **`go run main.go`**
2. In 20 seconds, **`/health`** will start returning 500, simulating a failure.
3. In Kubernetes, a failing **`/health`** would trigger an **auto-restart** of the pod, completing the recovery loop. (Refer to yaml configuration example for the liveness probe in the health monitoring section)

Auto-restart policies

Sometimes, applications crash due to panics, memory leaks, or unhandled exceptions. Instead of waiting for human intervention, cloud orchestrators can **automatically restart failed containers or VMs** based on pre-defined rules.

Example of k8s restart policies:

- **Always:** Restart the container on all failures.
- **OnFailure:** Restart only if it fails (non-zero exit).
- **Never:** Used mostly in jobs or test pods.

It is useful for auto-restarts and helps manage transient errors that are not indicative of systemic problems. Think of them as a fast **turn it off and on again**.

Also, monitoring is very important and critical in the above case, as any crash due to bad code i.e, **`NullPointerException`** especially in Golang can cause panic and the system can go in crash loop mode.

Circuit breaker pattern

The **circuit breaker** pattern acts like a fuse in your architecture. When one service starts failing (**e.g., 5xx errors or timeouts**), the circuit opens, temporarily stopping calls to that service and avoiding a cascading failure.

The states are as follows:

- **Closed:** Everything is normal.
- **Open:** Too many failures, cut off traffic.
- **Half-open:** Limited traffic sent to test if the service has recovered.

To implement a circuit breaker, use the following steps:

1. Monitor the success/failure rate of calls to a service.
2. If the failure rate exceeds a threshold, *trip* the circuit breaker.
3. When tripped, fail fast without attempting to call the service.
4. After a timeout period, allow a few requests through to test if the service has recovered.

Let us understand the circuit breaker pattern in a bit more detail with a practical hands-on implementation.

Implementing circuit breakers in distributed systems requires careful consideration. Here are some key points to keep in mind:

- **Failure thresholds:** Determine what constitutes a failure (e.g., timeouts, specific error codes) and how many failures should occur before opening the circuit.
- **Timeout duration:** Decide how long the circuit should stay open before transitioning to half-open.
- **Fallback behavior:** Define what should happen when the circuit is open. This might involve returning cached data, default values, or gracefully degrading functionality.
- **Monitoring and alerting:** Implement monitoring to track the state of your circuit breakers and alert when they trip frequently.

Considerations for cloud environments

When implementing circuit breakers in cloud environments, there are some additional considerations:

- **Distributed configuration:** In a microservices architecture, you might want to centralize your circuit breaker configuration so it can be easily updated across all instances.
- **Cloud-native solutions:** Many cloud providers offer services that can act as circuit breakers. For example, AWS API Gateway has throttling limits that can act as a form of circuit breaker.
- **Auto-scaling interaction:** Be aware of how your circuit breakers interact with auto-scaling policies. An open circuit breaker might prevent instances from receiving traffic, potentially triggering a scale-down event.

The code snippet is as follows:

- **`main.go`:**

```go
)

// Define breaker states
type State int

const (
  Closed State = iota
  Open
  HalfOpen
)
```

```
// CircuitBreaker struct
type CircuitBreaker struct {
 state           State
 failureCount    int
 successCount    int
 failureThreshold int
 retryTimeout    time.Duration
 lastFailureTime time.Time
 mutex           sync.Mutex
}

func NewCircuitBreaker(failureThreshold int, retryTimeout time.
Duration) *CircuitBreaker {
 return &CircuitBreaker{
  state:            Closed,
  failureThreshold: failureThreshold,
  retryTimeout:     retryTimeout,
 }
}

func (cb *CircuitBreaker) Call(fn func() error) error {
 cb.mutex.Lock()
 defer cb.mutex.Unlock()

 switch cb.state {
 case Open:
  if time.Since(cb.lastFailureTime) > cb.retryTimeout {
   fmt.Println("Retry timeout expired. Trying Half-Open state...")
   cb.state = HalfOpen
  } else {
   return errors.New("circuit breaker is OPEN")
  }
 case HalfOpen:
  // allow one trial
  err := fn()
  if err != nil {
   cb.trip()
   return errors.New("Half-Open trial failed. Going back to OPEN")
  }
  cb.reset()
  fmt.Println("Half-Open trial successful. Back to CLOSED state.")
```

```
		return nil
	}

func (cb *CircuitBreaker) trip() {
	cb.state = Open
	cb.lastFailureTime = time.Now()
	cb.failureCount = 0
	fmt.Println("Circuit Breaker tripped to OPEN state!")
}

func (cb *CircuitBreaker) reset() {
	cb.state = Closed
	cb.failureCount = 0
	cb.successCount = 0
}

func externalServiceCall() error {
	resp, err := http.Get("http://localhost:8081/downstream")
	if err != nil || resp.StatusCode != 200 {
		return errors.New("service call failed")
	}
	return nil
}

func main() {
	breaker := NewCircuitBreaker(3, 10*time.Second)

	http.HandleFunc("/ping", func(w http.ResponseWriter, r *http.Request) {
		err := breaker.Call(externalServiceCall)
		if err != nil {
			http.Error(w, "Downstream service unavailable: "+err.Error(), http.StatusServiceUnavailable)
			return
		}
		w.WriteHeader(http.StatusOK)
		w.Write([]byte("Pong from upstream service!"))
	})

	fmt.Println("Starting Circuit Breaker Demo on :8080...")
	log.Fatal(http.ListenAndServe(":8080", nil))
}
```

- **downstream.go**:

```
package main

import (
 "fmt"
 "log"
 "net/http"
)

var fail = true // Simulate failure state

func main() {
 http.HandleFunc("/downstream", func(w http.
 ResponseWriter, r *http.Request) {
  if fail {
   http.Error(w, "Simulated downstream failure", http.
 StatusInternalServerError)
   return
  }
  fmt.Fprintln(w, "Success from downstream!")
 })

 fmt.Println("Downstream service running on :8081")
 log.Fatal(http.ListenAndServe(":8081", nil))
}
```

To test this, perform the following actions:

1. Run the downstream service: **`go run downstream.go`**
2. Run the circuit breaker service: **`go run main.go`**
3. Use curl to test: **`curl http://localhost:8080/ping`**

The code demonstrates a simple circuit breaker pattern in Golang that:

- Monitors failures of a downstream service.
- Prevents calling the failing service when it is unstable.
- Recovers once the service is healthy again. This is useful when building resilient microservices.

Retry with backoff and dead letter queues

Failures in distributed systems are inevitable. What matters is *how you handle retries.*

Retry with exponential backoff: Rather than retrying immediately after a failure (which can worsen congestion), wait progressively longer between attempts. This gives the downstream component breathing room to recover, while increasing the chance of success over time.

Dead letter queues (DLQs): When retries are exhausted, messages are sent to a DLQ. This ensures:

- Data is not lost.
- Consumers of the queues can inspect and reprocess failed jobs.

Advantages and disadvantages

The following table provides a quick comparison of recovery mechanisms with their pros and cons:

Mechanism	Advantages	Drawbacks
Health checks and restarts	Fast recovery, no human needed	May restart too often without fixing root cause
Auto-restart policies	Keeps system alive after crashes	Does not address app-level failures
Circuit breaker	Protects system-wide failure	May lead to service unavailability temporarily
Retry + DLQ	Prevents data loss	Can create retry storms if not throttled carefully

Table 6.2: *Quick comparison of recovery mechanisms*

In reality, automated recovery is not about picking just one technique; it is about **layering** these strategies intelligently. Think of it like building an immune system:

- Probes detect sickness.
- Restarts kick in for minor issues.
- Circuit breakers prevent the spread of the infection.
- DLQs act as the body's memory to avoid repeating mistakes.

These methods, when composed thoughtfully, create resilient, reliable, and self-sustaining cloud-native systems that your customers will never notice, but always trust, and yes, this all comes with regular practice, as there is no single silver bullet for every problem.

Use case, payments microservice in a SaaS platform

Scenario: Your payment microservice frequently calls a 3rd-party payment gateway. Occasionally, the API returns 503 errors.

Without recovery: The pod crashes due to unhandled timeout exceptions. Customers see payment failures.

With automated recovery:

- The circuit breaker temporarily halts outbound calls.
- Kubernetes liveness check restarts the pod if it hangs.
- Retries with backoff and DLQ ensure transactions are eventually processed.
- Alerts trigger only if the system cannot recover within the SLA window.

Result? Users are unaffected. Engineers get to sleep.

Designing for failure is not a choice; it is now a prerequisite and paramount.

Automated recovery mechanisms make your architecture more dependable, scalable, and sleep-friendly. Whether you use health probes, circuit breakers, or retry strategies, the key is to build systems that do not rely on luck or late-night engineers.

Also, the key to effective automated recovery is to design your system so that individual components can be easily replaced without affecting the overall functionality. This leads us nicely into our next topic: **redundancy**.

Redundancy

Imagine you are streaming your favorite show, making a payment, or placing a last-minute order, and suddenly, the app crashes. Frustrating, correct? Now imagine if you are the one responsible for that app. This is where **redundancy** enters the scene, your invisible safety net, quietly ensuring that things continue to work even when something breaks behind the scenes. Essentially, it is all about backups, and perhaps backups of your backups.

Let us explore redundancy, what it is, why it matters, how to implement it, and how it plays out across cloud platforms.

Introduction to redundancy

Redundancy in cloud architecture refers to the strategic duplication of critical components or functions of a system to increase reliability and fault tolerance. Simply put, it is the art of having backup systems ready to take over when primary systems fail.

Redundancy ensures that a single point of failure does not bring down your application. It is not just about uptime, it is about building resilient, graceful systems that deliver consistent user experiences, any time, any day, any week, any month and any year.

In the cloud, this often means having multiple instances of your services running across different **Availability Zones** (**AZs**) or even regions.

It may so happen that one might design multiple instances of the services, but if all these instances are in the same data center and the data center faced major outages the application/system will go down and not be available, so it is imperative to have redundancy at multiple levels.

Value of redundancy

In cloud-native applications, downtime is not just a nuisance; it can be expensive too. According to *Gartner*, the average cost of IT downtime is $5,600 per minute. Redundancy can be a lifesaver here and helps in:

- Minimize downtime
- Ensure business continuity
- Protect user trust
- Comply with SLAs
- Enable **high availability** (HA)

When combined with observability and automation, redundancy transforms your system into a self-healing architecture.

Methods of implementing redundancy

In this subsection, we will look at methods to implement redundancy.

Infrastructure-level redundancy

At the foundation of every cloud system is the infrastructure's compute, storage, and network. If any one of these fails, your entire app could go down. Infrastructure redundancy protects against such failures by duplicating essential components across AZs or regions.

The types are as follows:

- **Zonal redundancy:** Replicate across multiple AZs within the same region. (**multi AZ**)
- **Regional redundancy:** Deploy the app across multiple regions for disaster recovery and compliance. (**multi regions**)
- **Multi-cloud redundancy:** Operate across different cloud providers (e.g., AWS + Azure). (**multi cloud**)

Some examples are as follows:

- An **Auto Scaling Group** in AWS with instances spread across 3 AZs.
- **S3** in AWS, by default, stores redundant copies of data across AZs.

When to use:

- For high-availability apps requiring near-zero downtime.
- Mission-critical systems with high SLA guarantees.

The cloud tools are as follows:

- AWS Auto Scaling, Azure Availability Zones, Google Instance Groups
- S3 / Azure Blob / GCS (redundant storage by default)

Application-level redundancy

Applications themselves can fail due to memory leaks, bugs, or resource exhaustion. To mitigate this, run redundant service instances behind a load balancer or API gateway.

The patterns are as follows:

- **Active-active:** All instances are online and serve traffic simultaneously.
- **Active-passive:** Primary handles traffic, while the backup remains idle until failure.

Let us look at an example:

- In a **Kubernetes** setup, multiple replicas of a microservices pod run behind a service and ingress controller.

The use case is as follows:

- Microservices where individual services that can independently fail or restart.
- High-throughput APIs that require horizontal scaling.

The cloud tools used are as follows:

- Kubernetes deployments with multiple replicas
- AWS Elastic Load Balancer + ECS/Fargate
- Azure App Gateway + AKS

Data-level redundancy

Data is the most valuable and vulnerable asset in the cloud. You need to ensure that it is available and consistent, even when a storage node or database instance fails.

The strategies are as follows:

- **Synchronous replication:** It is about writing to the primary node and replicating the same simultaneously on the secondary node. (**high consistency**)
- **Asynchronous replication:** Used for better performance, and where possible, delay in recovery is acceptable. (**eventual consistency**).

The technologies used are as follows:

- AWS RDS Multi-AZ (**synchronous**).
- Read replicas for scaling and redundancy (**asynchronous**).
- MongoDB Atlas with regional clusters.
- Cosmos DB with automatic multi-region writes.

The trade-off is provided as follows:

- **Synchronous:** Advised for consistency, but lowers the performance.
- **Asynchronous:** Advised for speed, but possible data loss in extreme scenarios.

Network-level redundancy

The network is the circulatory system of your application. A broken network connection, DNS outage, or traffic surge can break your system without any issue in your code.

The methods are as follows:

- **Multi-region DNS failover:** Automatically redirect traffic to healthy endpoints.
- **Global load balancers:** Direct users to the closest healthy deployment.
- **Redundant VPN/Direct Connect connections:** For hybrid cloud setups.

The cloud services are:

- AWS Route 53 Failover + Global Accelerator.
- Azure Traffic Manager + Front Door.
- GCP Cloud Load Balancing + Cloud DNS.

The use case is as follows:

- Global apps need edge redundancy.
- Financial or healthcare systems with guaranteed low latency.

Redundancy in containers

With the rise of Kubernetes and Serverless, redundancy now scales dynamically. Here, the infrastructure auto-recoveries from failure using **desired state reconciliation**:

- **Kubernetes:**
  - **Replicas** ensures a specified number of running pods.
  - **Liveness/readiness** probes restart unhealthy containers.
  - Pods are distributed across AZs using **topologySpreadConstraints**.

- **Serverless:**
  - AWS Lambda has built-in redundancy across AZs.
  - Use step functions with fallback paths for function failures.
  - Azure Functions + Durable Tasks enable resilient workflows.

The following table compares the redundancy layers in terms of offerings, implementation details and use case scenarios:

Redundancy layer	Key component	Example implementation	When to use
Infrastructure	AZ/Region Replication	ASG + ELB across AZs in AWS	General HA needs
Application	Replicas + Load Balancer	K8s deployments, ECS tasks with ALB	Service-level fault tolerance
Data	Synchronous/ Async Replication	RDS Multi-AZ, MongoDB Atlas Regional Clusters	Preserve critical user data
Network	DNS + Global Load Balancing	Route 53 Failover + Azure Front Door	Edge and network resilience
Cross-Cloud	Active-Active Multi-Cloud	AWS + Azure deployments with failover DNS	Extreme fault tolerance, compliance needs

***Table 6.3**: Quick summary of redundancy layers*

The following table compares the redundancy layers in terms of their pros and cons, that help in decision making while choosing what to opt:

Redundancy layer	Advantages	Disadvantages
Infrastructure-level	High availability, fast failover	Costly, requires infrastructure orchestration
Application-level	Improved performance, easy scaling	Risk of data inconsistency, complex routing
Data redundancy	Data protection, low read latency	Replication lag, eventual consistency issues
Network redundancy	Resilient connectivity, global reach	DNS propagation delays, complex networking setup

***Table 6.4**: Pros and cons of redundancy layers*

The following table compares the redundancy offered by various cloud providers for quick summarization:

Feature	AWS	Azure	GCP
Multi-AZ deployment	Supported via ASG, RDS, S3	Supported via Availability Sets/ Zones	Supported via regional managed services
Global load balancing	Route 53 + Global Accelerator	Azure Front Door	Cloud Load Balancer
Active-active multi-region setup	Available via Route 53, ELB, Lambda@Edge	Traffic Manager + App Gateway	Global HTTP(S) Load Balancer
Managed failover tools	Elastic Disaster Recovery, Route 53 failover	Azure Site Recovery	Cloud DNS with failover

***Table 6.5:** Cloud provider's comparison offering redundancy*

Hands-on redundancy in AWS

Let us say you are deploying a stateless web app that must remain available during failures. We have:

- **Set up Multi-AZ auto scaling group:**

```
aws autoscaling create-auto-scaling-group \
  --auto-scaling-group-name my-app-asg \
  --launch-template LaunchTemplateName=my-launch-template \
  --min-size 2 --max-size 6 \
  --desired-capacity 3 \
  --vpc-zone-identifier «subnet-abc123,subnet-def456»
```

- **Deploy Elastic Load Balancer (ELB):**

```
aws elbv2 create-load-balancer \
  --name my-app-lb \
  --subnets subnet-abc123 subnet-def456 \
  --security-groups sg-123456
```

- **Use Multi-AZ RDS database:**

```
aws rds create-db-instance \
  --db-instance-identifier mydbinstance \
  --multi-az \
  --engine mysql \
  --allocated-storage 20 \
  --db-instance-class db.t3.micro \
  --master-username admin \
  --master-user-password password
```

- **Enable Route 53 health checks + failover:** Set up a health check and define a failover policy in your Route 53 DNS configuration.

The following figure depicts an example of layered architecture on how redundancy can be accommodated at various layers of deployment:

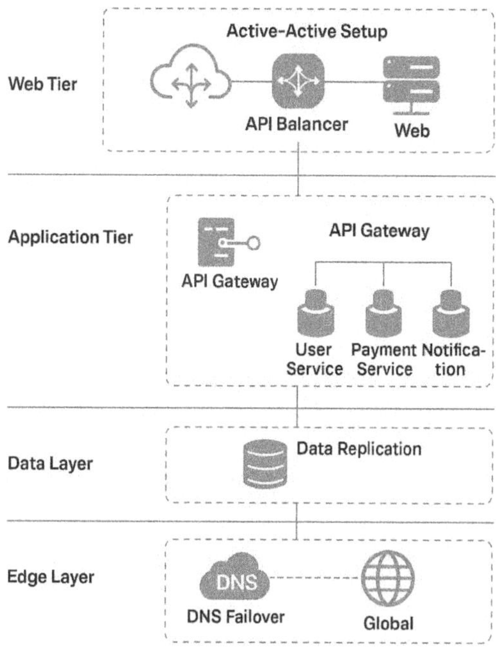

Figure 6.2: Layard architecture depicting redundancy at various components

Redundancy is not just a backup plan, it is a design philosophy. It is the cloud's equivalent of a safety net for digital experiences. And while it introduces complexity and cost, the **peace of mind and customer trust** it brings is priceless.

Whether you are deploying a single-page app or a globally distributed service mesh, designing with redundancy in mind will always be a smart bet.

Failover capabilities

Redundancy is a great tool, but it is completely effective once it is paired with appropriate failover mechanisms and allows for seamless switching to backup systems whenever necessary. So basically, it is a capability to switch to a secondary system from the primary when the need arises.

Imagine launching a mission-critical application that abruptly stops working due to a server crash or network outage. For modern businesses, downtime is not just inconvenient; it is expensive and can damage brand trust. Failover capabilities form the cornerstone of resilient cloud architectures, ensuring that services remain available and performant even when parts of the system fail.

Failover mechanisms ensure continuity by automatically switching to a redundant or standby (**secondary**) system when a **primary** component fails. In today's always-on digital world, whether it is an e-commerce checkout system, a live video stream, or a logistics platform, failover is essential in meeting the **Service Level Agreements** (**SLAs**), maintaining user experience, and protecting revenue.

The methods to achieve failover capabilities are as follows:

- **Active-passive failover:** In this type of setup, **a secondary (passive)** instance remains on standby. When the active instance fails, the passive instance is promoted to take over operations.
    - **Use case:** Database failover clusters (e.g., PostgreSQL or SQL Server with a warm standby).
    - **Cloud example:** AWS RDS Multi-AZ deployment
- **Active-active failover:** In this type of setup, nodes are active and serving traffic simultaneously. If one node fails, the others continue without disruption.
    - **Use case:** Load-balanced web servers or stateless microservices.
    - **Cloud example:** Azure Load Balancer with auto-scaling web app instances.
- **Geo-redundant failover:** This approach places infrastructure in multiple geographic regions. If a region goes down, traffic is routed to a healthy region.
    - **Use case:** Mission-critical applications with strict DR requirements.
    - **Cloud example:** Google Cloud's global load balancing or AWS Route 53 with latency-based routing.
- **DNS-based failover:** A domain name service is used to redirect users to a healthy endpoint when a primary service is down.
    - **Use case:** Static sites or simple app endpoints.
    - **Cloud example:** AWS Route 53 Health Checks with failover routing.
- **Service mesh-based failover:** At the microservices level, service meshes like **Istio** or **Linkerd** enable dynamic routing and retries in case of failures.
    - **Use case:** Kubernetes-native service-to-service failover.
    - **Cloud example:** Istio on **Google Kubernetes Engine** (**GKE**).

Method	Advantages	Disadvantages
Active-passive	Simple to implement, cost-effective	Failover time is higher due to warm standby
Active-active	High availability, no downtime	Complex synchronization, higher cost
Geo-redundant	Disaster-proof, region-level resilience	Expensive, requires global architecture

Method	Advantages	Disadvantages
DNS-based	Lightweight, easy to configure	Slow DNS propagation, not ideal for low RTO
Service mesh	Granular control, traffic routing at service level	Requires deep understanding of mesh configuration

***Table 6.6**: Pros and cons of failover mechanism*

Industrywide comparison of cloud providers

As cloud-native applications scale and operate globally and the ability to provide robust failover capabilities becomes a key differentiator among cloud providers. While most of the leading providers offer failover mechanisms out of the box, their implementation strategies, granularity of control, global reach, and automation features can vary significantly.

AWS is widely recognized for its extensive and mature failover toolset, offering everything from region failover using Route 53 to multi-AZ databases with automatic failover.

Azure focuses heavily on routing and global traffic distribution with services like Traffic Manager and Azure Front Door, making it ideal for multi-continent applications.

Google Cloud, on the other hand, excels in invisible, infrastructure-level failover through global load balancing, offering minimal configuration with high reliability.

Oracle and IBM Cloud also provide competent options, particularly for enterprise and hybrid workloads, though often with more manual configuration requirements.

The following table shows a comparison of the top cloud providers and their respective failover capabilities:

Cloud provider	Failover services offered	Highlights	Limitations
AWS	Route 53, **Elastic Load Balancing** (**ELB**), Auto Scaling, Global Accelerator, Multi-AZ RDS, S3 Cross-Region Replication	Broadest failover tools, native auto-failover, DR playbooks	Complex setup for custom multi-region failover
Azure	Azure Traffic Manager, Azure Load Balancer, Azure Front Door, AZs, Zone Redundant Storage	Deep integration with Microsoft stack, strong global traffic management	Slightly steeper learning curve for configuring front-door routing

Cloud provider	Failover services offered	Highlights	Limitations
Google Cloud	Global HTTP(S) Load Balancer, Cloud DNS, Multi-Region Storage, GKE Multi-Zone Clusters	Seamless global failover, built-in intelligence in routing	Fewer manual failover controls for advanced use cases

***Table 6.7**: Cloud provider comparison over various cloud vendors*

Failover-ready service implementation

Here is an AWS Cloud Formation template to simulate the failover scenario.

Implementing failover capability in AWS typically involves a combination of services like:

- Amazon Route 53 for DNS-level health checks and routing.
- ELB to distribute traffic within a region.
- Multi-AZ deployment (e.g., RDS or EC2) for availability.
- Auto Scaling Groups for automatic recovery.
- S3 or EFS replication for storage redundancy.

The following is a working end-to-end example using Route 53 health checks and failover routing between two EC2-based web servers, one in the primary region (e.g., us-east-1) and one in the secondary (e.g., us-west-2):

```
AWSTemplateFormatVersion: '2010-09-09'
Description: Route53 Failover Setup for EC2 Instances in Two Regions
Parameters:
  PrimaryInstanceIP:
    Type: String
    Description: Public IP of the Primary EC2 Instance
  SecondaryInstanceIP:
    Type: String
    Description: Public IP of the Secondary EC2 Instance
  DomainName:
    Type: String
    Description: DNS name (e.g., app.example.com)
  HostedZoneId:
    Type: String
    Description: Route53 Hosted Zone ID
Resources:
  PrimaryHealthCheck:
    Type: AWS::Route53::HealthCheck
```

```
    Properties:
      HealthCheckConfig:
        IPAddress: !Ref PrimaryInstanceIP
        Port: 80
        Type: HTTP
        ResourcePath: "/"
        RequestInterval: 30
        FailureThreshold: 3
  PrimaryRecordSet:
    Type: AWS::Route53::RecordSet
    Properties:
      HostedZoneId: !Ref HostedZoneId
      Name: !Ref DomainName
      Type: A
      SetIdentifier: "Primary"
      Failover: PRIMARY
      TTL: 60
      ResourceRecords:
        - !Ref PrimaryInstanceIP
      HealthCheckId: !Ref PrimaryHealthCheck
  SecondaryRecordSet:
    Type: AWS::Route53::RecordSet
    Properties:
      HostedZoneId: !Ref HostedZoneId
      Name: !Ref DomainName
      Type: A
      SetIdentifier: "Secondary"
      Failover: SECONDARY
      TTL: 60
      ResourceRecords:
        - !Ref SecondaryInstanceIP
```

You can upload this template to AWS CloudFormation and provide parameters like:

- Primary and Secondary EC2 public IPs
- Hosted zone ID
- Domain name (e.g., app.example.com)

Failover is not just about backups; it is about trust, experience, and reliability. Whether you are building a high-throughput SaaS app, a healthcare platform, or a fintech system, failover mechanisms are your safety net.

Investing in intelligent, well-architected failover designs ensures your cloud infrastructure gracefully handles the unexpected, because failure is inevitable, but user satisfaction does not have to suffer.

Graceful degradation

In an ideal world, every component of the system would work perfectly all the time. However, we do not live in an ideal world, do we? That is where graceful degradation comes in. It is the art of ensuring that your system can continue to function, albeit with reduced functionality, even when some components fail. Let us understand it in a bit more detail.

Imagine you are using your favorite food delivery app. You place an order, but suddenly, the live tracking map does not load. Annoying? Sure, but you still get the order confirmation, estimated delivery time, and support contact, all the essentials still work. That is graceful degradation in action.

Graceful degradation is the ability of a system to continue functioning, even when parts of it fail. Instead of going dark, your application trims the fat and delivers the core experience. This design philosophy is not about perfection; it is about prioritizing user experience when things go wrong, which, in the unpredictable world of cloud computing, they eventually will.

Cloud-native systems, by nature, are distributed, and every network call is a potential point of failure. Degradation is not failure; it is a strategy to fail smart.

Various methods to achieve graceful degradation

In cloud-native architectures, failures are not a question of **if** but **when**. But a smart system does not let those failures bubble up to users. It handles them quietly and elegantly. That is where graceful degradation comes in. Let us explore a few very practical and widely used methods to design cloud systems that do not break under pressure, but bend strategically, and help applications weather the storm without crashing and burning.

Dynamic feature management or feature toggling

Feature toggling (or feature flags) allows enabling/disabling specific functionality in real-time without deploying new code. This is like having dimmer switches for parts of your system.

The following points explain how it supports degradation:

- During high latency or partial outage of a dependent service, you can toggle off non-essential features (e.g., Recently Viewed Items) to preserve core functionality (e.g., checkout).
- You can also programmatically disable features based on system load, error rates, or A/B test outcomes.

Real-world example: Netflix disables personalization layers when recommendation services are slow, while keeping content streaming unaffected.

The tools used are as follows:

- AWS AppConfig
- LaunchDarkly
- Azure App Configuration
- Unleash

Best practice: Wrap all non-critical components in toggles; externalize the toggle config so it can be changed without redeploying.

Fallback mechanisms

When a dependent system fails, fallbacks allow the application to serve a secondary (less precise) result, so users are not left staring at a blank screen or an error.

Common fallback types:

- **Static fallback:** Serve a static or cached response.
- **Stub response:** Show *most popular instead of personalized.*
- **Graceful redirect:** Point the user to another pathway (e.g., redirect to a help article when live chat is down).

Example: If a weather API fails in a travel booking app, fall back to a generic weather widget or yesterday's cached data.

Implementation tip: Use libraries like [**Hystrix (Java)**] or [**resilience-go**] to automate fallback behaviors in microservices.

Read-only mode or data-safe degradation

Switch the application into read-only mode to protect data integrity during backend service outages or database recovery.

Why it works: Users can still access their history, view dashboards, or download reports, even if creating/updating records is temporarily disabled.

Use case: A banking app may allow users to view past transactions but block transfers temporarily if the core ledger system is in recovery mode.

How to implement:

1. Detect database write failures or replication lag.
2. Flag the system as degraded and redirect all POST/PUT/DELETE to a *Service Unavailable* response with context.
3. Maintain a consistent read cache.

Asynchronous processing

Offload non-critical operations to background jobs or queues, so the main workflow can continue even if a sub-process fails.

Use case: A user signs up. Email confirmation and welcome notification are queued instead of processed inline. If the notification system is down, the signup is not blocked.

Common tools are as follows:

- Amazon SQS / SNS
- Azure Service Bus
- Apache Kafka
- RabbitMQ

Important tip: **Use dead letter queues (DLQs) and retries to avoid silent loss of important tasks and events.**

The following table summarizes the pros and cons of graceful degradation methods, giving a decision framework:

Method	Advantages	Disadvantages
Feature toggling	Fast control, non-intrusive updates	Misuse can lead to code complexity
Fallback mechanisms	Seamless user experience	Requires solid caching & prediction strategies
Read-only mode	Protects data integrity	Reduces user interaction; may frustrate power users
Asynchronous processing	Improves system responsiveness	Complexity in error handling and observability

***Table 6.8**: Pros and cons of methods of graceful degradation*

The following table features the cloud providers on graceful degradation support:

Provider	Feature flags	Resilience toolkit	Observability stack	Notable edge
AWS	AppConfig, CloudWatch Alarms	AWS Resilience Hub	X-Ray, CloudWatch	Deep integration and automation
Azure	Azure App Configuration	Azure Chaos Studio	Azure Monitor	Hybrid support is strong
Google Cloud	Firebase Remote Config	GCP Fault Injection	Stackdriver	Strong real-time analytics

***Table 6.9**: Cloud providers on graceful degradation support*

Practical implementation of graceful degradation in Go

Let us look at a simple microservice example where the primary recommendation engine fails, and it degrades to a static list of popular products:

```
package main

import (
    "encoding/json"
    "log"
    "net/http"
    "time"
)

type Product struct {
    ID    int    `json:"id"`
    Name  string `json:"name"`
    Price string `json:"price"`
}

// Static fallback list
var fallbackProducts = []Product{
    {ID: 1, Name: "Wireless Mouse", Price: "$25"},
    {ID: 2, Name: "Mechanical Keyboard", Price: "$70"},
    {ID: 3, Name: "USB-C Hub", Price: "$40"},
}

// Calls the recommendation service with timeout
func fetchRecommendations() ([]Product, error) {
    client := http.Client{Timeout: 2 * time.Second}
    resp, err := client.Get("http://localhost:9090/recommend")
    if err != nil {
        return fallbackProducts, err // graceful fallback
    }
    defer resp.Body.Close()

    var products []Product
    if err := json.NewDecoder(resp.Body).Decode(&products); err != nil {
        return fallbackProducts, err
```

```
    }
    return products, nil
}

func handler(w http.ResponseWriter, r *http.Request) {
    products, err := fetchRecommendations()
    if err != nil {
        log.Println("Using fallback due to error:", err)
    }
    json.NewEncoder(w).Encode(products)
}

func main() {
    http.HandleFunc("/products", handler)
    log.Println("Server started at :8080")
    log.Fatal(http.ListenAndServe(":8080", nil))
}
```

How to test:

1. Simulate downtime by stopping the **`/recommend`** service.
2. The service will automatically degrade to serving the fallback list, without a crash or error to the user.

Additionally, always keep in mind the following points, as they are important for graceful degradation:

- **Prioritize features:** Identify which features are critical and which are nice-to-have. Ensure that non-critical features can be disabled without affecting core functionality.
- **Degrade incrementally:** Instead of a binary *working* or *not working* state, consider multiple levels of degraded functionality.
- **Provide clear feedback:** When features are degraded or disabled, provide clear information to users about what is happening and what they can still do.

In a world where users expect 99.999% uptime and instant access, graceful degradation is not a luxury, it is table stakes. Whether you are building a multi-tenant SaaS platform or a content delivery network, the goal is clear: **Fail predictably, fail safely, and keep the user in control**.

A great digital experience does not mean nothing ever goes wrong; it means users rarely feel it when it does.

Resilient cloud architecture as a sample blueprint

After this tour of different resiliency patterns, let us see how the pieces fit together and we can build a strong cloud architecture.

Layered resiliency

Resiliency should have layers. Think of it as an onion. The layers that we have to arrange are:

- **Application level:** This is where you implement circuit breakers, retries, and graceful degradation in your application code.
- **At the service layer:** Perform health checks and enable automated recovery mechanisms.
- **Infrastructure layer:** Ensure redundancy with multi-AZ and multi-region deployments.
- **Data layer:** Ensure data resilience through replication and backup strategies.

Example of a resilient architecture

There are number of resiliency patterns we could apply and let us take a look at how it might look like in practice in a hypothetical e-commerce application:

- **Frontend:**
  - Deploy across multiple regions using a CDN.
  - Implement circuit breakers for API calls.
  - Fall back to local storage for when backend services are down.
- **API gateway:**
  - Rate limiting: Use AWS API Gateway with usage plans.
  - Caching to reduce load on the backend services.
- **Application servers:**
  - Multi-AZ deployment.
  - Turn on auto-scaling for elasticity.
  - Use health checks and automatic instance replacement.
- **Database:**
  - Deploy a multi-AZ deployment for high availability.
  - Create read replicas to increase performance and failover.

- **Caching layer:**
  - o Use a distributed cache such as Redis across more than one node.
  - o Implement fallback mechanisms for cache failures.
- **Message queue:**
  - o Decouple components using a managed service like Amazon SQS.
  - o Use dead-letter queues for failed message processing.

Conclusion

As we conclude this chapter with some resiliency patterns, please take a moment to reflect on the journey we have been on. We have covered health monitoring, redundancy, failover capabilities, graceful degradation, and the circuit breaker pattern in detail, too. We have witnessed how these patterns can come together and compose to create a resilient, fault-tolerant system capable of withstanding the trials of cyberspace.

However, resilience is a mindset as much as it is a collection of techniques. It is about preparing for failures, planning for the things you least expect, and always searching for improvement. As you keep going on the journey of your cloud architecture, it is also encouraged that you adopt this mentality in all of your endeavors.

We must remember that building resilient systems is not just about keeping them up or achieving SLAs. It is about delivering trustworthy, predictable experiences to users, regardless of hardship. It is about building trust and confidence in your services. And at the end of the day, it is about helping your business succeed in an increasingly digital world.

Throughout your work, be it developing new features, resolving incidents, or planning future strategies, continually reflect on the question: *How can this be made more resilient?* Let resilience serve as the guiding principle in every decision you make.

We will cover how to handle and manage data patterns in our next chapter, and learn to defend against threats to one of your biggest assets, your data.

Join our Discord space

Join our Discord workspace for latest updates, offers, tech happenings around the world, new releases, and sessions with the authors:

https://discord.bpbonline.com

CHAPTER 7
Data Management Patterns

Introduction

Welcome to another paramount concept on cloud application architecture. In this chapter, we will begin to explore one of the most critical components of application architecture: data management. This chapter covers several data management patterns that can help make cloud systems more effective, scalable, and reliable. We will also go through practical strategies and techniques that have been successfully deployed in real-world scenarios, approaches that others can adopt to navigate the complex landscape of cloud data management.

Before diving into individual patterns, it is important to set the stage. Imagine a scenario where a lead architect is building a high-growth e-commerce platform. Initially, the application uses a single database to meet all its data requirements. However, as the user base scales, performance issues begin to surface. The database becomes a bottleneck, unable to handle the increasing load, a situation all too familiar in the cloud world.

This is a common challenge that almost all architects and developers have encountered multiple times. Fortunately, data management patterns come to the rescue, offering solutions for key concerns such as scaling, consistency, and availability in a cloud environment. The chapter proceeds to explore these patterns in detail, one by one.

Structure

In this chapter, we will go over the following topics:

- Data partitioning
- Eventual consistency
- Data replication
- Data backup and disaster recovery
- Data lakes and data warehouses
- Data governance

Objectives

After finishing this chapter, you will be well versed with key points and concepts of data management, what constitutes creating a backbone for managing data in the cloud, and making sure the data is not accidentally shared. You will also realize the importance of strong data governance, **disaster recovery** (**DR**), and control points, and navigating through data bottlenecks via synchronization and backups.

Data partitioning

In today's cloud-native era, where data is generated at unprecedented speed and volume, managing data effectively is not just a performance concern; it is an architectural necessity. One of the unsung heroes of scalable cloud systems is data partitioning. While it may sound technical, at its core, it is about organizing data in a way that your system can breathe, scale, and grow gracefully. Whether you are building a SaaS platform for millions, or streamlining your internal systems, partitioning is the secret sauce that keeps things smooth under load.

Importance of data partitioning

Think of your database as a high-speed highway. Initially, with a few cars, everything runs fine. But as traffic increases, say millions of requests per second, that one-lane road gets jammed. Partitioning is like adding more lanes to that highway.

Here is why partitioning matters:

- **Scalability:** Efficiently distributes data and load across multiple servers or nodes.
- **Performance:** Reduces latency by querying smaller chunks of data.
- **Manageability:** Easier backups, restores, and maintenance.
- **Fault isolation:** Issues in one partition do not necessarily impact others.
- **Cost optimization:** Partitioning can optimize storage costs in pay-per-use cloud models.

- **Security:** Isolate data into separate partitions, allowing applications to enable strict security policies.

The following table depicts various use cases and the appropriate rationale behind the techniques used in the corresponding use cases:

Use case	Best method	Rationale
User management at scale	Horizontal (Sharding)	Scales linearly as the user base grows
Large table with frequent reads	Vertical partitioning	Optimizes performance and cost
Multi-tenant SaaS apps	Directory-based	Allows tenant-specific partitioning
Event logs or IoT data	Range partitioning	Efficient time-based queries
Distributed system with high concurrency	Hash partitioning	Even load distribution

Table 7.1: *Use cases of partitioning*

Methods of data partitioning

Partitioning is not a one-size-fits-all concept. Depending on your business case, you will need different strategies. Let us discuss some of the major methods.

Horizontal partitioning or sharding

Horizontal partitioning, often called **sharding**, is like dividing a large pizza into slices. Each slice (or shard) contains a subset of your data, typically based on a key such as the user ID or geographic location.

For example, let us say you are running a social media platform. Instead of storing all user data in one database, you could shard it based on user ID ranges. Users with IDs 1-1,000,000 go to Shard A, 1,000,001-2,000,000 to Shard B, and so on. The benefits include improved performance and scalability. Each shard handles fewer requests, reducing the load on individual databases. Moreover, you can easily add more shards as your data grows. However, be warned: sharding is not without its challenges. It can complicate queries that need data from multiple shards, and you will need to carefully design your sharding strategy to avoid hotspots (shards that receive disproportionately high traffic).

The benefits of horizontal partitioning are as follows:

- **Scalability:** You can scale out by adding more machines to store and handle new data slices.
- **Improved performance:** Queries hit only a portion of the data (that is,, one shard), reducing load.

- **Easier archiving:** Old partitions (for example, based on dates) can be archived or deleted without touching the entire table.
- **Fault isolation:** A failure in one shard does not bring down the entire data system.

The challenges of horizontal partitioning are as follows:

- **Complex joins:** Performing joins across partitions becomes costly or requires data duplication.
- **Data skew:** Poor partition key choice can lead to uneven load distribution (some shards are hotter).
- **Complex query routing:** Requires application logic or middleware to route to the right shard.
- **Operational overhead:** Maintaining multiple shards increases deployment, backup, and monitoring complexity.

Vertical partitioning

While horizontal partitioning splits data rows, vertical partitioning splits columns. It is like taking that pizza and separating the toppings onto different plates. In practice, this might mean storing different types of data in separate databases.

For example, in an e-commerce application, you might keep product information in one database, user profiles in another, and order history in a third. This approach can improve performance by allowing you to optimize each database for its specific data type. It also enhances security by allowing you to apply different access controls to different data types.

The benefits of vertical partitioning are as follows:

- **Performance optimization:** Narrower rows improve cache hits and I/O speed, especially for OLTP queries.
- **Separation of concerns:** Sensitive or rarely-used data can be isolated for security or cost-saving purposes.
- **Improved maintainability:** Smaller tables are easier to manage, alter, and index.

The challenges of vertical partitioning are as follows:

- **More joins:** Reconstructing complete records requires joins, which can hurt performance.
- **Increased schema complexity:** More tables lead to higher development and testing effort.
- **Cross-table consistency:** More tables mean higher development and testing effort.
- **Data consistency:** Multiple vertical partitions pose greater challenges in data consistency.

Directory-based partitioning

Directory-based partitioning, also known as **look-up-based** partitioning, uses a central directory (or routing mechanism) to determine where a specific data element lives. Think of it like a receptionist at the front desk of a hotel, and based on your reservation, they tell you which floor and room to go to.

Instead of relying on a static rule like hashing or ranges, this method uses a lookup table or metadata service, to dynamically route incoming data requests to the correct partition or database node.

For example, imagine a multi-tenant SaaS platform that manages separate data silos for each enterprise client. Company A's data resides in **`db_company_a`**, and Company B's in **`db_company_b`**. A central directory service uses the **`tenant_id`** to determine which database connection to route to.

The benefits of directory based partitioning are as follows:

- Fine-grained control over tenant isolation.
- Easy to enforce data residency/compliance.
- Flexibility to migrate tenants independently.

The challenges are as follows:

- Directory service must be **highly available**.
- Lookup latency can introduce performance issues.
- Managing the consistency of routing metadata adds complexity.

Functional partitioning

In functional partitioning, the system is split into domain-driven components, and each domain owns its data. Rather than all services pulling from a monolithic database, each microservice has its own bounded context and data schema.

This is commonly found in microservices architecture.

For example, a digital marketplace has multiple modules:

- **Auth service** manages users and roles.
- **Inventory service** tracks products and availability.
- **Payment service** handles transactions.

Each of these services owns its data store and interacts through APIs or async queues.

The benefits of functional partitioning are as follows:

- Clear ownership of data with simpler domain modeling.
- High fault isolation (payment outage does not affect auth).
- Easier scaling per domain (for example, scale payment only).

The challenges of functional partitioning are as follows:

- Cross-domain queries are hard (need de-normalization or async joins).
- Eventual consistency is the norm.
- Requires robust observability to trace across domains.

Range partitioning

In range partitioning, data is split across partitions based on a sequential range of values—such as dates, alphabetical strings, or numeric IDs.

This method is particularly efficient when **querying ranges** of data, for example, logs, transactions, time series.

For example, a FinTech application stores transaction data and partitions it based on **`transaction_date`**:

- Jan–Mar → Partition 1
- Apr–Jun → Partition 2
- Jul–Sep → Partition 3

The benefits of range partitioning are as follows:

- Ideal for time-based analytics.
- Data pruning improves performance.
- Easy to archive or delete old partitions.

The challenges of range partitioning are as follows:

- Uneven data distribution if traffic is bursty (hot partitions).
- Querying across ranges can hit multiple partitions.
- Need automation to manage and rotate partitions (for example, create one per month).

Hash partitioning

Hash partitioning distributes data across partitions using a hashing algorithm applied to a key (like **`user_id`** or **`order_id`**). This ensures a more uniform distribution, avoiding skewed loads.

The hash function is used on a partition key to determine at which partition corresponding data belongs to.

For example, in a social media platform, users are assigned to DB shards using a hash of their user ID.

```
userID = 12334567
partition = userID % 10 -----→ 10 shards
```

The benefits of hash partitioning are as follows:

- Excellent for horizontal scaling.
- Avoids hotspotting.
- Simple to implement and scale.

The challenges of hash partitioning are as follows:

- Harder to support range queries (for example, *users who joined in Jan*).
- Rebalancing partitions requires careful planning.
- Not human-readable (opaque data-to-node mapping).

Let us look at the following table explaining and summarising the partition types on the basis of various parameters as listed:

Partitioning type	Distribution	Query performance	Complexity	Use case fit
Horizontal	Even/Manual	High if well-sharded	Moderate to High	User-centric systems
Vertical	Manual	High for focused queries	Medium	Analytics, profile data
Directory-based	Lookup table	High	High (managing lookup)	Multi-tenant SaaS
Functional	Service-driven	High	High	Microservices
Range	Sequential	Medium to High	Low	Time-series, logs
Hash	Uniform	Consistent	Medium	Any distributed data

Table 7.2: *Comparison of partitioning method*

In the world of cloud-native, distributed, and multi-region applications, data partitioning is no longer optional; it is fundamental. It empowers your systems to handle more, cost less, and perform better, especially when designed with awareness of the methods and their trade-offs.

Whether you are scaling a startup or modernizing enterprise systems, it is important to choose the right partitioning pattern tailored to your architecture and domain. This will set you on the path to reliable, resilient, and high-performing systems.

Eventual consistency

Let us understand consistency first.

Consistency refers to a database query returning the same data each time the same request is made. Strong consistency means the latest data is returned, but, due to internal consistency methods, it may result in higher latency or delay. With eventual consistency, results are less consistent early on, but they are provided much faster with low latency. Early results of eventual consistency data queries may not have the most recent updates because it takes time for updates to reach replicas across a database cluster.

Let us now dig deep into the concept that seems to be very confusing when developers first come across it: **Eventual consistency**.

In distributed systems (the nature of the cloud), achieving perfect consistency on all nodes at all times, is often impractical if not outright impossible.

Eventual consistency, on the other hand, is a model that states that it is fine if data is not immediately consistent across all nodes, unless it eventually becomes consistent. That may seem like a dangerous gamble, but in a lot of cases, it is a reasonable trade-off that enables improved performance and availability.

Let us look at an example. Consider a well-known social media site. When you post a status update, does it matter if your friend on the other side of the world sees it a few seconds off from somebody who is located in the same city as you? Probably not. This deferral gives the platform the space to prioritize availability (allowing you to post quickly) over immediate global consistency.

Systems today are distributed across continents, data centres, and services. And while we crave instant synchronization, achieving strong consistency everywhere, all the time, is like trying to get five toddlers to agree on pizza toppings; it is unrealistic and expensive.

That is where eventual consistency steps in as a pragmatic hero.

Eventual consistency is a consistency model used in distributed computing where the system guarantees that, given enough time without new updates, all replicas of a data item will converge to the same value. Unlike strong consistency, it does not enforce immediate synchronization across nodes.

It is not about laziness; it is about availability, resilience, and speed. For many real-world applications (social media, e-commerce carts, IoT), eventual consistency is good enough and makes the system more performant and fault-tolerant.

However, before deep diving into eventual consistency ways and methods, let us take a step back and understand the CAP theorem.

CAP theorem

Before we get into what eventual consistency actually means, we need to cover the foundational principle that lays out how distributed systems are designed: the CAP theorem. Fundamentally, the CAP theorem, as articulated in a Google paper by *Eric Brewer*, claims that a distributed system can provide only two of the following three properties at any point:

- **Consistency (C):** All reads return the latest write, and / or an error.
- **Availability (A):** Each request will receive a (non-error) response but not guaranteed to contain the latest write.
- **Partition Tolerance (P):** The system will not fail even if the network drops or delays an arbitrary **Number** (**N**) of messages.

Consider a traffic light system in a city. When a network cable gets cut (a partition), the signal controller must make a choice: should it stop working (sacrificing availability) or keep working without correct coordination (sacrificing consistency)? In cloud-native systems, where partition tolerance is a non-negotiable (networks inherently suck), architects usually do trade-offs on consistency vs. availability.

Here is where the eventual consistency just steps in, a pragmatic trade-off that selectively prefers availability and partition tolerance to consistency, enabling the latter to happen eventually rather than immediately.

Methods of achieving eventual consistency

Achieving eventual consistency in a distributed system is not a one-size-fits-all problem. It requires a mix of patterns, algorithms, and smart engineering trade-offs. Let us explore the core methods used by cloud-native architectures to ensure that all replicas eventually converge to the same state, even in the presence of network partitions, delayed writes, or concurrent updates.

Conflict-free Replicated Data Types

Conflict-free Replicated Data Types (**CRDT**) are mathematically designed data structures that allow updates from different replicas to be merged automatically and deterministically, without requiring coordination. This makes them ideal for distributed systems where latency and availability are prioritized.

Here is how CRDTs work:

- CRDTs rely on commutative, associative, and idempotent operations.
- For example, if two users concurrently add elements to a CRDT-based set on two different nodes, when they sync, both elements will be present—no data loss, no conflicts.

Some common CRDT types are:

- **G-Counter** (grow-only counter)
- **PN-Counter** (increment / decrement)
- **OR-Set** (observed-remove set)

Let us consider a practical example. In real-time collaboration tools like Google Docs, Notion, or Figma, where users edit content simultaneously, CRDTs ensure that every user's view converges, regardless of the sequence of operations.

Vector clocks and version vectors

Vector clocks are used to track the causal history of data updates across multiple nodes. Each node maintains a vector (an array of counters), and updates are tagged with the current vector state. This helps detect whether two versions of data are:

- Causally related (one happened before the other)
- Concurrent/conflicting (need to be reconciled)

Here is how it works:

- When a node updates a data item, it increments its own counter.
- Upon syncing, nodes compare their vectors to determine consistency or conflicts.

Here is a real-world example. Amazon Dynamo and Riak use vector clocks to detect conflicting updates. Conflicts can then be resolved through client-side logic, version merges, or custom resolution strategies.

Last-Write-Wins

Last-Write-Wins (**LWW**) is the most straightforward (and blunt) consistency strategy. In LWW, each data update is tagged with a timestamp, and the system retains the version with the most recent timestamp in case of conflicts.

The pros are:

- Simple and easy to implement.
- Low-latency, suitable for systems with frequent writes.

The cons are:

- Risk of data loss in concurrent updates.
- Relies on clock synchronization, which may drift in real-world deployments.

Here is a use case:

- IoT telemetry, status flags, user presence indicators where precision is less critical than responsiveness.

For example, in a shopping app, if two microservices update a user's shipping status simultaneously, LWW ensures the most recent status (*Shipped vs Delivered*) wins.

Quorum-based replication

This method leverages the mathematics of majority agreement to balance consistency and availability. It is the foundation of many distributed databases (like Cassandra and DynamoDB).

The key terms are as follows:

- **N:** Total number of replicas.
- **W:** Number of nodes that must acknowledge a write.
- **R:** Number of nodes to read from.

As long as **W + R > N**, you guarantee that at least one node contains the most recent write.

The different types of the quorum-based replication are as follows:

- **Read quorum:** Reads from R replicas to ensure a recent value.
- **Write quorum:** Requires W replicas to accept the write.

For example, if *N=3*, a common quorum configuration might be *W=2* and *R=2*. This ensures overlap and helps reconcile data discrepancies over time.

Here is a real-world scenario. Apache Cassandra allows configuring the consistency level per operation: ONE, QUORUM, or ALL.

The following table features the various use cases of eventual consistency techniques:

Method	Use case
CRDTs	Collaborative platforms (Google Docs, Notion), real-time chat apps
Vector clocks	Conflict resolution in distributed databases (Cassandra, DynamoDB)
LWW	Caching layers, shopping cart updates, IoT telemetry feeds
Quorum Replication	Financial ledgers, distributed logs, globally-distributed web apps

***Table 7.3:** Use cases of eventual consistencies*

The following table depicts the comparison of eventual consistency techniques over various parameters:

Method	Complexity	Conflict handling	Latency	Use case suitability
CRDTs	High	Automatic	Low	Real-time collaboration
Vector Clocks	Medium	Manual/Custom	Medium	Databases, logs
Last-Write-Wins	Low	Timestamp-based	Low	Simple data overwrite
Quorum Replication	Medium	Avoids Conflicts	Higher	Read-heavy apps

***Table 7.4:** Eventual consistency techniques comparison*

Now let us look into how and what services and support various cloud providers offer for eventual consistency:

Cloud provider	Service	Eventual consistency support
AWS	DynamoDB, S3	Yes – configurable consistency in DynamoDB (eventual or strong), S3 offers read-after-write eventual consistency
Azure	Cosmos DB, Blob Storage	Yes – Cosmos DB supports multiple consistency models including eventual
Google Cloud	Firestore, Cloud Storage	Yes – Firestore supports eventual for global reads, Cloud Storage is eventually consistent for certain metadata
Cassandra (Self-managed)	Apache Cassandra	Strong support – relies heavily on eventual consistency and tunable consistency

Table 7.5: *Cloud provider's services for eventual consistency*

Each major cloud platform embraces eventual consistency where it makes sense. For high-availability scenarios, such as object storage (S3, Blob, GCS) or globally distributed NoSQL databases (Cosmos DB, DynamoDB, Firestore), eventual consistency is the default behavior. They also offer tunable consistency levels, so that developers can choose between strong, bounded staleness, session, or eventual, depending on the workload.

Eventual consistency implementation in MongoDB Atlas with Golang

Let us walk through an actual implementation using **MongoDB Atlas** and **Golang**, simulating eventual consistency across two microservices writing to a shared collection with potential conflict.

Scenario

Two services concurrently update the status of a shipment. We resolve the conflict using LWW strategy based on timestamps. Refer to the following code:

main.go

```
package main

import (
  "context"
  "fmt"
  "time"
```

```

	"go.mongodb.org/mongo-driver/bson"
	"go.mongodb.org/mongo-driver/mongo"
	"go.mongodb.org/mongo-driver/mongo/options"
)

type Shipment struct {
	ID        string    `bson:"_id"`
	Status    string    `bson:"status"`
	UpdatedAt time.Time `bson:"updated_at"`
}

func main() {
	ctx := context.TODO()
	client, err := mongo.Connect(ctx, options.Client().ApplyURI("<Your MongoDB Atlas URI>"))
	if err != nil {
		panic(err)
	}
	defer client.Disconnect(ctx)

	collection := client.Database("<DBname>").Collection("<collectionname>")

	// Simulated concurrent update
	updatedStatus := record{
		ID:        "recordID",
		Status:    "CustomStatus",
		UpdatedAt: time.Now(), // each service sets its own timestamp
	}

	// Use Update with $max to implement Last-Write-Wins (based on timestamp)
	filter := bson.M{"_id": updatedStatus.ID}
	update := bson.M{
		"$max": bson.M{
			"updated_at": updatedStatus.UpdatedAt,
			"status":     updatedStatus.Status,
		},
```

```
}

result, err := collection.UpdateOne(ctx, filter, update)
if err != nil {
 panic(err)
}

fmt.Printf("Matched %v, Modified %v\n", result.MatchedCount, result.
  ModifiedCount)
}
```

Here is how it works:

- Each service attempts to update the same record.
- The $max operator ensures the update only proceeds if the **updated_at** value is newer.
- This avoids stale data overwrites, a simple yet effective way to implement LWW.

Eventual consistency is not a compromise; it is a strategic choice for modern, distributed cloud systems. It powers everything from messaging apps to global retail platforms, balancing availability and performance while accepting brief inconsistencies. With the right strategy, be it CRDTs, vector clocks, or quorum voting, you can build scalable, resilient systems that do not break the bank or your sleep.

Remember, eventual consistency is not appropriate for all scenarios. For financial transactions or critical health data, you might need stronger consistency guarantees. Always consider your application's specific needs when choosing a consistency model.

Data replication

Data replication might sound like a dry operational detail, but in reality, it is the unsung hero that keeps today's digital world spinning. Whether you are streaming your favorite show on a cross-continental flight or collaborating live on a shared document with teammates around the globe, replication is working quietly in the background, making sure your data is always available, synchronized, and resilient. At its core, it is the practice of copying data from one system to another, often across regions or cloud zones, to ensure redundancy, fault tolerance, and faster access. But modern replication is not just about making backups; it is about designing for continuity, delivering performance at scale, and future-proofing applications against latency, outages, or even geopolitical regulations. For architects, it is a balancing act of consistency, availability, and cost. For students, it is a gateway to understanding distributed systems, eventual consistency, and real-world engineering trade-offs. In a world that never sleeps, data replication ensures that your architecture does not sleep either.

Historical context

Imagine the early 90s: clunky on-premise servers humming in cold data centres, backup tapes being carted around like prized possessions, and nightly cron jobs praying not to fail. In that world, **data lived dangerously**. In one place, one format, often isolated from everything else. If a hard disk crashed, you were not just dealing with downtime. You were staring into the gorge of permanent data loss.

Then came distributed systems and the rise of the internet economy. With businesses expanding across continents, the idea of having just **one golden copy** of the data became a liability. Enter data replication, the idea that your data should not only be duplicated but should live in harmony across systems and geographies.

As early as the mid-2000s, systems like MySQL and Oracle supported **master-slave replication** models. However, those setups were often complex to configure and brittle under pressure. Now, fast forward to the cloud era. AWS, Azure, GCP, and modern distributed databases like Cassandra and MongoDB made replication seamless, programmable, and often invisible.

In today's world of real-time streaming, globally distributed users, and AI workloads, data replication is not just a way to survive failure; it is the way we scale trust.

Importance of data replication

In today's cloud-driven world, data replication is your insurance policy. It ensures that when things go sideways (which they often do), your application does not go down with the ship.

Let us break this down:

- **High Availability (HA):** Data replication allows systems to stay up even when parts of the infrastructure fail. If one node or region becomes unavailable, requests can be routed to a replica.
- **Disaster recovery (DR):** Replicated data across geographically distant regions means you are not dependent on a single data centre. Even if there is a natural disaster or outage, operations can resume from another region.
- **Improved read performance:** By placing read replicas closer to the user geographically, latency can be significantly reduced.
- **Data locality compliance:** Certain regions (like the EU with GDPR) require data to be stored within geographic boundaries. Replication lets you meet these legal and compliance requirements effortlessly.
- **Seamless upgrades and maintenance:** With replicated systems, you can perform updates, schema changes, and maintenance on one node while traffic continues on another, without downtime.

It is no longer about whether you should replicate data; it is about how well you do it.

Let us imagine a scenario. You run a global e-commerce site. Your customer, let us name her Maria in this case, is in New York, clicks on **Buy Now**. That transaction better not go down a black hole because your US-East server hiccupped. That is where **replication** shines.

Data replication is not just a resilience tactic; it is a **business enabler**. Here is why it matters more than ever:

- **Business continuity:** If your primary region experiences a power outage or a disaster, a replica in another region can seamlessly continue serving traffic. Your customers stay happy.
- **Geographic distribution:** Replication enables low-latency access for users worldwide. No more data traversing oceans and waiting seconds to respond.
- **Real-time analytics:** Want to run heavy queries without stressing the production database? Replication makes it possible by offloading reads to replicated nodes.
- **Hybrid cloud and multi-cloud:** As businesses hedge their bets across cloud providers, replication is what makes data flow between them fluidly.
- **Data sovereignty:** In some countries, legal regulations demand data be stored locally. Replication helps maintain global architecture while respecting local rules.

Without replication, cloud-native systems would be like skyscrapers without fire exits. It is not just about scaling; it is about surviving, thriving, and delivering delight 24x7x365.

Methods of data replication

Replication is not one-size-fits-all. The method you choose depends on trade-offs: speed vs. consistency, simplicity vs. flexibility, and cost vs. availability. Here is a deeper dive into the primary methods.

Synchronous replication

Writes are committed to both the primary and secondary nodes simultaneously. A client request is considered successful only after **all** replicas confirm the write.

Here are some use cases:

- Financial systems (banks, trading apps).
- Inventory management where accuracy is mission-critical.

Here are some key benefits:

- **Strong consistency:** Everyone sees the same data, always.
- **Minimal data loss:** If a failure happens right after a write, the replica has your back.

Here are some challenges:

- Slower write performance due to network latency.
- Higher cost due to redundant writes and resource utilization.

For example, in PostgreSQL, enabling synchronous replication ensures that data committed to a primary node waits for acknowledgment from a standby node before the transaction is marked as complete.

Asynchronous replication

Data is written to the primary node and then propagated to replicas **afterward**. The client is notified of success before replication completes.

Here are some use cases:

- Social networks (likes, comments).
- Content delivery platforms.
- Mobile gaming backends.

Here are some key benefits:

- **Faster writes:** No waiting around.
- Higher throughput and reduced latency.

The challenges are as follows:

- Risk of stale reads during replication lag.
- Possibility of data loss if the primary fails before sync completes.

For example, in MongoDB, secondary nodes replicate data from the primary asynchronously using the operation log, ensuring performance at scale.

Multi-master replication

Multiple nodes can handle writes and sync changes across the system. Conflict resolution is typically done based on timestamps or custom logic.

Here are some use cases:

- Global SaaS apps (Google Docs, Slack).
- Collaborative tools.
- Mobile applications with offline support.

Here are some key benefits:

- Global write availability.
- No single point of failure.

The challenges are as follows:

- Complex conflict resolution (what if two users edit the same thing simultaneously?)
- Increased operational complexity.

For example, AWS DynamoDB Global Tables offer a multi-master model where each AWS region acts as a writer and reader, syncing changes with eventual consistency.

Peer-to-peer replication

All nodes are equal. Each can act as both source and destination for data changes. Common in decentralized or hybrid systems.

Here are some use cases:

- Edge computing scenarios.
- IoT networks.
- Blockchain applications.

The key benefits are as follows:

- Decentralization boosts resilience.
- No central point of failure.

The challenges are as follows:

- Conflict resolution logic can become intricate.
- Network overhead is higher.

For example, CouchDB uses a peer-to-peer replication protocol, which makes it ideal for devices operating in disconnected or offline-first environments.

Each replication method shines under different circumstances. Here is how organizations typically use them in the following scenarios:

Replication method	Real-world use case
Synchronous replication	Stock trading platforms require absolute accuracy of records. If a trade is placed, it must be visible across all nodes in real-time. There is no room for lag.
Asynchronous replication	Media streaming services like Netflix replicate viewing history asynchronously; if a user pauses on their phone, it syncs to their smart TV a few seconds later.
Semi-synchronous replication	Online marketplaces like Amazon need a balance, order confirmation is fast, yet durable across multiple zones.
Multi-master replication	Collaborative platforms like Notion or Google Docs let users make updates from any region, with instant visibility to others.

Table 7.6: Data replication use cases

Let us also examine the comparison of data replication techniques in a summarised form:

Replication type	Consistency	Latency	Complexity	Fault tolerance
Synchronous	Strong	High	Medium	High
Asynchronous	Eventual	Low	Low	Medium
Semi-synchronous	Medium	Medium	Medium	High
Multi-master	Eventual (with conflict resolution)	Low	High	Very High

Table 7.7: *Date replication techniques comparison*

Moreover, each provider offers nuanced advantages; choosing one depends on performance SLAs, compliance requirements, and cost efficiency. Here is a quick comparison for the same for reference:

Cloud provider	Replication options	Unique features	Ideal for
AWS	Multi-AZ, Multi-Region, Global Datastore (DynamoDB), Aurora Replicas	Global tables in DynamoDB with low-latency cross-region writes	High-performance, global SaaS apps
Azure	Geo-Replication (for Blob, SQL), Zone Redundant Storage	Read-access geo-redundant storage (RA-GRS), Cosmos DB with 5 consistency models	Enterprise apps, compliance-heavy systems
GCP	Cloud Spanner, Bigtable replication, Multi-region buckets	True horizontal scaling with strong consistency in Spanner	Global transactional apps
MongoDB Atlas *(Cloud-agnostic)*	Built-in replica sets across zones and regions	Self-healing clusters, Global clusters, zone-based sharding	Apps needing geo-aware writes/reads

Table 7.8: *Cloud provider offerings for data replication*

Now, let us look the data replication in action with a practical example.

For this, we will use Mongo DB replica set and Golang code base to write on. Follow the given steps:

1. Spin up a MongoDB Atlas Cluster. Then:
    a. Go to MongoDB Atlas.
    b. Create a new cluster.
    c. Select **Cloud Provider & Region** (Choose AWS/GCP/Azure with multiple availability zones).
    d. Under **Cluster Tier**, select an instance size with **3 nodes** (replica set).

2. Use this sample Golang Code to Connect to replica set.

main.go

```
package main

import (
    "context"
    "fmt"
    "log"
    "time"

    "go.mongodb.org/mongo-driver/mongo"
    "go.mongodb.org/mongo-driver/mongo/options"
)

func main() {
    ctx, cancel := context.WithTimeout(context.Background(), 10*time.Second)
    defer cancel()

    uri := "mongodb+srv://<username>:<password>@<cluster-url>/test?retryWrites=true&w=majority"
    clientOpts := options.Client().ApplyURI(uri)

    client, err := mongo.Connect(ctx, clientOpts)
    if err != nil {
        log.Fatal(err)
    }
    defer client.Disconnect(ctx)

    collection := client.Database("replication_demo").Collection("logs")

    doc := map[string]interface{}{
        "timestamp": time.Now(),
        "message":   "This is a replicated log entry",
    }

    res, err := collection.InsertOne(ctx, doc)
    if err != nil {
        log.Fatal(err)
    }

```

```
    fmt.Printf("Inserted document with ID: %v\n", res.InsertedID)
}
```

This app connects to a replica set and inserts a document. MongoDB Atlas automatically replicates it across nodes.

Thus, data replication is no longer just an operational strategy; it is a **resiliency superpower**. Whether you are building a global SaaS product or an internal analytics engine, replicating data effectively can be the difference between a good user experience and a service outage.

Each method, synchronous, asynchronous, semi-sync, and multi-master, serves a purpose depending on your system's needs. Moreover, with cloud providers offering native support for sophisticated replication, it is easier than ever to architect for scale and reliability.

Data backup and disaster recovery

The story of backup and DR mirrors the evolution of technology itself. In the 1960s and 70s, when computers were massive and data was precious but scarce, backups were literally handwritten records, magnetic tapes, and carefully stored paper copies. The mindset back then was simple: *If the mainframe dies, we retype everything.*

As businesses became increasingly dependent on digital systems, the 80s and 90s shepherded in slightly more sophisticated methods: floppy disks, tape libraries, and mirrored hard drives. DR plans, however, were often informal, handwritten notes or basic procedures that sat untouched in dusty filing cabinets.

By the 2000s, everything changed. As digital-first companies like Amazon and Google emerged, and with cyber threats growing exponentially, the value of data skyrocketed. A hardware failure or cyberattack could now bankrupt a business overnight. Thus, backup and DR became strategic necessities, not just technical best practices.

Today, with public cloud infrastructure at the forefront, DR is almost entirely automated, geographically distributed, and integrated with AI-driven predictive analytics.

Importance of backup and recovery

In today's hyper-connected world, downtime is not measured in hours. It is measured in seconds and dollars lost per second. The importance of a solid backup and DR strategy cannot be overstated, and the following parameters are key motivators for the same:

- **Business continuity:** Having a backup strategy ensures that your business operations can survive crises, whether there are cyberattacks, ransomware, fires, floods, or human errors. A well-prepared organization can switch over to backup systems seamlessly, without losing customer trust.
- **Data integrity and trust:** Backup systems ensure that your data remains accurate, untampered, and retrievable even if your production environment is compromised.

- **Regulatory compliance:** Compliance standards like GDPR, HIPAA, and PCI-DSS require businesses to have proper data recovery and business continuity plans. Failure to comply can result in hefty fines and reputational damage.
- **Resilience to modern threats:** With sophisticated threats like ransomware attacks encrypting entire networks, having an isolated, tamper-proof backup is often the only way to avoid catastrophic data loss.
- **Competitive advantage:** In a crisis, companies with robust DR can continue operations while competitors are stuck scrambling. Customers remember who stayed reliable during chaos.

In short, backup and DR are not just about surviving disasters, they are about building a resilient, trustworthy brand in an unpredictable digital world.

Methods of backup and recovery

Organizations today have a range of methods to suit different operational needs, budgets, and risk profiles. Let us dive deeper into them:

- **Full backup:** A full backup is the most straightforward approach. A complete copy of all data at a certain point in time. Its features are:
  - **Practical example**: Backing up an entire customer database to AWS S3 Glacier every week.
  - **Real world fit**: Best suited for static datasets that do not change frequently.
  - **Pros**: Simplicity in restoration (one file, no dependency chains).
  - **Cons**: High storage and bandwidth consumption.
- **Incremental backup:** Here, after an initial full backup, only the changes (deltas) since the last backup are saved. Its features are:
  - **Practical example:** Daily incremental backups for an e-commerce site's orders database.
  - **Real world fit:** Fast-changing datasets where daily full backups would be too costly.
  - **Pros:** Saves storage and speeds up backup processes.
  - **Cons:** Restoration may be complex; you have to restore the full backup plus every subsequent incremental.
- **Differential backup:** A blend of full and incremental approaches. Differential backups capture all changes since the last full backup. Its features are:
  - **Practical example**: Corporate email system backing up all new or changed emails since last Sunday's full backup.

- **Real world fit**: Ideal when quicker restores are needed, but storage can accommodate some redundancy.
- **Pros**: Easier to restore than incremental backups.
- **Cons**: Backup sizes grow with each passing day after a full backup.

- **Point-in-time snapshots:** Cloud platforms make it easy to capture snapshots of databases, storage volumes, or even entire virtual machines. Its features are:
  - **Practical example:** Snapshots of AWS RDS databases every 6 hours.
  - **Real world fit:** Critical for applications needing frequent recovery points, such as fintech apps.
  - **Pros:** Fast, automated, storage-efficient.
  - **Cons:** May not capture "in-flight" transactions unless combined with quiescing techniques.
- **Geo-redundant replication:** Data is simultaneously replicated to multiple geographic locations. Even if one region burns down (literally), your operations can continue from another region. Its features are:
  - **Practical example:** Replicating customer data from AWS US-East to AWS US-West.
  - **Real world fit:** Mission-critical applications, regulated industries (healthcare, finance).
  - **Pros:** Ultimate protection against regional disasters.
  - **Cons:** Higher complexity and too much cost.
- **Disaster Recovery as a Service (DRaaS):** DRaaS providers offer fully managed backup, replication, and failover services, often via SaaS platforms. Its features are:
  - **Practical example**: Using Azure Site Recovery to auto-failover workloads from on-prem to Azure Cloud during outages.
  - **Real world fit**: Mid-sized enterprises without deep in-house DR expertise.
  - **Pros**: Offloads heavy lifting; quick to implement.
  - **Cons**: Vendor lock-in risks and potential SLA mismatches.

With the given points, let us view a summarised version of the given techniques in quick tabular snapshot for easy reference:

Method	Pros	Cons	Ideal use case
Full backup	Complete protection, easy to restore	High storage costs, time-consuming	Static or infrequently changing datasets

Method	Pros	Cons	Ideal use case
Incremental backup	Storage efficient, faster daily backups	Restoration can be complex (needs chaining)	Rapidly changing environments
Differential backup	Simpler restoration than incremental	Grows in size until next full backup	Medium-change rate datasets
Point-in-time snapshot	Quick recovery, low overhead	Not always a full backup (metadata risk)	Cloud-native applications
Geo-redundant replication	Survives regional failures	Higher costs, needs more planning	Critical business applications
DRaaS	Fastest recovery time, offloads management	Vendor dependency, recurring costs	Small-medium businesses without large IT teams

***Table 7.9:** Comparison of data backup methods*

Data lakes and data warehouses

Very often, we are asked this question: Should we use a data lake or a data warehouse? The answer is, as with many other things in technology is, that it depends on the situation.

To appreciate the evolution of data lakes and warehouses, we must rewind a bit back to when business decisions were driven by gut feeling more than data. As businesses grew, they realized that their operational data (sales, inventory, transactions) held valuable insights. This sparked the development of **data warehouses** in the late 1980s and early 1990s. These were purpose-built systems, optimized for querying and reporting structured data.

Enterprises would extract data from operational systems (like ERP and CRM), transform it into a unified format, and load it into a centralized warehouse. This process, also called **Extract, Transform, Load** (**ETL**), enabled executives to answer questions like: How were our Q4 sales in the North-East region compared to last year.

Data warehouses were a big deal. They helped banks detect fraud, retail chains forecast sales, and telecom companies reduce churn. Think of it as a high-end wine cellar: you did not throw in any random bottle. Only the best, most organized vintages made it in, after being cleaned, labeled, and categorized.

However, with the explosion of unstructured data in the 2000s, such as social media, logs, IoT, and multimedia, warehouses started to feel constrained. They were significant for structured data, but cumbersome and expensive for storing and processing raw, diverse formats. There was a need for a more flexible, scalable solution.

Enter the data lake, a more relaxed, no-judgment zone for data, powered by big data technologies such as Hadoop and later, cloud-native storage like AWS S3 and so on. Unlike the warehouse, which demanded you clean up before entry, the lake said: Come as you are. Dump everything in raw, whether structured, semi-structured, or even binary blobs. Hence, data scientists and ML engineers finally had a place to experiment freely.

Let us look at both in them greater detail:

- **Data warehouses:** Structured and processed. Think of a data warehouse as a library where all the books are neatly categorized, indexed, and placed on specific shelves. It is a repository for structured, processed data that is organized for a specific purpose.
  - Data warehouses are great when:
    - You need to perform complex queries and analytics on structured data.
    - You have well-defined, consistent data models.
    - You need to support business intelligence and reporting tools.
  - For example, a retail company might use a data warehouse to store historical sales data, customer information, and inventory levels. This structured approach allows for quick and efficient analysis of business performance.
- **Data lakes:** Raw and diverse. A data lake, on the other hand, is more like a vast reservoir where you can pour in data of all types and formats. It is a storage repository that holds a large amount of raw data in its native format until it is needed.
  - Data lakes shine when:
    - You need to store large volumes of diverse data (structured, semi-structured, and unstructured).
    - You want to keep data in its raw form for future use cases you have not yet defined.
    - You are dealing with big data and need to support data scientists and machine learning workflows.
  - For instance, a social media company might use a data lake to store user-generated content, clickstream data, and server logs. This allows them to retain all potentially valuable data and figure out how to use it later.

Importance of data lakes and data warehouses

In today's cloud-native world, the difference between a reactive and a proactive enterprise often lies in its data architecture. Both data lakes and warehouses play critical, complementary roles in this story. Let us go over them:

- **Data warehouses** are essential when accuracy, speed, and analytics on structured data are paramount. Think financial forecasting, marketing dashboards, or supply chain optimization. They are like polished dashboards; they do not care about every drop of oil, just the refined stuff. They are fast, reliable, structured and built for dashboards, financial models, and operational KPIs.

- **Data lakes**, on the other hand, are the staging grounds for innovation. They allow teams to explore raw data, perform machine learning experiments, run real-time analytics on log streams, or even process video and sensor data, all in one place. They are like open oil fields, you collect everything you possibly can, without immediate plans for all of it. Maybe today you are focused on web traffic logs, but tomorrow those same logs could train your recommendation engine or feed anomaly detection models. Data lakes give your future self-options.

Together, they power everything from KPI dashboards to AI-driven personalization, forming the backbone of modern business intelligence and digital transformation strategies.

Where it gets even more interesting is the convergence of both, which is powering modern analytics platforms. If your query is how many items we are selling per region, use a warehouse. If you want to train a neural net to predict what customers will buy next, use data lake.

So, whether you are answering to what happened, or trying to predict what could happen, you are going to need both.

Methods of implementing data lakes and data warehouses

Let us break this down practically and learn how we actually build these systems in the cloud.

Data lake implementation methods

The different data lake implementation methods are:

- **Raw data ingestion to object storage**
    - Data from various sources, such as mobile apps, IoT devices, and logs, is dumped into object storage (like Amazon S3 or Azure Data Lake Storage).
    - In terms of formats, everything is fair game: JSON, CSV, images, Parquet, Avro, etc.
- **Schema-on-read querying**
    - You apply schema at query time using tools like AWS Athena, Apache Presto, or Databricks SQL.
    - This means you do not have to know what your data looks like when you ingest it.

- **Metadata cataloging**
  - Tools like AWS Glue Data Catalog or Apache Hive Metastore help you organize datasets for easier discovery.
- **ETL/ELT pipelines**
  - You can run Spark, Airflow, or Glue pipelines to clean and transform lake data, sometimes feeding it into downstream warehouses.

Data warehouse implementation methods

The different data warehouse implementation methods are:

- **Data modelling first (Schema-on-write)**
  - Before ingestion, you define strict schemas: what tables, columns, data types, and keys your system expects.
  - This enforces data integrity but requires upfront planning.
- **ETL pipelines**
  - Raw operational data is extracted, cleaned (nulls removed, types cast), and transformed (aggregated, filtered), then loaded into your warehouse.
  - Tools like Fivetran, dbt, Snaplogic, and Talend are common here.
- **Columnar storage engines**
  - Most modern warehouses (for example, Redshift, BigQuery, Snowflake) use columnar formats to compress and query data faster.
  - Great for SELECT-heavy workloads with large datasets.
- **Federated querying**
  - Warehouses are now smart enough to reach into your data lake and query raw data directly, so you do not always need to move it.

Use cases of data lakes and data warehouses

Understanding when and where to use a data lake or data warehouse often comes down to the type of data you are handling, your team's goals, and the agility your business demands.

The use cases for data lakes are:

- **Machine learning and data science:** Data scientists thrive in data lakes. They need raw, unfiltered, diverse datasets to experiment with predictive models and training pipelines.
- **Real-time analytics:** Logs, IoT sensor streams, and clickstream data are ideal for ingestion into a lake where tools like Apache Kafka and Flink can process them in near real-time.

- **Multimedia and IoT data:** Images, videos, JSON blobs, and other semi-structured formats are not ideal for traditional warehouses, but a data lake handles them with ease.

The use cases for data warehouses are:

- **Business intelligence dashboards:** When the CFO wants last quarter's financials or the VP of Sales needs a dashboard comparing conversion rates, the data must be reliable and instantly available.
- **Regulatory and compliance reporting:** Warehouses offer immutability and consistency, making them ideal for audits, tax calculations, and legal reporting.
- **Operational reporting:** From performance metrics to inventory summaries, warehouses support high-speed aggregation and querying of structured data.

With the understanding, let us have a quick summarization in tabular format for data lake and warehouse comparison:

Feature/Attribute	Data lake	Data warehouse
Data Types Supported	Structured, semi-structured, unstructured	Structured
Storage Cost	Low (object storage like S3, Blob)	High (columnar DBs with compute/storage)
Schema Type	Schema-on-read	Schema-on-write
Performance for Queries	Slower (depends on data prep)	Fast (optimized for SQL queries)
ETL vs ELT	ELT (load first, transform later)	ETL (transform before loading)
Ideal Use Cases	ML, IoT, Big Data exploration	BI, Reporting, Regulatory compliance
Tooling Examples	AWS Athena, Spark, Databricks	Snowflake, BigQuery, Redshift
Data Governance	Complex, evolving	Mature and centralized

Table 7.10: *Data lake vs data warehouse*

Moreover, each major cloud provider offers solutions across the spectrum. Here is a bird's eye view of their capabilities:

Cloud provider	Data lake offering	Data warehouse offering	Integrated stack support	Notable feature
AWS	Amazon S3 + Glue + Athena	Amazon Redshift	Yes (Lake Formation, Spectrum)	Seamless querying from Redshift to S3
Azure	Azure Data Lake Storage	Azure Synapse Analytics	Yes	Hybrid queries across lake + warehouse

Cloud provider	Data lake offering	Data warehouse offering	Integrated stack support	Notable feature
Google Cloud	Google Cloud Storage + Dataproc	BigQuery	Yes	Serverless warehouse & ML integration
Snowflake	Indirect (external table access)	Snowflake Warehouse	Partial	Cross-cloud querying, native ML
Databricks	Delta Lake (on any cloud)	Partner-integrated (with Snowflake or BigQuery)	Yes (via Unity Catalog, Lakehouse)	Unified Lakehouse vision

Table 7.11: *Cloud provider offering for data lake and warehouses*

Choosing between data lakes and data warehouses

Let us understand a decision framework that helps when deciding between a data lake and a data warehouse by considering the following factors:

- **Data structure:** If your data is highly structured and you have well-defined schemas, a data warehouse might be more appropriate. For diverse, unstructured data, a data lake is often better.
- **Query patterns:** Data warehouses excel at complex SQL-based analytics queries. If you need to support ad-hoc exploration of raw data, a data lake might be preferable.
- **Data volume and velocity:** Data lakes are better suited to handling extremely large volumes of data and high-velocity data streams.
- **Cost:** Data lakes are generally less expensive for storage but may require more processing work to derive insights.
- **User base:** Data warehouses are typically easier for business analysts to use directly. Data lakes often require more technical expertise to extract value.
- **Flexibility:** If you are not sure how you will use the data in the future, a data lake provides more flexibility to adapt to new use cases.

Remember, these are not mutually exclusive. Many organizations use both data lakes and data warehouses as part of a comprehensive data strategy.

Data governance

In an era where data fuels every strategic decision, the idea of *governance* may sound like red tape. But let us be honest, without it, organizations can easily end up in data chaos. Imagine your cloud ecosystem as a bustling city, data governance is the city planning, zoning, and public safety all rolled into one. It is not just about control; it is about enabling data to safely reach its potential.

Before cloud-native environments, data governance was largely a boardroom checkbox. In the 1980s and 90s, businesses were driven by mainframe and relational database systems. Governance, back then, meant periodic audits, managing access at the database level, and maintaining Excel sheets for documentation.

With the rise of distributed systems and the explosion of internet-scale data in the 2000s, this passive approach failed. Enterprises suddenly found themselves flooded with disparate data from CRMs, ERPs, e-commerce platforms, and third-party sources, all with different structures and standards.

The situation escalated with regulations like SOX (2002) in the U.S. and GDPR (2018) in Europe. Organizations could no longer afford data ambiguity. They had to prove ownership, lineage, access control, and proper handling of every single byte of personal or financial data.

With the advent of cloud era, services like AWS, Azure, and GCP offered scalability, they also made governance harder. Data now lived in buckets, streams, blobs, warehouses, and lakes. This shift elevated data governance from IT's backroom to a **mission-critical capability**. Today, it is not just about managing data, it is about securing trust and enabling compliance at scale.

Importance of data governance in the cloud

Think of cloud data as water flowing through a city, without governance, it either floods or gets wasted. Here is why strong data governance matters:

- **Data trust and quality:** In a cloud ecosystem, different teams rely on shared data for decisions. Governance ensures that this data is accurate, up-to-date, and consistent across tools. Without it, one marketing dashboard might say sales went up 5%, while finance reports a 10% drop, because they are using different versions of the same dataset.

- **Security and risk mitigation:** With remote work and global teams, data is accessed from everywhere. Governance enforces who gets to see what and when. It prevents a junior analyst from accidentally viewing customer credit card info or modifying critical inventory datasets.

- **Regulatory compliance:** Whether it is **GDPR**, **HIPAA**, **CCPA**, or **PCI-DSS**, regulations require organizations to prove they know the following:

    - Where data comes from,

    - Who accessed it,

    - How it is stored and transformed,

    - How long is it retained,

  - o Moreover, governance provides the audit trails and classification systems that make this possible.
- **Operational efficiency:** Good governance minimizes data duplication and misinterpretation. Imagine avoiding five versions of a "customer record" by having one governed source, saving time, reducing integration overhead, and streamlining operations.

Here is a quick snapshot on the key metrics and KPIs for data governance:

Category	Metric / KPI	Definition	Why it matters
Data quality	Data Accuracy Rate	% of data entries that are correct and free from errors.	Inaccurate data can lead to poor decision-making and customer dissatisfaction.
	Data Completeness Score	% of data fields populated as required per schema or business rule.	Ensures required data is available for operations, analytics, and compliance.
	Data Consistency Index	% of data that aligns across systems (e.g., master data consistency).	Prevents conflicting information across platforms and reduces redundancy.
Data security	Access Control Effectiveness	% of data assets with proper **Role-Based Access Control** (**RBAC**).	Ensures only authorized users can access sensitive data.
	Sensitive Data Exposure	Number of unauthorized access attempts to sensitive datasets.	Helps detect and prevent data breaches and compliance violations.
Policy and compliance	Policy Compliance Score	% of data assets compliant with internal and regulatory policies.	Critical for meeting standards like GDPR, HIPAA, SOC 2, etc.
	Audit Trail Completeness	% of systems or datasets with complete audit trails enabled.	Required for compliance and forensic investigations.

***Table 7.12:** Metrics and KPIs for data governance*

Methods of implementing data governance

Data governance is a layered discipline involving technical tools, organizational processes, and cultural alignment. Here is a look at how governance is established in cloud-native environments:

- **Metadata management:** Metadata is *data about data*. It provides critical context about who created a dataset, what it contains, what it connects to, and how it has changed over time. Metadata management acts as the foundation for governance, enabling users to understand data without directly inspecting its content.

    - **Example:** In AWS Glue Data Catalog, every dataset (like an S3 object or a Redshift table) is tagged with metadata: column names, data types, classification (like PII), last updated date, and lineage.
    - **Benefit:** Enhances discoverability, data democratization, and reduces tribal knowledge bottlenecks.

- **Data lineage and provenance:** Think of this as GPS tracking for your data, lineage maps where data comes from, the transformations it goes through, and where it ends up. It is essential for debugging errors, ensuring auditability, and understanding impact analysis.
    - **Example:** In an ETL pipeline built with Apache Airflow, data lineage tools can track transformations from MongoDB to BigQuery via Apache Beam, providing complete traceability.
    - **Benefit:** Critical for root cause analysis, compliance reporting, and model reproducibility in AI workflows.

- **Access control and masking:** This involves controlling who can access what data based on their role, department, or location. Masking ensures sensitive information like Social Security Numbers or passwords; is hidden from unauthorized users, even if they access the dataset.
    - **Example:** Using Lake Formation in AWS, you can restrict access to only specific columns of a table for marketing analysts, while giving finance users full access.
    - **Benefit:** Protects sensitive data and aligns with privacy laws like GDPR and HIPAA.

- **Stewardship and ownership:** Governance without human responsibility quickly falls apart. Stewardship assigns **people to data**. Each dataset should have an owner, someone responsible for its quality, documentation, and access controls.
    - **Example:** A data steward in HR owns employee records and enforces policies on retention, usage, and updates.
    - **Benefit:** Creates accountability and improves data lifecycle management.

- **Data quality monitoring:** This is about catching problems before they snowball. Quality rules ensure data conforms to standards, no missing values, valid formats, no duplicates, no schema drift.
    - **Example:** Great expectations or AWS Deequ can be used to validate data as part of the pipeline and alert users on anomalies.
    - **Benefit:** Prevents bad data from entering downstream systems or business dashboards.

Let us connect these methods to real-world scenarios via the following table:

Use case	Governance method applied	Outcome
Finance team accessing PII	Role-based access + Data masking	PII is protected, only visible to approved users
M&A integrating two data pipelines	Data lineage + Metadata management	Clear map of transformations avoids data corruption
Customer data audit (GDPR)	Metadata catalog + Lineage	Traceable customer data for legal reporting
Automated nightly reports failing	Data quality rules + Lineage	Detects faulty transformations or missing sources
Business glossary misalignment	Metadata management + Stewardship	Unified terminology across departments

Table 7.13: *Data governance use cases*

Data governance in the cloud is not just about rules and restrictions. It is about **unlocking trust** in your data. When done right, governance does not slow you down; it is the invisible scaffolding that allows your business to scale, innovate, and move fast **without breaking things**.

As cloud ecosystems evolve with AI/ML, real-time analytics, and data democratization, governance will only become more critical. Think of it as moving from *manual audits* to *automated integrity checks*. The future lies in automated, adaptive, and policy-driven governance systems that empower, not restrict, data innovation.

Conclusion

As we end this chapter, you now must have gained a deeper understanding of different data management patterns that you can take advantage of in cloud architecture. From distribution patterns that enable you to scale, to consistency patterns that balance availability and correctness, to hot topics such as data lakes, warehouses and data governance, these lessons are from first-hand experience, and many of the patterns have grown organically and are the backbone of robust cloud architecture and systems.

Keep in mind, there is no one-size-fits-all answer to data management. The right method for you will depend on your needs, constraints, and goals. One should assess and mix and match these patterns, and to adapt the approach as per the need and as the application scales and changes with time.

As you continue on your trip with cloud architecture, do not forget these in your toolbox. They will enable you to build systems that can accommodate the scale, the complexity, and the dynamic nature of the modern cloud. Most importantly, they will help you provide value to your users by ensuring that your data is always available, consistent, and fast.

In the next chapter, we turn to another important dimension of cloud architecture: security patterns. We will take a look at how to secure your data and systems in the cloud based on the data management foundation we laid here.

Join our Discord space

Join our Discord workspace for latest updates, offers, tech happenings around the world, new releases, and sessions with the authors:

https://discord.bpbonline.com

CHAPTER 8
Security Patterns

Introduction

As we venture deeper into the world of cloud computing, one aspect stands out as both a principal concern and a critical enabler, **security**. In this chapter, we will explore the intricate landscape of security patterns in cloud architecture. Often when one first starts working with cloud systems, security feels like an intimidating labyrinth. But as you will soon discover, with the right patterns and practices, it becomes a powerful tool in your cloud architect's toolkit.

When we talk about building in the cloud, it is easy to get caught up in the thrill of scalability, resiliency, data management, and speed. The cloud feels almost magical as you click a few buttons and suddenly have access to enormous compute power, endless storage, and global networks, but none of that magic matters if your application is not secure.

Security in cloud architecture is not a feature you add at the end, like a fancy spoiler on a sports car. It is the chassis, seatbelt, airbags, and brakes, woven into the very design of the vehicle. Without it, your cloud platform is less of a Ferrari and more of a crash waiting to happen.

In traditional on-premises systems, you might have been able to build a moat around your servers, a castle-and-moat security model. But the cloud blows that model apart. Your data can live across multiple continents, your services can interact with hundreds of external

APIs, and your users can log in from anywhere. A blessing for agility, but a nightmare when it comes to all the risks involved.

Cloud security today is about rethinking everything. You no longer trust **inside** vs **outside**, you validate every request. Additionally, you no longer guard a few castle gates; you build invisible fences everywhere. Also, you do not just prevent breaches; you assume breaches will happen and design systems to limit the damage.

This shift demands a new security mindset, one that is proactive, layered, automated, and embedded into every layer of the architecture. From identity management to encryption, from network design to compliance frameworks, cloud security touches every decision, every day.

But here is the upside: getting cloud security right does not just keep you out of the headlines. It enables faster innovation. It builds customer trust. It allows companies to embrace the future without fear. Since in the cloud, speed is important, innovation is important, but nothing is more important than *trust*.

Structure

In this chapter, we will go over the following topics:

- Identity management
- Data encryption
- API security
- Network security
- Threat modeling
- Compliance and regulatory aspects

Objectives

By the end of this chapter, you will have a solid grasp of the foundational pillars that underpin powerful cloud security, from identity management and data encryption to API protection, network design, and regulatory compliance. More importantly, you will understand how these components interlock to create a cohesive, resilient defense strategy. You will also be able to recognize the most common threats and vulnerabilities that surface in modern cloud environments, and how to counter them before they escalate proactively. With the help of real-world patterns and proven best practices, you will learn how to architect secure, trustworthy cloud systems that do not slow down innovation but rather empower it. In the cloud, security is not about building a wall and hoping for the best; it is about engineering systems that are intelligent, responsive, and inherently aware of who and what is accessing them. At the core of any effective cloud security posture lies one powerful idea: in today's landscape, identity is the new perimeter.

Identity management

Imagine your cloud architecture as a vast, bustling city. Identity management is the system of gates, checkpoints, and identification cards that ensures only the right people access the right places. It is the foundation of cloud security, and getting it right is very crucial.

In the early days of technology, securing a company's assets meant fortifying a single location, much like building thick walls around a castle. If you could control who got inside the network, you could sleep easily at night. Fast forward to today's cloud-driven world, and the **castle walls** have vanished. Users access systems from coffee shops, airports, remote islands, and home offices. Applications sprawl across multiple clouds. Devices multiply like rabbits. In this environment, identity, not location, has become the new security perimeter.

Instead of asking, *are you inside the network?*, the cloud security now asks, *who are you? Can I trust you? What exactly should you have access to?* Identity is no longer just a first step; it is a living, breathing layer that needs to be constantly verified and monitored. A strong identity management strategy is the only way to ensure that the right people and systems have the right access, at the right time, for the right reasons.

In essence, the old doors and walls are gone, but if we treat identity as the new gate, lock, and guard, we have new ammunitions and fighting chance to keep our cloud environments secure.

Core components of identity management

Now let us look into the core components that constitute the identity management and make this an important security perimeter against the external threats we need to safeguard our cloud applications from.

Authentication

Authentication is the act of confirming that users, devices, or applications are who they claim to be. It is your first line of defence, like a passport ID at the airport, proving who you are claiming to be. In cloud systems, we often use **Multi-factor authentication** (**MFA**), i.e., combining something you know (**password**), something you have (**authenticator app**), and something you are (**biometrics**).

Modern authentication also embraces **OAuth, OpenID Connect** (**OIDC**), and **SAML** to enable **Single Sign-On** (**SSO**) across apps without needing multiple passwords.

The following are some key authentication techniques:

- **Username and password:** Traditional but now considered weak if used alone.
- **Multi-factor authentication:** Combines two or more authentication factors:

  - Something you know (password)
  - Something you have (phone, security token)
  - Something you are (biometrics like fingerprints)

  Example: AWS Management Console enforces MFA using a virtual authenticator app like Google Authenticator. Even if an attacker steals your password, they cannot log in without your phone.

- **Single Sign-On (SSO):** With SSO, users log in once and gain access to multiple systems without re-authenticating.

  Example: A user logs into Gmail once and instantly gains access to Google sheets, Google docs, Google drive, etc., without needing to remember multiple passwords.

- **Passwordless authentication:** Emerging trend where biometric login or device-based authentication removes the need for passwords altogether (**Apple FaceID**).

The following are some advantages and disadvantages of authentication:

- **Advantages:**
  - Reduces password fatigue (especially with SSO).
  - Drastically improves security posture with MFA.
  - Supports seamless user experience with federated identity.
- **Disadvantages:**
  - MFA fatigue if overused (constant prompts), many a time a UX detractor.
  - Password resets and SSO outages can ripple across systems.
  - Integrating legacy apps into SSO can be painful.

Authorization

After authentication, authorization ensures users only access what they are permitted. It acts like a smart access badge that only opens the doors you are allowed to enter.

While authentication answers *Who are you?*, authorization answers *What can you do*? Authorization mechanisms decide what data a user can access and what operations they can perform based on the permissions assigned.

Cloud services often use policy engines like AWS IAM Policies or Azure RBAC to enforce these rules dynamically.

A few common authorization models are as follows:

- **Role-Based Access Control (RBAC):** Assign access based on the job title, like admin or a user role. Instead of manually assigning permissions to every user, you create various roles and assign permission to these. Once it is done, it is just a matter of assigning the user a particular role.

- **Attribute-Based Access Control (ABAC):** Assign access based on dynamic attributes instead of static roles. Attributes can be like **Read**, **Modify,** or it can be like department (HR, Finance), etc., and is more fine-tuned way to manage permissions as compared to RBAC.
- **Policy-Based Access Control (PBAC):** Assign access based on complex organizational policies. Think of it like a full legal contract (policy) that spells out access rights, instead of just checking someone's job title or attributes alone.

Let us look at a quick comparison of the preceding authorisation models on various relevant parameters in *Table 8.1:*

Model	Granularity	Complexity	Ease of implementation	Security
RBAC	Coarse-grained; permissions are tied to roles.	Low; easy to manage but less flexible.	Very easy; predefined roles and simple management.	Basic security; easy to assign, but limited by the number of roles.
ABAC	Fine-grained; access decisions can be made based on multiple attributes.	Medium to high; more complex but very flexible.	Moderate; requires defining and managing attributes.	High; dynamic, context-aware, and adaptable.
PBAC	Very fine-grained; access is defined by customizable policies.	High; policies can become complex depending on the conditions.	Complex; requires setting up policies and evaluation systems.	High; customizable, context-aware, and granular.

Table 8.1: *Authorisation model comparison*

The following is a summary of strengths for authorization models:

- **RBAC:** Perfect for traditional, static environments with clear roles (for example, enterprise applications, internal tools). It is simple and effective, but lacks the flexibility needed for modern cloud or SaaS environments.
- **ABAC:** Great for cloud-native, multi-tenant systems where access needs to be dynamic, fine-grained, and context-aware (for example, SaaS platforms, APIs, or any system that requires conditional access based on attributes like location, time, or device).
- **PBAC:** Ideal for complex, policy-driven environments where you need to express sophisticated access rules (for example, microservices architectures, policy-driven platforms, and systems where contextual conditions are critical).

Table 8.2 is a summary of the advantages and disadvantages of these models:

Model	Advantages	Disadvantages
RBAC	• Simple to implement • Easy to manage with few roles • Suitable for static environments with clear roles	• Can become inflexible with complex systems and many roles • Roles can lead to privilege creep and insufficient granularity • Difficult to support dynamic, context-sensitive access control
ABAC	• Very flexible and context-aware • Fine-grained control over access • Expandable and adaptable for large systems	• Can become complex to manage at scale • Policies may be harder to write and maintain • Requires continuous monitoring and maintenance
PBAC	• Highly customizable, adaptable in real-time • Expandable and dynamic across multiple services • Policy enforcement is centralized, making it easier to manage across multiple services	• Can become difficult to manage as policies grow in complexity • Performance can degrade with large sets of complex rules • Requires specialized tools for policy enforcement and evaluation

***Table 8.2**: Advantages and disadvantages of authorization models*

The following are some advantages and disadvantages of authorization:

- **Advantages:**
  - Granular, targeted access control minimizes security breaches.
  - Helps enforce compliance (HIPAA, GDPR, SOC2).
  - Automated policy application across massive user bases.
- **Disadvantages:**
  - Incorrect permission settings can cause **privilege creep**.
  - Overly permissive roles can become security landmines.
  - In multi-cloud setups, maintaining consistency is tricky.

Principle of least privileges

One key aspect that should always be kept in mind, while dealing with authorization models is to stick to the principle of least privileges always. This principle is straightforward. Give users the minimum level of access they need to do their job. It is like giving the cleaning staff access to offices, but not to the server room. The following points should always be adhered to while specifying the privileges:

- Start with zero access and add permissions as needed.
- Regularly review and audit access rights.
- Use time-bound access for temporary needs.

This can sometimes be a massive undertaking in large organisations switching to this principle but always pays off in longer run.

User lifecycle management

Managing a user's journey from onboarding, internal movement, to off-boarding is vital for cloud security. Without proper lifecycle management, ghost accounts and excessive permissions are often exploited by attackers.

It includes the following stages:

- **Provisioning:** Create user accounts, assign initial access.
- **Updates/changes:** Update access as job roles evolve.
- **De-provisioning:** Instantly remove access when users leave.

Example: In Microsoft Azure AD, when an employee resigns, workflows automatically remove them from SharePoint groups, disable Office365 access, and archive their OneDrive.

Here are a few of the advantages and disadvantages of lifecycle management, to be kept in mind to help make decisions:

- **Advantages:**
  - Immediate lockout reduces insider threat risk.
  - Seamless onboarding improves employee productivity.
  - Audit trails help with compliance reporting.
- **Disadvantages:**
  - Manual provisioning increases human error risk.
  - Automation errors can accidentally de-provision active users.
  - Cross-app integration (Salesforce, AWS, internal tools) can be tedious.

Before wrapping this topic up, let us understand some common identity threats in cloud environment and a few strategies to keep in mind to avert these threats.

Common identity threats and risks

As we understood above, with enterprises shift to cloud-native architectures, identity becomes the new security perimeter. While firewalls once protected perimeters, now it is identity that gates access. However, this centrality also makes it a prime target. Let us look at some of the most pervasive identity threats:

- **Credential theft:** The most common risk in identity security, where attackers gain access to usernames and passwords through phishing, malware, or data breaches. Once stolen, these credentials can be used to impersonate users and access sensitive systems. In 2024, Roku shared that it had been hit by two separate attacks where hackers used stolen usernames and passwords from other websites to break into people's accounts. The first attack hit about 15,000 users, and the second one was much bigger—impacting over half a million accounts. Out of those, roughly 400 users saw suspicious purchases made without their permission. This kind of **credential stuffing** is rampant in systems that do not implement MFA.
- **Privilege escalation:** In this attack, adversaries exploit a low-level user account or misconfiguration to gain higher privileges and access more sensitive systems or data. A misconfigured IAM policy in AWS that grants overly permissive rights (*:*) can allow an attacker to go from read-only to full administrative control.
- **Session hijacking:** By stealing a user's session token or exploiting weak session management, attackers can masquerade as legitimate users without even needing credentials.

Imagine a SaaS dashboard where tokens are cached in local storage. If an attacker exploits an XSS vulnerability, they can steal tokens and operate under an active session.

Key identity management strategies

To guard against the risks mentioned in the preceding section, cloud-native identity strategies must be multilayered, dynamic, and policy-driven. Let us discuss some proven methods and architectural patterns for identity management.

Implement multi-factor authentication

Do not rely on passwords alone. MFA adds a second layer, usually a time-sensitive code or biometric to verify identity.

Use case: An admin logs into AWS Console. In addition to password, they are prompted with a **Time-based One-Time Password** (**TOTP**) app.

Mentioned are few of the advantages and disadvantages of MFA, to be kept in mind to help make decisions:

- **Advantages:**
    - o Drastically reduces the risk of credential theft.
    - o Easy to roll out with most IDaaS platforms.

- **Disadvantages:**
  - o Adds friction to the user experience if not implemented smartly.
  - o May require device access or user training.

Adopt Principle of Least Privilege (PoLP)

Users or entities should have only the access to data, resources and applications necessary for their role, nothing more, nothing less.

Example: In GCP, a developer only gets access to Dev environment resources and cannot read from production storage buckets.

Here are few of the advantages and disadvantages of PoLP, to be kept in mind help make decisions:

- **Advantages:**
  - o Limits lateral movement for attackers.
  - o Enforces clean RBAC models.
- **Disadvantages:**
  - o Complex to audit and maintain in large orgs.
  - o Can hinder productivity if too restrictive.

Use Identity Federation and SSO

Integrate corporate identity providers (like Okta, Azure AD) with cloud platforms using SAML, OIDC, or OAuth.

Use case: An enterprise enables SSO across AWS, GCP, and internal apps via Okta. Employees log in once and get access to all authorized services.

Mentioned are a few of the advantages and disadvantages of SSO, to be kept in mind to help make decisions:

- **Advantages:**
  - o Unified identity across services.
  - o Easy de-provisioning upon user exit.
- **Disadvantages:**
  - o Federation misconfigurations can introduce vulnerabilities
  - o Relies on uptime of external IDP

Enable Just-In-Time (JIT) access and auditing

Temporary privilege escalation when needed (for example, during an incident), followed by auto revocation and full audit logging.

Example: Using Azure **Privileged Identity Management** (**PIM**), a user requests access to production environment, valid for 2 hours, with alerts sent to auditors.

Mentioned are few of the advantages and disadvantages of JIT, to be kept in mind to help make decisions:

- **Advantages:**
    - Minimizes persistent access.
    - Enables accountability and forensic readiness.
- **Disadvantages:**
    - Requires strong process discipline and tooling integration.

Identity is the latest security perimeter in cloud computing. Authentication and authorization are no longer just technical chores; they are the trust anchors that ensure only the right person does the right thing at the right time. Managing identities well means you are not just guarding the doors; you are also defining who can access only the resources they are entitled to.

Data encryption

If identity management is about controlling access to your cloud city, encryption is about securing the valuables within it. It is crucial for protecting data both at rest and in transit.

In the cloud, data does not just sit quietly in a locked drawer. It travels across networks, gets processed, and is often stored on multi-tenant infrastructure. This dynamic, distributed nature brings immense power, but it also widens the attack surface dramatically. Without encryption, you are essentially sending your private messages on postcards instead of sealed envelopes, and anyone who intercepts them can read everything. Without encryption, your data is as exposed as an unlocked phone in a crowded space. Encryption acts as a digital cloak, converting data into unreadable gibberish unless the right key is available.

Key reasons for encryption

In this section, we will discuss some key critical factors that make data encryption non-negotiable.

Pervasive cyber threat landscape

From ransomware attacks to sophisticated nation-state espionage, cloud environments are attractive targets because of the sheer volume and value of data stored. Encryption ensures that even if data is accessed or stolen, it remains unintelligible without the decryption keys, essentially making the breach less valuable to the attacker.

Regulatory compliance mandates

Governments and industry bodies have drawn a hard line on data privacy. Regulations like:

- **GDPR (EU):** Mandates protection of personal data with strong privacy controls.
- **HIPAA (U.S.):** Requires encryption of health data during transmission and storage.
- **PCI-DSS (Global):** Requires cardholder data encryption for financial transactions. Not using encryption in such regulated spaces can lead to penalties, legal issues, and reputational harm.

Shared responsibility model

Cloud providers secure the infrastructure, but customers are responsible for securing the data. Encryption is your armor in this shared-responsibility battlefield, it empowers organizations to retain control of their data confidentiality, even within third-party infrastructure.

Zero trust and multi-tenant cloud models

In a zero-trust world, you assume that no actor or system, internal or external, is inherently trustworthy. Encryption enforces that mindset by making access tightly scoped and authenticated, even for internal services. This is especially crucial in **multi-tenant clouds**, where your data may share physical resources with other customers.

Cloud-native threat vectors

Encryption is the last line of defence against:

- Snapshot leaks from cloud storage.
- Misconfigured S3 buckets.
- API exfiltration of sensitive information.
- Compromised admin credentials. These are not hypothetical risks. They have made headlines and cost companies millions in damages.

Even though the preceding factors pose compelling reasons for data encryption and the importance of it, let us look further at some use cases of data encryption, further strengthening the need.

Use cases of data encryption

With some business-relevant use cases, let us make this even more real by walking through them in detail.

Healthcare SaaS with PHI data

The following are the details:

- **Scenario:** A platform storing **Electronic Health Records** (**EHRs**) on AWS.
- **Encryption need:** HIPAA compliance mandates all data must be encrypted at rest and in transit.
- **Implementation:**
  - o Encrypting at rest using AWS KMS-managed keys (SSE-S3 for object storage).
  - o Encrypting APIs with TLS 1.2 or higher.
  - o Database field-level encryption for sensitive fields like Social Security Numbers and patient diagnoses.
- **Outcome:** Even if the S3 bucket were accidentally exposed, data would remain unreadable without access to the encryption keys.

eCommerce platform handling payments

The following are the details:

- **Scenario:** A cloud-native commerce engine processes credit card transactions.
- **Encryption need:** PCI-DSS compliance, plus consumer trust in payment security.
- **Implementation:**
  - o HTTPS endpoints secured via TLS/SSL certificates.
  - o Customer card data tokenized and stored using envelope encryption.
  - o Payment gateways use client-side encryption to avoid raw card info even reaching the backend.
- **Outcome:** Fraud risk reduced, compliance met, and customer confidence improved.

Global file storage SaaS

The following are the details:

- **Scenario:** A multi-cloud file sharing service allows users to upload and share sensitive documents.
- **Encryption need:** Cross-region legal compliance (for example, GDPR in Europe, CCPA in California).
- **Implementation:**
  - o Client-side encryption using user-generated keys before data is uploaded to the cloud.
  - o AES-256 with public/private key encryption for sharing.

- **Outcome:** Service becomes regionally compliant without needing to change infrastructure drastically.

Secrets management for CI/CD pipelines

The following are the details:

- **Scenario:** A DevOps team managing hundreds of deployments across AWS and Azure.
- **Encryption need:** Store and retrieve credentials, API keys, and tokens securely during builds.
- **Implementation:**
    - o Use of AWS Secrets Manager or HashiCorp Vault with encrypted at-rest storage.
    - o Tight IAM roles to control access and audit logs for visibility.
- **Outcome:** Clean pipeline security with zero plaintext secrets checked into source code.

These use cases show that encryption is not a one-size-fits-all tool, it is a custom-made solution that aligns with specific business goals, compliance needs, and threat models. Choosing **how** and **where** to apply encryption can be the difference between a newsworthy breach and a non-event.

Encryption types

Encryption in the cloud happens at different stages and layers. In this subsection, we will discuss the most widely used methods:

- **Encryption in transit:**
    - o **What:** Secures data as it moves between clients, services, or servers.
    - o **How: Transport Layer Security** (**TLS**), HTTPS, VPN tunnels.
    - o **Use case:** Protecting API traffic or internal microservice communication.
- **Encryption at rest:**
    - o **What:** Secures data stored on disks or cloud storage services.
    - o **How:** AES-256 encryption via cloud provider-native solutions (for example, AWS KMS, Azure SSE).
    - o **Use case:** Securing S3 buckets, RDS databases, or file blobs.
- **Client-side encryption:**
    - o **What:** Data is encrypted before it even hits the cloud.
    - o **How:** Handled by client applications using custom libraries and keys.

    - **Use case:** When regulatory environments mandate zero-trust on third-party platforms.

- **Application-level encryption:**
    - **What:** Encrypting specific fields or payloads within an app (for example, encrypting SSNs in a JSON).
    - **How:** Encryption libraries in programming languages like Go, Java, or Node.js.
    - **Use case:** Tokenizing user information before storing in NoSQL databases.

Let us take a look at a quick, summarized comparison of advantages and disadvantages of encryption approaches in *Table 8.3*:

Method	Advantages	Disadvantages	Best fit use case
In-transit	Easy to implement; widely supported	Does not protect at-rest or internal access	Web apps, REST APIs
At-rest	Strong layer of defense	Key mismanagement risks	Databases, Object storage
Client-side	Full control over data security	Harder to manage keys, more complexity	Zero-trust environments
App-level	Fine-grained encryption	Performance impact, more code handling	PII/PHI field-level encryption

***Table 8.3**: Encryption approaches comparison*

Encrypting data in Go using AWS KMS

The following is a hands-on example of encrypting a text message using AWS KMS in a Go microservice:

1. Install AWS SDK for Go

```
go get github.com/aws/aws-sdk-go/aws
go get github.com/aws/aws-sdk-go/service/kms
```

2. Encrypt and decrypt example

```
package main

import (
    "fmt"
    "os"

    "github.com/aws/aws-sdk-go/aws/session"
    "github.com/aws/aws-sdk-go/service/kms"
```

```
)

func main() {
    keyID := "arn:aws:kms:us-east-1:123456789012:key/your-kms-key-id"

    sess := session.Must(session.NewSession())
    svc := kms.New(sess)

    // Encrypt
    plaintext := []byte("Top Secret Cloud Data")
    encryptInput := &kms.EncryptInput{
        KeyId:     &keyID,
        Plaintext: plaintext,
    }

    encryptOutput, err := svc.Encrypt(encryptInput)
    if err != nil {
        fmt.Println("Encrypt error:", err)
        os.Exit(1)
    }

    fmt.Println("Encrypted Data:", encryptOutput.CiphertextBlob)

    // Decrypt
    decryptInput := &kms.DecryptInput{
        CiphertextBlob: encryptOutput.CiphertextBlob,
    }

    decryptOutput, err := svc.Decrypt(decryptInput)
    if err != nil {
        fmt.Println("Decrypt error:", err)
        os.Exit(1)
    }

    fmt.Println("Decrypted Text:", string(decryptOutput.Plaintext))
}
```

Data encryption is not just a checkbox on a compliance form; it is a fundamental pillar of trust, especially in cloud-native ecosystems where data is highly distributed and accessed globally. Whether you are securing a healthcare API, anonymizing user analytics, or implementing zero-trust strategies, understanding and correctly applying encryption methods is what keeps sensitive data private in a very public infrastructure.

API security

In the cloud world, APIs are no longer just technical conveniences; they are business-critical interfaces. They expose functionality to external partners, internal services, mobile apps, and even third-party marketplaces. Every login, file upload, payment, or IoT command is likely routed through an API.

And here is the truth: if your API is not secure, your entire cloud architecture is vulnerable. APIs are the most exposed surface area in modern applications and the most targeted by attackers.

In fact, recent industry studies show *API-related breaches have grown faster than traditional web app attacks*, simply because attackers know APIs often lack the visibility and enforcement that web frontends typically have.

Why API security is non-negotiable

In cloud-native architectures, APIs expose both internal and external services. Think of them like doors and windows to your digital home, wide open, unless you lock them properly. A weakly secured API is a hacker's favorite entry point. *Gartner* estimates that *by 2025, over 90% of web-enabled applications will have more surface area exposed through APIs than through the user interface*. That is a massive shift in the security landscape.

The following are the vulnerabilities of APIs:

- Broken authentication (anyone gets the keys)
- Injection attacks (like SQL injection)
- Excessive data exposure
- Rate limiting bypass (DoS)
- Cross-site scripting (XSS)
- Misconfigured access controls

Table 8.4 is a broad comparison of how APIs can be compromised in multiple ways:

Threat type	Description	Example
Broken authentication	Poorly secured login tokens or sessions	APIs that do not expire access tokens when passwords change
Excessive data exposure	APIs returning more data than necessary	`/user/info` returns full SSN when only name is needed
Rate limiting bypass	Absent throttling lets attackers brute-force	Password reset endpoint can be hammered with OTP attempts
Mass assignment	Automatic binding exposes unintended fields	Attackers update internal flags like **`isAdmin: true`**

Threat type	Description	Example
Injection attacks	User input is not sanitized	SQL or NoSQL injection via API query parameters
Insecure direct object references (IDOR)	IDs exposed without an authorization check	Accessing `/user/12345/invoice.pdf` without ownership check

Table 8.4: Broad comparison of API threats

Core principles of API security

As we have discussed the common threat models for APIs, let us understand the core principles we can deploy to make the API secure and safeguard it against the threats listed in the preceding section.

Authentication

We have gone through the same previously, as to how important authentication is, so having authentication implemented via the following points is key:

- Enforce strong OAuth 2.0 or OpenID Connect protocols.
- Never rely on weak API keys alone.
- Use MFA especially for administrative APIs.

Example: Require access tokens issued by a trusted identity provider (for example, Auth0, AWS Cognito), and enforce token expiration and refresh policies.

Authorization

Similarly, authorization was also explained previously, as to how important authorization is, and having this to implemented via the following points is important:

- Implement RBAC or ABAC at the resource level.
- Apply **least privilege** policies and do not let one endpoint have excessive powers.
- Validate scopes and permissions **per API call**, not just once at login.

Example: A user with the *viewer* role should not be able to call `/api/deleteAccount`.

Scope validations for APIs are done by defining OAuth scopes.

In large-scale cloud-native systems, OAuth scopes are essential for implementing strict API security models. They allow you to break down monolithic permissions into granular, service-specific access rights. This becomes vital in microservices architectures, where services authenticate via delegated tokens. Scopes let you enforce strong boundaries between what different services or even different modules within a service, can access. It is crucial to design these scopes in a way that supports scalable permissioning, clear audit trails, and dynamic policy updates, all while ensuring that user data remains protected and access is tightly controlled across the ecosystem.

Input validation and output filtering

Input validation ensures that data coming into your API is clean, correctly formatted, and safe, preventing injection attacks or malformed data errors. Output filtering, on the other hand, ensures that your API does not unintentionally expose sensitive information when responding. The following are the key points for the same:

- All inputs (**headers, query params, bodies**) must be validated against **API contracts** (for example, OpenAPI schema).
- Sanitize output to avoid overexposing sensitive data. It should not throw back the entire database collection, but spit out only relevant and non-sensitive fields.
- Use **allow-lists** not block-lists, as this is stricter policy then open everything and then removing from it.

Example: Implement schema-based validation using libraries like `Joi` in Node.js or **`FluentValidation`** in .NET.

Rate limiting and throttling

Rate limiting and throttling control the number of API requests a client can make within a given time frame, helping prevent abuse, **denial-of-service** (**DoS**) attacks, and resource exhaustion while maintaining service reliability. The following are the key points for the same:

- Enforce quotas per IP, user, or API key.
- Implement burst control to prevent sudden spikes.
- Return **HTTP 429 (Too Many Requests)** instead of failing silently.

Example: Use Amazon API Gateway's built-in throttling rules or NGINX rate limiting for private APIs.

Secure data transmission

Secure data transmission uses encryption protocols like TLS/HTTPS to ensure that data exchanged between clients and APIs cannot be intercepted or tampered with during transit, protecting against man-in-the-middle attacks. The following are the key points for the same:

- Always enforce **HTTPS** (TLS 1.2 or above).
- Avoid transmitting sensitive data in query parameters.
- Use **HMAC** or signed tokens for payload verification.

Example: Avoid `https://api.example.com/send?password=abc123`. Use POST with encrypted body instead.

Auditing, monitoring, and logging

Auditing involves systematically recording API activities and changes. Monitoring keeps a real-time pulse on API behavior, performance, and usage patterns, allowing teams to detect anomalies, slowdowns, or suspicious activities before they escalate into incidents. Logging captures detailed information about API requests, responses, errors, and system events, forming the backbone for debugging, analysis, and incident response. The following are the key points for the same:

- Every API call should be **logged**, tagged with user context and timestamp.
- Use **distributed tracing** (for example, OpenTelemetry) to track requests across services.
- Monitor for anomalous behavior — for example, sudden spikes or access from unexpected geographies.

Example: Pair logs with tools like Prometheus, Sumologic, or AWS CloudTrail for real-time alerting.

Figure 8.1 is a logical flow of API security in actions, with the preceding principles in mind:

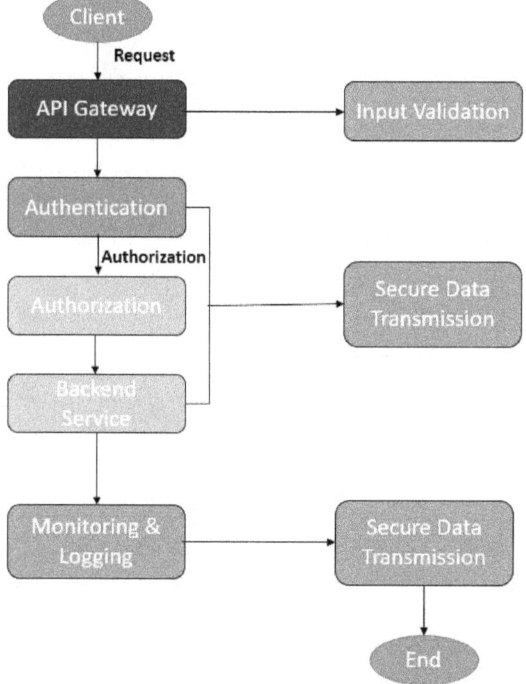

***Figure 8.1:** API security logical flow*

With the aforementioned understandings in mind, let us look at a practical code implementing a secure API in Golang using JWT for authentication:

```
package main

import (
 "fmt"
 "net/http"
 "github.com/golang-jwt/jwt/v5"
 "time"
)

var jwtKey = []byte("my_secret_key")

func GenerateJWT(username string) (string, error) {
 claims := &jwt.RegisteredClaims{
  Subject:   username,
  ExpiresAt: jwt.NewNumericDate(time.Now().Add(time.Hour * 2)),
 }

 token := jwt.NewWithClaims(jwt.SigningMethodHS256, claims)
 return token.SignedString(jwtKey)
}

func AuthMiddleware(next http.HandlerFunc) http.HandlerFunc {
 return func(w http.ResponseWriter, r *http.Request) {
  tokenStr := r.Header.Get("Authorization")
  claims := &jwt.RegisteredClaims{}

  token, err := jwt.ParseWithClaims(tokenStr, claims, func(token *jwt.Token) (interface{}, error) {
   return jwtKey, nil
  })

  if err != nil || !token.Valid {
   http.Error(w, "Unauthorized", http.StatusUnauthorized)
   return
  }

```

```
    next.ServeHTTP(w, r)
  }
}

func ProtectedEndpoint(w http.ResponseWriter, r *http.Request) {
  fmt.Fprintf(w, "Welcome to the secure API!")
}

func main() {
  http.HandleFunc("/secure", AuthMiddleware(ProtectedEndpoint))
  http.ListenAndServe(":8080", nil)
}
```

Test this by generating a JWT token using **GenerateJWT**, passing it in the **Authorization** header, and hitting the **/secure** endpoint.

The following table lists best practices in a nutshell for API security:

Practice	Purpose	Tooling/Solution
OAuth2 and JWT	Secure authentication	Auth0, Okta, Cognito, custom JWT
API Gateway Policies	Throttling, validation, routing	AWS API Gateway, Apigee, Kong
Schema validation	Input validation	JSON Schema, OpenAPI spec
Monitoring	Anomaly detection	CloudWatch, Datadog, New Relic
Rate limiting	Abuse prevention	Redis tokens, API Gateway, Envoy
Encryption (TLS)	Secure transport	Let's Encrypt, Cloudflare, ACM

***Table 8.5**: API security practices in nutshell*

Securing APIs is not a **set it and forget it** strategy. It is an ongoing practice of monitoring, validating, and evolving because attackers adapt, and so should your defenses. In the world of cloud-native development, API security is not just about locking the front door, it is about knowing every window, tunnel, and chimney attackers might use, and guarding them with vigilance.

Network security

Imagine your cloud infrastructure as a modern city. Skyscrapers filled with sensitive data, highways transferring information, and entry gates handling countless requests. Without proper security checkpoints, traffic rules, and surveillance, chaos (and attacks) are inevitable.

In the cloud, this **city** spans across the internet. That means your data is not just moving across internal wires; it is exposed to public networks, making it a prime target for malicious actors. Network security in cloud architecture ensures that every bit of data traveling in and out of your virtual infrastructure is protected from unauthorized access, tampering, or interception.

With one more analogy to better understand, think of your cloud environment as a digital airport. Data is like passengers, arriving, departing, and transferring between gates. Now imagine if there were no security screenings, fire exits, or air traffic control. Chaos, right?

That is what an unsecured cloud network looks like. Attackers exploit any open ports, misconfigured routers, or weak segmentation like smugglers finding an unguarded runway. Strong network security ensures only authorized **flights** take off and land, while threats are grounded before they cause harm.

Key principles of network security

Let us examine some key principles of network security, which make it truly stand against the external threats looming in the cloud environment.

Defense in-depth

A layered approach where each component (**firewalls, encryption, segmentation**) adds a layer of protection, like concentric castle walls.

Each layer, DNS, firewall, endpoint protection, and access policies, should independently provide protection. If one fails, the others still defend.

Zero Trust Architecture

Do not assume everything is trustworthy, even inside your network. Every user, device, and service must be continuously verified. Assume a breach at every step and validate continuously.

Least privilege access

We have touched on this principle multiple times, (and yes, this is a very important principle from security perspective). You would not give the janitor access to the CEO's safe. Similarly, ensure every entity in your cloud has only the access it truly needs. Only allow access to what is strictly necessary. If your app does not need to talk to a DB, it should not be able to do so.

Micro-segmentation

Split your cloud environment into small zones with strict access controls, like hotel floors needing keycards. If one area is compromised, others stay isolated. Similarly break down networks into isolated zones to prevent lateral movement in case of a breach.

Core network security components

Table 8.6 shows the components of network security in a summarized format for easy reference:

Component	Description	Example use case
Firewalls (Traditional and **Next Generation Firewalls** (**NGFWs**))	Control incoming/outgoing traffic based on rules.	Blocking suspicious IPs from accessing the app.
Security groups	Virtual firewall for cloud resources.	AWS EC2 instance only accepts port 443 traffic.
Network **Access Control Lists** (**ACLs**)	Act as stateless firewalls controlling traffic at the subnet level.	Denying all traffic from a CIDR range.
VPNs and Direct Connect	Provide encrypted/private tunnels into cloud environments.	Securing on premise to cloud communication.
Intrusion Detection/Prevention Systems (**IDS/IPS**)	Monitor and stop suspicious traffic patterns.	Detecting brute force login attempts.
Web Application Firewall (**WAF**)	Protects against web-based attacks like XSS, SQLi, etc.	Blocking malicious payloads from web form inputs.

Table 8.6: Components of network security

Best practices

The following are some best practices associated with network security:

- **Establish a strong perimeter**
  - Use WAFs and firewalls to protect public-facing assets. Pair them with rate limiting and geofencing to reduce risk exposure.
- **Secure internal communication (east-west traffic)**
  - Just because it is inside your network does not mean that it is safe. Implement service mesh with **mutual TLS** (**mTLS**) and enforce strict API communication policies.
- **Secure and inspect external communication (north-south traffic)**
  - All ingress and egress points must be tightly controlled using firewalls, **Intrusion Detection/Prevention Systems** (**IDS/IPS**), and secure web gateways. Ensure all external-facing APIs and applications are fronted by API gateways and protected via TLS, authentication, and rate-limiting.

- **Use DNS-level security**
  - o Many attacks start with a malicious domain. Cloud DNS firewalls and external services like Cisco Umbrella or Google Safe Browsing help filter traffic at the root.
- **Automate threat detection**
  - o Use native cloud services (like AWS GuardDuty, Azure Defender) and plug into a SIEM for real-time correlation, anomaly detection, and alerts.
- **Rate limiting and throttling**
  - o Protect APIs and services from **distributed denial of service** (**DDoS**) and abusive usage.
- **Do not forget network hygiene**
  - o Rotate keys and secrets regularly.
  - o Avoid hardcoding credentials.
  - o Periodically review security group and firewall rules.
  - o Disable unused ports/services immediately.

Table 8.7 provides a snapshot of cloud provider comparison on network security features:

Feature	AWS	Azure	GCP
Network Firewall	AWS Network Firewall	Azure Firewall	VPC Firewall Rules
DDoS Protection	AWS Shield	Azure DDoS Protection	Google Cloud Armor
VPC Flow Logging	VPC Flow Logs	NSG Flow Logs	VPC Flow Logs
Web Application Firewall	AWS WAF	Azure WAF	Cloud Armor (with WAF)
Private connectivity	AWS Direct Connect	Azure ExpressRoute	Cloud Interconnect

***Table 8.7**: Network security features among cloud providers*

Real-world use case

Let us look at the details:

- **Scenario:** A growing e-commerce platform hosted on AWS experiences multiple attack vectors, DDoS attacks, SQL injection attempts, and unauthorized port scans.
- **Network security strategy:**
  - o **WAF** filters all HTTP(S) traffic at the edge using managed rulesets to block injection attempts.

- **AWS Shield Advanced** provides automatic DDoS mitigation.
- **VPC Peering** isolates backend and database subnets from the public internet.
- **VPC Flow Logs** are fed into **Amazon GuardDuty** for real-time threat detection.
- **Security Groups** restrict access to ports only from whitelisted IPs and services.
- **Transit Gateway** helps route traffic securely across multiple VPCs without exposing internal workloads to the public internet.

Network security in cloud architecture is not just about keeping intruders out, it is about controlling how data moves, who can see it, and what can be done with it. As cloud environments become more complex and distributed, adopting a proactive and layered network security posture becomes not just important but also equally essential.

Like putting locks on your doors, setting up alarm systems, and having watchtowers around your city, cloud network security ensures that your digital kingdom stays secure, resilient, and responsive.

Threat modelling

Threat modelling is one of the most crucial but often under-discussed areas in cloud security architecture. If done right, it shifts the mindset from reactive to proactive, helping teams anticipate and counter threats before they turn into costly breaches.

At its core, threat modelling is the practice of identifying, analyzing, and mitigating potential security risks within a system, before attackers can exploit them. It is a proactive exercise that helps you think like a threat actor, enabling you to anticipate weak points in design, misconfigurations, or integration flaws that could otherwise be overlooked during development.

In cloud environments, where APIs, containers, microservices, and infrastructure scale rapidly and dynamically, threat modelling becomes an imperative practice, one that evolves alongside your cloud architecture. It is not a one-time checklist, but a mindset woven into the **software development lifecycle** (**SDLC**), ensuring security is embedded from the ground up.

Think of it like planning security for a bank. You do not just build vaults, you sketch out all the ways someone could try to rob it, from picking the lock to bribing the guard or digging a tunnel. Threat modelling in the cloud works the same way; it is about thinking like an attacker **before** they show up.

Unlike traditional on-premises systems with clear network perimeters, cloud applications exist in distributed, often borderless environments. A single misconfigured S3 bucket or over-privileged IAM role can open a door wide enough for a data breach that costs millions in damage, reputation, and compliance fines.

Threat modelling offers:

- **Predictive risk management:** By mapping out what can go wrong before deployment.
- **Reduced remediation costs:** Fixing vulnerabilities in the design or development phase is exponentially cheaper than patching post-production.
- **Improved compliance:** Many frameworks (for example, **ISO 27001, SOC 2, HIPAA**) require evidence of risk assessments, threat modelling delivers that visibility.
- **Collaboration:** It forces cross-functional discussions between engineering, product, and security teams, leading to holistic security outcomes.

Key components of threat modelling

Let us look into some of the key components, of threat modelling, which are crucial at early phases:

- **Assets:** Assets are anything of value. Data, services, systems, and users, everything that your organization wants to protect. In the cloud, assets are not static. Databases spin up and down, compute resources scale automatically, and secrets rotate. Understanding and classifying assets (**public, internal, restricted, sensitive**) helps prioritize protection mechanisms.
- **Actors:** These include both human users (**developers, admins, external users**) and non-human entities (**CI/CD pipelines, serverless functions, third-party APIs**). Knowing who (or what) interacts with your system helps in defining access scopes and enforcing least privilege.
- **Entry points:** These are basically the points from where does data enters or exit the system. These include RESTful APIs, CLI tools, admin consoles, mobile apps, cloud storage endpoints, and even logs. Entry points are where most attacks begin (for example, SQLi, XSS, brute force).
- **Trust boundaries:** Trust boundaries separate different levels of privilege or control. For example, the boundary between a public web app and a backend API is critical. Each crossing of a trust boundary needs validation, authentication, and possibly data transformation or inspection.

Mapping threats involves anticipating how assets could be targeted or compromised. For example:

- **Spoofing** identity to access admin consoles.
- **Tampering** with application configurations via exposed interfaces.
- **Information disclosure** via public S3 buckets.
- **DoS** through unthrottled APIs or unprotected endpoints.

There are controls like input validation, MFA, encryption, network segmentation, zero-trust principles, and IAM role hardening. The mitigation strategy must be layered and defense-in-depth, covering people, processes, and technologies.

Table 8.8 are some examples and techniques to deal with common threats, as a part of threat modelling:

Threat type	Example	Mitigation strategy
Spoofing	Fake user logs in using leaked credentials	Enforce MFA and credential hygiene
Tampering	Customer alters order data via insecure API	Use input validation, integrity checks
Repudiation	Admin deletes logs to hide refund abuse	Immutable logs with centralized logging (SIEM)
Info disclosure	Sensitive data exposed via misconfigured S3	Block public access, encrypt at rest and in transit
DoS	Bot overwhelms the payment endpoint	Implement rate limiting and WAF protection
Privilege escalation	Low-privy user accesses admin APIs	Use IAM policies, scoped tokens, and API gateway authorization.

Table 8.8: Threat types and mitigation modelling

Best practices

The following are some best practices to incorporate, but not limited to what is mentioned, when it comes to threat modelling:

- **Start early:** Bake threat modelling into design, not after go-live.
- **Make it collaborative:** Involve developers, ops, security, and product managers.
- **Prioritize threats:** Not all threats are equal, rank them by likelihood and impact.
- **Review regularly:** Cloud is dynamic. So should be your threat model.
- **Automate where possible:** Use tools to flag misconfigurations, IAM risks, and public exposures, like (OWASP, Anchore etc)
- **Embed in agile:** Conduct threat modeling during sprint planning and architectural reviews.

Compliance and regulatory aspects

In the cloud, where data often resides across borders and systems operate in shared environments, compliance is more than a box to check. It's a competitive differentiator and a legal safeguard. Whether you are managing sensitive healthcare data, processing financial transactions, or running a SaaS platform for **small and medium business** (**SMBs**), regulatory obligations shape the way you store, process, transmit, and protect data.

Failing to comply does not just result in fines. It can destroy customer trust, attract lawsuits, and halt operations. For example:

- **Meta** was fined €1.2 billion in 2023 for violating EU data transfer laws.
- **Equifax** suffered one of the most infamous breaches due to poor patching and was fined several million dollars.

Compliance frameworks are not just about penalties, they embody **proven security and privacy best practices** to protect individuals, intellectual property, and businesses.

Common compliance frameworks

The following are some common compliance frameworks.

- **General Data Protection Regulation, or GDPR (EU):**
  - **Focus**: Personal data privacy and protection for EU citizens.
  - **Key elements**: Consent management, right to be forgotten, data localization, breach notification within 72 hours.
  - **Cloud focus:** Data residency, encryption, DPA agreements with cloud providers.
- **Health Insurance Portability and Accountability Act, or HIPAA (USA)**
  - **Focus**: Protecting healthcare information (PHI).
  - **Key elements**: Access controls, audit logging, secure data transmission.
  - **Cloud focus:** Signed **Business Associate Agreements (BAA)** with cloud vendors.
- **Payment Card Industry Data Security Standard, or PCI DSS:**
  - **Focus**: Security, availability, processing integrity, confidentiality, and privacy of customer data.
  - **Key elements**: Continuous monitoring, control effectiveness over time.
  - **Cloud focus:** Central to SaaS business credibility, commonly requested in vendor reviews.
- **ISO/IEC 27001:**
  - Focus: Information Security Management System (ISMS) standards.
  - Key elements: Risk management, internal audits, continuous improvement.
  - Cloud focus: Sets a foundational baseline for mature security practices.

- **Federal Risk and Authorization Management Program, or FedRAMP**
  - **Focus**: US federal cloud adoption security standard.
  - **Key elements**: Strict authorization, continuous monitoring.
  - **Cloud focus:** Mandatory for federal cloud providers, costly but high trust.

Other than the ones listed in the preceding sections, there are many other compliances like StateRAMP, CCPA and many others, which when obtained instill much more trust, security and confidence in the cloud applications and platforms, but are beyond the scope of the book to cover.

Cloud specific challenges in compliance

As the saying goes, there is no such thing as a free lunch—and the same holds true for compliance. While it plays a critical role in earning customer trust and instilling confidence, navigating compliance in the cloud comes with its own set of complexities and challenges.

Data residency and sovereignty

Cloud providers often store data across multiple geographic locations to ensure availability and redundancy. But regulations like GDPR or India's DPDP Act enforce strict rules around where data can be stored and how it's transferred across borders.

Solution: Use region-specific storage options (for example, AWS Regions or Azure Geo Zones) and configure strict geofencing rules in infrastructure policies.

Shared responsibility confusion

Many companies falsely assume that the cloud provider handles all aspects of compliance. In reality, cloud providers secure the infrastructure, but you must secure your applications and data.

Use case: In AWS, S3 is secure by default, but misconfiguring access control policies can still expose data publicly. That is on the user.

Solution: Establish a clear responsibility matrix and enforce it during procurement and architecture reviews.

Audit and logging complexity

Cloud logs and microservices logs can be scattered across services and containers, making traceability and centralized compliance reporting difficult.

Solution: Use log aggregation platforms (for example, Sumologic, ELK Stack, Datadog) and correlate across services. Leverage cloud-native audit trails like AWS CloudTrail or Azure Activity Logs.

Best practices for maintaining cloud compliance

Table 8.9 summarizes the best practices with corresponding tools to use, when it comes to maintaining cloud compliance:

Practice	Description	Tools
Map regulations to cloud services	Build a matrix mapping regulatory clauses to specific cloud configurations.	AWS Artifact, Azure Compliance Manager
Implement continuous compliance monitoring	Automate checks for policy violations, misconfigurations, and unauthorized changes.	Fugue, Wiz, Azure Policy
Classify and tag data assets	Label PII, financial data, or confidential info for appropriate handling.	AWS Macie, Google DLP
Encrypt everything (at rest and in transit)	Use managed KMS (for example, AWS KMS, GCP KMS) or **customer-managed keys (CMKs)**.	AWS CloudHSM, HashiCorp Vault
Train development and DevOps teams	Provide role-specific training on compliance implications and tools.	A Cloud Guru, SANS, internal enablement

Table 8.9: Cloud compliance best practices

Also, each major cloud provider has invested heavily in building a strong compliance posture, but their approach, tooling, and ecosystem maturity differ slightly depending on their focus, enterprise history, and regulatory partnerships.

Amazon Web Services

Amazon Web Services (**AWS**) leads in breadth of compliance certifications and global deployment maturity. It offers fine-grained control, and tools like AWS Artifact and Macie provide easy access to audit reports and advanced data classification. Its outposts and hybrid offerings allow companies with data residency requirements to maintain workloads on-premises while still benefiting from cloud scale. AWS is generally preferred by government contractors and regulated industries for its FedRAMP High readiness and infrastructure breadth.

Microsoft Azure

Azure shines in enterprise compliance integration, especially for customers already using Microsoft's ecosystem (for example, Office 365, Dynamics). It offers strong compliance with data governance and privacy, with tools like Microsoft Purview and Azure Information Protection that map well to data classification, labelling, and governance. Its hybrid capabilities are the strongest due to Azure Arc and Azure Stack, making it ideal for complex compliance landscapes and multinational orgs.

Google Cloud Platform

Google Cloud Platform (**GCP**) is catching up quickly with a privacy-by-design architecture, strong DLP APIs, and tools like Assured Workloads that cater to specific regulatory needs. While its number of HIPAA-eligible services is lower than AWS and Azure, it compensates with simplicity and developer-first compliance APIs. GCP is favoured by data-centric teams and AI/ML-heavy startups that need embedded compliance tools during development.

So, with the aforementioned understandings, it is clear that compliance in the cloud is not just about ticking boxes; it is a strategic pillar for customer trust, market access, and operational security.

- Choose cloud providers that offer **certified services**, granular access controls, and transparent compliance documentation.
- **Automate wherever possible:** From encryption enforcement to misconfiguration alerts.
- Do not treat compliance as a project—treat it as a **continuous journey** embedded into your cloud lifecycle.

Conclusion

In this chapter, we have considered the aspects of identity, data, API security, threat models, and the regulation and compliance side. The topics mentioned in the preceding sections provide the entire picture of how to secure the cloud architecture. Solid identity management, strong encryption practice, secure APIs, as well as a well-established network architecture and maintaining compliance with the ever-changing laws and regulations are key to sustainable cloud environment security. Also, remember that security does not operate on a one-time principle. It needs to be constantly assessed and improved. While building your cloud city, never forget the basics of security. Periodically audit and enhance your security protocols, keep them updated on the current and emerging threats and security practices, as well as develop a culture of security vigilance in your organization.

In the upcoming chapter, we will discuss the messaging and integration patterns, covering how to ensure communication between the components of cloud architecture. Those patterns will further facilitate building more flexible, expandable, and resilient systems in addition to the security aspects we covered in this chapter.

CHAPTER 9
Messaging and Integration Patterns

Introduction

Imagine building a smart city. Streets are neatly laid out, power lines hum quietly beneath, and sensors dot every corner. But what truly brings this city to life is the real-time exchange of signals, traffic lights adjusting to flow, emergency alerts broadcasting instantly, and power grids balancing load dynamically. That invisible exchange of information is the city's nervous system.

Picture your cloud application. Whether it is a sprawling enterprise system, an e-commerce platform handling thousands of transactions per second, or a SaaS product with dozens of modular services, communication is what ties everything together. Without thoughtful integration and messaging patterns, even the most beautifully built services risk becoming isolated silos, even efficient on their own, but disconnected and brittle at scale.

Messaging and integration patterns are the glue, the signals, the nervous system of your architecture. They decide whether a service responds instantly or waits in a queue. They control how data flows, whether a system crashes or gracefully handles overload, whether a new feature rolls out seamlessly or breaks under pressure.

As we shift from monolithic applications to **microservices**, **serverless computing**, and **event-driven architectures**, the need for strong messaging models becomes more and more critical. Today's applications are not just running code, they are coordinating thousands of interactions, often in real-time, across distributed environments.

But designing those interactions is not trivial. Should services talk directly or through an intermediary? Is it better to broadcast events or push them one-to-one? How do you protect APIs from overload? Can your app scale seamlessly when demand spikes? And what happens when you are integrating with legacy systems that were not built for the cloud in the first place? Let us discover the answers to these questions in this chapter.

Structure

In this chapter, we will go over the following topics:

- Message queues
- Publish-subscribe system
- API gateways
- Streaming data and event pipelines
- Choreography
- Orchestration
- Hybrid cloud integration patterns

Objectives

This chapter intends to tackle and explore the foundational messaging models like message queues and pub-sub systems, talk about the operational smarts of API gateways, and elaborate upon high-speed use cases with streaming pipelines. We will unpack why choosing between orchestration and choreography might change how you build your next service. Finally, we will explore how hybrid integration patterns can bridge cloud-native designs with the stubborn but necessary on-premises systems that still drive many businesses.

By the end of the chapter, you will not only understand the theory but also know how to make practical, scalable, and secure choices in your cloud applications. Whether you are designing a startup MVP or architecting a legacy enterprise beast, these patterns are your blueprint.

Message queues

Imagine you are building an e-commerce platform. You have services for inventory management, order processing, payment handling, and customer notifications. Each of these services needs to communicate with the others, but they are all running on different instances, potentially in different geographic regions. How do you ensure that when a customer places an order, the inventory is updated, the payment is processed, and a confirmation email is sent, all in a coordinated and reliable manner?

This is where messaging and integration patterns come into play. They provide the mechanisms for these disparate services to communicate effectively, ensuring that your cloud application functions as a cohesive whole rather than a collection of isolated parts.

A **message queue** is a communication mechanism that enables services to talk to each other by sending messages through an intermediary queue. Instead of a service directly calling another and waiting for a response (*which creates tight coupling, also known as synchronous flow*), it can now send a message to a queue and move on with its tasks. The receiving service will process the message asynchronously, when ready. These are used majorly in scenarios of **point-to-point messaging**.

Think of a coffee shop. A barista does not take your order, make your coffee, and hand it to you immediately. Instead, a cashier takes your order and hands it to the coffee maker via a printed ticket, the queue. The coffee maker delivers the coffee when it is ready. This way, both roles work efficiently without holding up the other.

Importance of message queues

The following pointers highlight the importance of message queues:

- **Decoupling:** Producers and consumers do not need to know about each other's internals or availability.
- **Scalability:** You can scale the producer and consumer services independently.
- **Fault tolerance:** If the consumer crashes, messages can wait in the queue until it restarts.
- **Buffering:** Helps absorb load spikes. Producers can keep sending messages even if consumers are slow.
- **Guaranteed delivery:** Many queue systems ensure messages are delivered at least once, or exactly once with appropriate configurations.

Core components of message queueing systems

In this subsection, let us look at and understand the core components and functioning of message queues.

Producer

A **producer** is the source of messages. It creates and sends messages to the message queue (broker), primarily responsible for the following:

- Construct messages (payload + metadata).
- Sending it to the broker (with optional topic or queue name).
- Define delivery guarantees (at-most-once, at-least-once, exactly-once).
- Optionally assign message priority or headers.

Consumer

A **consumer** is a service or component that reads messages from a queue and processes them, responsible for:

- Connect to the queue.
- Pull or receive messages (depending on the queue type).
- Process message logic (for example, store in DB, call APIs).
- Acknowledge processing success/failure.

Broker

The **broker** is the middleware that handles the queuing system. It stores, routes, and delivers messages between producers and consumers, and its responsibilities are as follows:

- Receive and queue messages.
- Enforce policies (TTL, priority, retry).
- Route messages to appropriate consumers (based on queue type, topic, routing key).
- Ensure message delivery guarantees (persistence, retries, ordering).

A few examples of brokers are:

- RabbitMQ
- Apache Kafka
- Amason SQS

Acknowledgements

Acknowledgements confirm whether a message was successfully processed by the consumer. Without this mechanism, message loss or duplication may occur. These are of the following types:

- **Positive Acknowledgement (ACK):** Once message was processed successfully, broker can delete it.
- **Negative Acknowledgement (NACK):** If message failed processing, broker may retry or move to **dead letter queue** (**DLQ**).
- **Auto-acknowledge:** Automatically confirms receipt, even before processing, **not recommended** for critical systems.

Dead letter queue

It is a secondary queue where messages go when they cannot be successfully processed after a defined number of attempts. The triggers for **Dead Letter Queue** (**DLQ**) are as follows:

- Message exceeds the retry limit.
- Message format is invalid.
- Processing results in repeated errors.
- Consumer crashes before acknowledging.

DLQ are explicitly important in handling exceptions during message handlings, and hold key benefits like:

- Enables **debugging** and **root cause analysis**.
- Prevents **poison messages** from blocking the primary queue.
- Ensures observability into failed processing.

Figure 9.1 is a logical flow diagram of all these components in action, while handling a message:

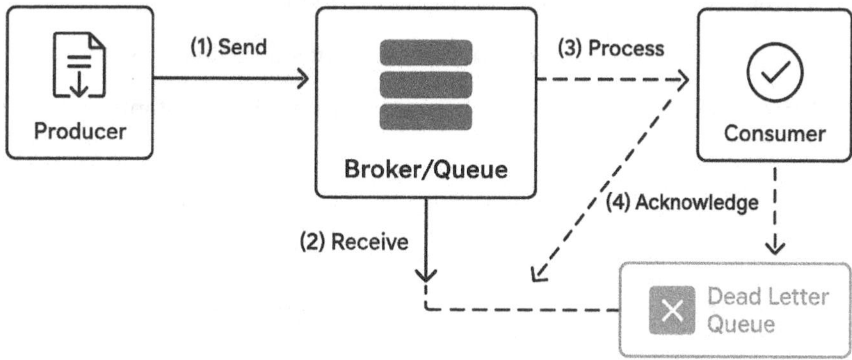

***Figure 9.1:** Logical diagram of message flow*

Message queue delivery types

Message queues essentially offer three types of deliveries as depicted in the following *Table 9.1:*

Delivery type	Description	Use case
At-most-once	Messages may be lost, but never delivered more than once	Real-time telemetry where occasional loss is okay
At-least-once	Messages are delivered one or more times	Payment processing (with idempotent design)
Exactly-once	Messages are guaranteed to be delivered just once	Financial transactions, audit logs

***Table 9.1:** Message queues delivery semantics*

Publish-subscribe systems

In a **pub-sub system**, publishers broadcast messages *without knowing who will read them*, while subscribers express interest in specific topics or message types. A message broker (*for example, Kafka, Redis Pub/Sub, Google Cloud Pub/Sub or Amazon SNS*) ensures the messages get delivered to all interested subscribers.

Think of a news agency. The publisher releases breaking news, and subscribers (**TV stations**, **apps**, **social feeds**) broadcast or act on it in their own ways. The publisher does not know who the viewers are, it just pushes out news. That is pub-sub in a nutshell.

Importance of pub-sub system

The following pointers highlight the importance of a pub-sub system:

- **Loose coupling:** Publishers and subscribers never need to know each other. This makes the architecture flexible and easier to evolve.
- **Scalability:** Broadcasts can reach thousands of subscribers instantly.
- **Real-time:** Great for scenarios where updates must be instantly pushed to many endpoints.
- **Extensibility:** New subscribers can join without any change to the publishing service.

Core components of pub-sub systems

Let us look at and understand the core components and functioning of pub-sub systems.

Publisher

A **publisher** is a producer of messages. It sends messages without knowing who will consume them, focusing only on pushing information to a **topic**. It is:

- **Decoupled from subscribers:** The publisher does not need to know who the subscribers are or how many exist.
- **Push-only:** Publishers publish events or messages to a topic.
- **Asynchronous:** Typically, it does not wait for acknowledgment from subscribers.

Topic

A **topic** is a named logical channel or category to which messages are published. It acts as the **bulletin board** or conduit between publishers and subscribers, with characteristics like:

- **Named entity:** For example, **`order.events.created`** or **`user.notifications`**.
- **Routing mechanism:** Allows subscribers to express interest in specific topics.
- **Broadcasts to multiple subscribers:** All subscribers to a topic receive all messages published to it.

Broker

The **broker** is the message-handling infrastructure that manages the flow of messages between publishers and subscribers. Its key responsibilities are as follows:

- **Message routing:** Ensures messages from publishers are delivered to the correct subscribers.
- **Persistence (optional):** Stores messages temporarily or permanently.
- **Retry mechanisms:** Resends messages if a subscriber fails.
- **Fan-out:** Distributes one message to multiple subscribers.
- **Decoupling layer:** Completely separates producers from consumers.

Example:

- Kafka
- Google Pub/Sub
- AWS SNS
- RabbitMQ (in pub/sub mode)

Subscriber

A **subscriber** is a consumer that expresses interest in messages of a specific topic and processes them, with the following characteristics:

- **Pull or push:** Can pull messages from the broker or receive them pushed.
- **Multiple subscribers per topic:** All receive a copy of the message.
- **Independent processing:** Each subscriber can handle the message differently.

Message

A **message** is the unit of data transmitted from publisher to subscriber, encapsulating an event or data payload, with following listed attributes:

- **Payload:** The actual content (for example, JSON, binary, Protobuf).
- **Metadata:** Headers, timestamps, routing keys, etc.
- **ID or key (optional):** For partitioning, duplication, or correlation.

Table 9.2 is a summary table for the preceding components, for quick and easy reference:

Component	Role	Real-world analogy
Publisher	Sends messages	News agency / YouTuber
Topic	Named channel	Radio frequency / Magazine
Broker	Manages and routes messages	Post office / News distributor
Subscriber	Receives and processes messages	Newspaper subscriber / Viewer
Message	The data/event itself	News article / Email

Table 9.2: *Pub-sub components with roles and use-cases*

Now that we have understood the components of pub-sub systems, let us look into the type of implementation patterns in publish-subscribe systems.

Fan-out pattern

The **fan-out** pattern is when a single event or message is **dispatched to multiple consumers/services**. This is a typical pattern in **event-driven** or **microservices architectures** using **publish-subscribe mechanisms**.

It works with the following scenario:

- One **producer** publishes an event.
- The event is sent to a **message broker** (like SNS, Kafka, or RabbitMQ).
- The broker then **delivers copies** of the event to **multiple subscribers/consumers**.

Topic filtering

Topic filtering allows consumers to **receive only specific messages** from a shared topic or stream **based on message content or labels (topics)**.

It works with the following scenario:

- Publishers **tag messages** with topics or attributes.
- Consumers **subscribe to specific topics** or use **filters** to receive only relevant messages.
- Works well with **Kafka topics**, **AWS SNS filtering policies**, or **Google Pub/Sub** with filtering.

Event sourcing

Event sourcing stores the **state of a system as a sequence of events**, rather than storing just the current state. Instead of updating rows in a database, you **persist every change** as an **immutable event**.

It works with the following scenario:

- Every state change emits an event: for example, **`AccountCredited`**, **`AccountDebited`**.
- To reconstruct current state, **replay all events** in order.
- Often paired with **Command Query Responsibility Segregation (CQRS)** for scalable reads.

Table 9.3 offers a comparative analysis of the preceding implementation pattern for easy reference:

Pattern	Fan-out	Topic filtering	Event sourcing
Primary use	Distribute one event to many consumers	Route messages selectively by topic	Store state as an event stream
Architecture fit	Event-driven, microservices	Pub/Sub, IoT, logging, alerting	Domain-driven design, transactional apps
Decoupling	High – Consumers do not depend on each other	High – Filtered subscribers	Medium – All consumers need to understand event structure
Storage need	Minimal (just queues/buffers)	Minimal	High – requires persistent event store
Latency	Low (parallel consumers)	Low (filtered at broker level)	Moderate (due to replay for state)
Auditing/ Traceability	Low to Medium	Low to Medium	Very High – perfect audit trail
Scalability	High	High	Medium to High (with smart design)

***Table 9.3**: Patterns comparative analysis*

Message queues and **publish-subscribe systems** form the backbone of modern, extendable, and loosely coupled cloud architectures. While message queues shine in task distribution and reliable work execution with one-to-one delivery, publish-subscribe systems excel in broadcasting events to many receivers, fueling event-driven ecosystems. Together, they enable fault-tolerant communication between services, decouple system components, and make architectures future-proof. Choosing the right pattern depends on the problem at hand, whether it is streamlining backend job processing or broadcasting real-time updates to a global audience. Mastery over these patterns equips architects and developers to design systems that are not just reliable and extensible but also adaptive to change.

API gateways

In the microservices world, an API gateway acts as the intelligent entry point to your application. Think of it as the concierge at a high-end hotel. Instead of customers wandering around trying to find their room (or service), they go to one place, where they are directed appropriately, authenticated, and even offered a warm welcome.

An **API gateway** is a server that sits between clients and backend services. It handles routing, authentication, load balancing, request transformation, response aggregation, and rate limiting, all in one centralized layer. This allows developers to decouple the service consumers from the implementation details of backend microservices.

Without a gateway, clients would need to keep track of all microservices, their locations, protocols, and how to authenticate with each one individually. That is neither scalable, nor secure.

Key functions of an API gateway

Let us look at some key functions of the API gateway, which are not just technical bells and whistles; they are central for building secure, adaptable, and maintainable cloud-native architectures. The deeper orchestration of traffic, identity, rate control, and transformation empowers teams to iterate quickly without risking stability or performance.

Request routing and protocol translation

The gateway intelligently routes each incoming client request to the correct microservice, often based on URL path, request headers, or HTTP method. It can also perform protocol bridging—for example, converting a REST call to a gRPC call.

Importance

It abstracts away the complexity of knowing service locations, versions, and protocols from clients. Without this, client apps would need to be tightly coupled to backend APIs.

Key insights

Here are the details of routing and protocol translation, and how to achieve the same:

- **Smart routing** can include rules based on API versioning (/v1/orders, /v2/orders) or user type (admin vs. regular user).
- **Protocol translation** enables legacy systems to coexist with newer microservices. For example, an external system may send XML over SOAP, which the gateway converts into JSON REST for backend services.

Use case

A logistics company supports external tracking via REST while internally using gRPC services for speed. The API gateway handles translation so that external partners never need to know the internal protocol.

Authentication and authorization

API gateways serve as the first line of defense, verifying the identity of the caller (authentication) and checking what they are allowed to access (authorization).

Importance

Centralized security enforcement ensures that unauthorized access is blocked before it reaches backend services. This helps maintain zero-trust principles.

Key insights

Mentioned are the various authorization strategies and examples, with their use case:

- **Supports various auth strategies, such as:**
  - OAuth 2.0 for delegated access.
  - JWT validation for stateless identity.
  - API keys for simple client authorization.
  - Mutual TLS for service-to-service authentication.
  - Can delegate complex authentication to identity providers (for example, Auth0, Azure AD).

Use case

An eCommerce platform integrates with 3rd-party vendors. Each vendor gets an API key. The gateway validates this key and ensures that vendor A cannot access vendor B's order data.

Rate limiting and throttling

Limits the number of API requests from a single user or app within a specified time window.

Importance

Protects backend systems from overload due to abuse, misconfigurations, or bot attacks. Helps maintain performance and fairness across clients.

Key insights

Mentioned are the scenarios in which rate limiting and throttling comes in handy:

- **Rate limiting** sets the total cap (for example, 1000 requests/hour).
- **Throttling** controls how fast requests are served (for example, 5 requests/sec).

The techniques include:

- Token bucket algorithms
- Leaky bucket algorithms
- Sliding window counters

Use case

A mobile banking app limits login attempts to 5 per minute per IP. Any excess is blocked by the API gateway, mitigating brute-force attacks.

Caching

Temporarily stores responses to repeated requests, reducing the need to hit the backend services every time.

Importance

Improves performance, reduces latency, and decreases load on downstream services, especially for frequently accessed but rarely updated data.

Key insights

Here are scenarios in which the caching mechanism can be used:

- **Supports:**
  - **Time-to-live (TTL)** settings to control cache expiration.
  - **ETags** and **Last-Modified headers** for conditional caching.
- Gateways like **NGINX**, **Cloudflare**, or **Amazon API Gateway** offer fine-grained cache control.

Use case

An airline's flight status API caches responses for 30 seconds. Customers get near-instant updates without overloading the backend every time they refresh.

Load balancing and failover

Distributes incoming requests across multiple backend service instances and reroutes traffic if one instance fails.

Importance

Ensures high availability, improved response times, and fault tolerance.

Key insights

The following are the scenarios where load balancing plays a critical role:

- Implements round-robin, least-connections, or weighted balancing.
- Detects unresponsive services and removes them from the rotation until healthy again.
- Can integrate with service discovery tools like Consul, Eureka, or Kubernetes DNS.

Use case

An API gateway sends traffic across five payment processing instances. When one goes down during a deployment, traffic is automatically rerouted to healthy nodes with zero disruption.

Monitoring, logging, and observability

Captures telemetry (logs, metrics, traces) for all API traffic, helping developers detect issues and understand usage patterns.

Importance

Essential for debugging, SLA monitoring, and incident response. What you cannot see, you cannot fix.

Key insights

The following points when achieved, reinforces the importance mentioned previously:

- Generates access logs, error logs, and latency metrics.
- Supports distributed tracing (for example, using OpenTelemetry, Jaeger, Zipkin).
- Can send logs to ELK, Datadog, or Sumo Logic.

Use case

A SaaS provider tracks a sudden rise in 500 errors from /checkout. Logs show malformed requests from a misbehaving client version. Gateway analytics help spot and isolate the issue quickly.

Request/Response transformation

Modifies requests or responses on-the-fly without requiring backend service changes.

Importance

Supports backward compatibility, data normalization, and smooth integration between mismatched systems.

Key insights

The following are the scenarios where transformations are handy to use:

- **Transform:**
  - Header injection/removal
  - Request/response body mapping
  - Path rewriting

- Enables API versioning and helps maintain contract consistency as backend services evolve.

Use case

A client expects **customer_id**, but the backend now uses **user_id**. Instead of changing the client or the service, the gateway rewrites the JSON response field transparently.

API gateway vs service mesh

It is also very important to understand the difference among API gateway and service mesh, as this contrast is pivotal for cloud-native architecture. It is crucial to understand where each pattern fits, how they complement (not replace) each other, and guide them in choosing the right tool for the right layer.

An API gateway is a reverse proxy that sits at the edge of your system, acting as a single-entry point for all external client requests. It manages north-south traffic, that is traffic coming into your system from the outside world. Think of it as the front door to your services, handling authentication, rate limiting, request routing, and security before anything hits your backend.

A service mesh manages east-west traffic, the internal service-to-service communication within your application. It ensures that microservices can talk to each other securely, reliably, and observably. Rather than embedding logic into services, the mesh introduces a sidecar proxy (for example, Envoy) alongside each microservice. These proxies handle things like retries, circuit breaking, traffic splitting, and mutual TLS, all without changing service code.

Key differences

Table 9.4 lists down key differences between API gateway and Service mesh in a concise manner, on various parameters:

Aspect	API Gateway	Service mesh
Traffic direction	Handles north-south traffic (external → internal)	Handles east-west traffic (internal → internal)
Deployment location	Deployed at the edge, as an entry point	Deployed within the cluster, alongside each service
Key use case	Client-to-service **communication**: routing, auth, rate limiting	Service-to-service **communication**: reliability, observability, mTLS
Security features	Centralized authentication/ authorization, API keys, JWTs	mTLS between services, policy enforcement, service identity verification

Aspect	API Gateway	Service mesh
Observability	Collects API metrics/logs from the client-facing side	Collects per-service telemetry, enables tracing of internal calls
Traffic control	Routing, caching, versioning, request/response transformation	Load balancing, retries, circuit breakers, traffic shadowing
Performance overhead	Slight overhead, typically one hop before entering the mesh	Heavier overhead due to sidecars in every pod
Coding requirement	Minimal changes in app code; config-driven	No code changes required; logic is offloaded to sidecars
Cost and complexity	Easier to adopt; less infrastructure, mostly config changes	Complex setup and learning curve; deeper cluster integration

***Table 9.4**: API gateway vs service mesh*

The following is a quick decision guidance table on when to use what, when it comes to API Gateway vs service mesh:

Use case	API Gateway	Service mesh
Client authentication and rate limiting	✓	✗
Observability across internal microservices	✗	✓
External API versioning and transformation	✓	✗
Automatic retries and traffic shifting	✗	✓
Secure service-to-service communication (mTLS)	✗	✓
External developer portal and API docs	✓	✗

***Table 9.5**: Decision framework for API gateway vs service mesh*

Understanding the distinction and synergy between API gateways and service meshes is crucial for designing resilient, secure, and scalable cloud applications. Rather than viewing them as alternatives, think of them as two halves of the same architectural coin, each solving different layers of communication and governance challenges.

Streaming data and event pipelines

Imagine you are managing a logistics platform with millions of active shipments, or a fintech app processing thousands of transactions per second. In either scenario, waiting for a daily data sync is not good enough. Delayed information means missed opportunities, inefficient operations, and poor user experience.

Welcome to the world of real-time.

Streaming data and event pipelines are not just technologies; they are the lifeblood of flexible, intelligent, cloud-native systems. They turn data from static snapshots into living, breathing signals. They make systems responsive, predictive, and fault-tolerant. Whether it is fraud detection, fleet tracking, or varied pricing, it is streaming pipelines doing the heavy lifting behind the scenes.

A streaming data pipeline is like the nervous system of a modern cloud-native application; it senses, transmits, processes, and reacts to stimuli continuously and with minimal latency.

Let us explore the architecture, key components, design patterns, and real-world implications of streaming data and event pipelines. We will also break down how they are transforming modern cloud architecture and where they fit in the broader picture of messaging and integration.

Streaming data

At its core, **streaming data** is simply information that flows continuously from a source to a destination. It arrives in **small, timestamped chunks**, often in milliseconds, and is meant to be consumed and acted upon quickly.

The following are the key characteristics of streaming data:

- **Real-time:** Processed as it arrives.
- **Continuous:** Never-ending flow of data.
- **Immutable:** Each event is a fact that does not change, like **user X clicked Y at time Z**.

This is fundamentally different from traditional **batch data**, which is collected over a period and processed afterward. Streaming systems **react** to each event, enabling decision-making within seconds or even milliseconds.

Event pipelines

An event pipeline is the infrastructure that:

- **Captures** raw events from producers.
- **Processes** them (filter, enrich, transform).
- **Distributes** them to appropriate consumers.
- Optionally **stores** them for analytics, audit, or replay.

In other words, it is a **multi-stage conveyor belt** that intelligently handles and routes real-time data. It is what allows your fraud detection system to analyze a credit card transaction the moment it happens or your recommendation engine to react to a user's browsing behavior instantly.

Let us unpack the essential building blocks of an effective streaming pipeline with the help of *Table 9.6:*

Component	Purpose
Producers	Emit events (for example, APIs, IoT devices, user interactions)
Ingestion layer	Buffers and queues incoming data (Kafka, Kinesis, Pub/Sub)
Processing engine	Applies real-time logic (Flink, Spark Streaming, Kafka Streams)
Storage	Archives for long-term access or analytics (S3, BigQuery, Snowflake)
Consumers	Use the output (alerts, dashboards, ML pipelines, microservices)

***Table 9.6**: Building blocks of event pipeline*

The following are some examples of tools that power real-time processing from streaming pipeline:

- **Apache Kafka:** The gold standard for high-throughput distributed event streaming.
- **AWS Kinesis:** A fully managed alternative tailored for AWS ecosystems.
- **Google Cloud Pub/Sub:** Reliable ingestion and fan-out on GCP.
- **Apache Flink:** Best-in-class stream processing engine with stateful capabilities.
- **Kafka Streams:** Lightweight and embedded in Java microservices.
- **Apache Beam:** Unified batch + streaming abstraction (runs on Flink, Dataflow, Spark).
- **NiFi:** Low-code, visual approach to building stream-based dataflows.

Each of these has unique strengths. For instance, Kafka excels at fault-tolerant ingestion, Flink at complex event processing, and NiFi at orchestrating multi-source pipelines.

Figure 9.2 is a sample architecture to explain the flow and processing of data using a streaming data architecture:

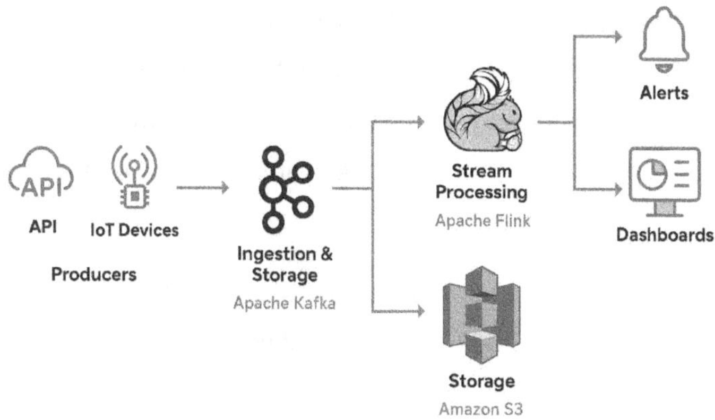

***Figure 9.2:** Sample streaming data architecture*

Let us look at the breakdown of this flow.

Data sources

These are the producers of data. They can be:

- Web/mobile apps generating user activity events.
- IoT devices pushing sensor readings.
- Microservices emitting logs or business events.
- Databases or legacy systems streaming **change data capture** (**CDC**) events.

Ingestion layer

This layer handles incoming streams, typically with:

- Apache Kafka, Amazon Kinesis, or Google Pub/Sub.
- It provides durability, fault tolerance, and buffering.
- Acts as a decoupling layer between producers and consumers.

Stream processing layer

This is where real-time computation happens. It can include:

- Apache Flink, Kafka Streams, or Spark Streaming.
- Tasks include filtering, enrichment, windowing, joins, anomaly detection.
- Enables transformation of raw data into actionable insights.

Output to multiple destinations

The processed or enriched data is routed to:

- Data lakes (like S3, GCS) for long-term storage.
- Data warehouses (like BigQuery, Redshift, Snowflake) for analytics.
- Dashboards or monitoring systems (for example, Grafana, Looker) for visualization.
- Downstream applications, like alerting systems or personalized services.

Key concepts in the flow

The following are the key concepts highlighted in the preceding flow of *Figure 9.2:*

- **Scalability and decoupling:** Producers and consumers do not need to know about each other.
- **Fault tolerance:** If one component fails, others can still function.
- **Real-time responsiveness:** Supports use cases like fraud detection, personalization, and live metrics.

Finally, *Table 9.7* is a quick comparison of batch processing vs stream processing, to provide a deeper insight into it:

Aspect	Batch processing	Streaming processing
Latency	Minutes to hours	Sub-second to seconds
Use cases	Reports, backups, historical analysis	Live dashboards, alerts, personalization
Architecture complexity	Simpler	More complex, requires real-time SLAs
Examples	Hadoop, Glue	Kafka, Flink, Spark Streaming

Table 9.7: *Batch vs streaming comparison*

Streaming is not just about speed, it is about **architecting your business for adaptability and insight**. It allows your systems to respond like living organisms, sensing, analysing, and acting faster than ever before.

From personalized UX and fraud prevention to live logistics and predictive maintenance, streaming pipelines represent a **shift in mind-set**. One where real-time data is not just a feature, it is a competitive advantage.

Choreography

Imagine a bustling city intersection with no traffic lights. Dozens of cars, pedestrians, and cyclists crisscross the junction, yet somehow manage to keep moving without collisions. How? Everyone follows shared rules, watches for signals from others, and self-regulates. This is, in essence, what service choreography is in cloud-native application architecture. A decentralized system where each component knows what it has to do and reacts to events without being micromanaged.

In a choreography-based integration model, there is no central conductor directing the flow. Each service listens for events and responds according to its own logic. It is elegant, loosely coupled, and efficient. Choreography shines in distributed systems where agility, fault tolerance, and independence of components are critical.

This decentralized nature aligns perfectly with the core philosophy of microservices. Autonomous, self-contained units that interact through well-defined interfaces. It is particularly appealing in event-driven architectures, where services publish and subscribe to events asynchronously. The beauty lies in the simplicity of collaboration, like dancers in a troupe who move in harmony, not because someone commands them, but because they understand the rhythm and play their part.

Need for choreography

Modern cloud applications are expected to be fast, fault tolerant, and independently deployable. The traditional monolithic approach where one large service controls everything fails to keep up with these expectations. This is what choreography addresses.

As systems scale, having a single orchestrator becomes a bottleneck and a risk. If it fails, the whole system can grind to a halt. Choreography sidesteps this by removing the dependency on a central controller.

This is especially crucial in domains that require high elasticity and responsiveness. For instance, in e-commerce systems during flash sales, services like inventory, payment, recommendation, and shipping must act quickly and independently based on real-time events. Choreography enables this independence while maintaining alignment through shared event protocols and contracts.

Choreography also allows for faster evolution of systems. Teams can independently build and release services without waiting on changes to a central orchestrator. This makes it ideal for agile development environments where speed and autonomy matter more than tight control.

Components of choreography

Choreography primarily hinges on **event-driven architecture (EDA)**. Services communicate by emitting events to a common message broker like *Apache Kafka, Amazon EventBridge, or RabbitMQ*. The following are some key techniques and components:

- **Event publishing and subscribing:** Event producers are services that emit events based on some internal state change or user action. Consumers are services that react to those events. For example, a service emits an event (for example, **`OrderPlaced`**), which is consumed by other services (for example, **`InventoryService`**, **`NotificationService`**) interested in that event.
  - Producers are completely unaware of who is listening. They simply emit events like **`OrderPlaced`**, **`PaymentConfirmed`**, **`InventoryReserved`**, etc.
  - Consumers implement handlers or subscribers to these events, performing actions when they receive them.
- **Event brokers:** Middleware that carries events from producers to consumers and decouple producers from consumer's Common brokers include Apache Kafka, RabbitMQ, AWS EventBridge, Google Pub/Sub, and NATS.
  - Brokers ensure **decoupling.** The producer need not know if anyone is listening, and consumers can join or leave at will.
  - They offer **durability**, **scalability**, and **ordering guarantees** in various degrees.
  - Kafka supports event replay and exactly-once semantics, making it ideal for event sourcing patterns.
- **Event schemas and contracts:** A formal definition of the structure of the event payload. Think of it as a contract between the emitter and the consumer. To prevent chaos, services must agree on event formats using schema registries or contract testing.

  - Tools like **Avro**, **Protobuf**, or **JSON Schema Registry** help enforce structure.
  - **Schema evolution is key**: Adding / removing fields must not break consumers.
  - Teams adopt **backward and forward compatibility** to keep the system resilient to changes.
- **Consumer-driven design:** Services subscribe to only the events they need and react accordingly. Example of such events are like:
  - **Event notification** (signal that something happened).
  - **Event-carried state transfer** (event contains full context needed).
  - **Event sourcing** (state changes stored as a series of events), enables auditing and rollback.
  - **CQRS** (separate read and write models), improves performance and allows scaling read / write layers independently.
- **Retry and idempotency:** Making event consumers robust against duplicate events and partial failures. Because events are asynchronous, services must be able to handle duplicates and failures gracefully.
  - Services often use **unique message IDs** to detect replays.
  - **At least once delivery** by brokers demands idempotent consumers.
  - Retry policies, circuit breakers (for example, Netflix Hystrix), and **dead letter queues** (**DLQs**) are crucial to prevent cascading failures.
- **Observability and tracing:** Monitoring choreographed flows through centralized logging, distributed tracing (for example, OpenTelemetry), and metric dashboards.
  - Tools like Jaeger, Prometheus, and ELK Stack help trace flow across services.
  - Correlation IDs are passed along event headers to tie related actions together.

This lightweight, scalable approach keeps systems responsive and makes on boarding of new services much easier to just plug them into the event stream.

Let us look at a practical example of putting together the preceding components to solve a business problem.

Problem

An e-commerce platform handling flash sales wants to manage orders, payments, inventory, and notifications, all independently and at scale.

Solution with choreography

The following steps display the solution with choreography:

1. **Customer places order** | **`OrderService`** emits | **`OrderCreated`** event.
2. **`PaymentService`** listens to **`OrderCreated`** | processes payment | emits **`PaymentSuccessful`** or **`PaymentFailed`** event.

3. **InventoryService** listens to **PaymentSuccessful** | reserves stock | emits **InventoryReserved** event.
4. **ShippingService** listens to **InventoryReserved** | schedules delivery.
5. **NotificationService** listens to all events | sends updates to the user.
6. **MonitoringService** aggregates events for dash-boarding and alerts.

No single service tells others what to do. They react to signals. This makes the system:

- **Scalable** (new services can subscribe without changing existing code)
- **Resilient** (failures in one service do not halt the entire flow)
- **Extensible** (for example, **LoyaltyPointsService** can subscribe to **PaymentSuccessful** and reward users)

Orchestration

If choreography is a jazz jam session, orchestration is a symphony led by a conductor. It is structured, predictable, and central to the performance. In cloud architecture, orchestration refers to a centralized approach where a single service, often called the orchestrator, controls the flow of interactions between different services.

This pattern is commonly used in workflows where coordination is essential. The orchestrator issues commands to each service, awaits responses, and proceeds to the next step accordingly. Tools like **AWS Step Functions, Netflix Conductor, and Apache Airflow** help automate and control such sequences.

While orchestration can seem rigid, its strength lies in clarity and control. It is ideal for long-running business processes that require strict sequencing, error handling, and rollback capabilities, something that can be hard to enforce with choreography alone.

Need for orchestration

Orchestration is necessary when business processes are **complex**, **sequential**, **and interdependent**. In such cases, allowing each service to make decisions independently can result in chaos. You need a reliable conductor to maintain order.

Consider a loan approval system at a bank. There is a sequence of steps strictly to be followed: credit check, risk analysis, compliance verification, and final approval. Each step depends on the outcome of the previous one. This kind of workflow, with specific decision points and branching logic, is best managed by a central orchestrator.

Orchestration is also valuable for tracking and monitoring complex workflows. Since the orchestrator is aware of the full process, it can generate audit logs, trigger compensations, and provide visibility into every state transition.

Components of orchestration

Orchestration is about having a **centralized conductor**, a dedicated service that directs the actions of other services in a predefined sequence. While it may sound more rigid than choreography, orchestration excels when workflows need strong coordination, retry logic, error handling, and visibility. Think of it as a symphony with a conductor ensuring every note is in perfect order.

Let us dissect its core components and then unify them with a real-world example.

Orchestration engine or workflow manager

A central service responsible for coordinating the execution of tasks and managing their lifecycle, with following functions:

- Defines workflows as state machines, **Directed Acyclic Graphs** (**DAG**), or event chains.
- Provides retry policies, timeouts, failure paths, parallel execution.
- Maintains workflow state and transitions.
- Can invoke APIs, Lambda functions, microservices, or containerized jobs.

Task workers or activity services

The distributed services or micro-services that perform actual business tasks when invoked by the orchestrator, with the following properties:

- These workers are stateless, modular, and reusable.
- Each worker is registered with the orchestrator and responds when called.
- Workers do not know who's calling them, they just do their job.

Workflow definition and DSL

Declarative or visual representation of workflows using **Domain Specific Languages** (**DSLs**) or graphical tools, with following functions:

- Describes flow logic: conditions, retries, parallelism.
- Enables non-engineering stakeholders to contribute (for example, BPMN for business users).
- YAML/JSON for AWS Step Functions, visual designer in Azure Logic Apps.

Control flow and decision handling

Ability to handle complex logic such as branching, looping, conditional execution, fan-out/fan-in patterns, with following functions:

- Ensures deterministic execution paths.
- Can incorporate dynamic decisions based on API responses or input data.
- Error boundaries allow graceful degradation or compensation flows.

Error handling and compensation logic

Mechanisms to handle task failures gracefully and roll back partial operations when needed, with the following functions:

- Retries with exponential backoff.
- Dead-letter queues for failed messages.
- Compensation logic, especially important in **saga patterns** to undo already completed steps (for example, **cancel payment if shipping fails**).

Monitoring, auditing, and observability

Central visibility into the status and health of workflows and tasks., with the following benefits:

- Dashboards show live and historical workflows.
- Logs and metrics help debug or optimize performance.
- Audit trails improve compliance and traceability.

Let us look at a practical example of putting together all of these components to solve a business problem.

Scenario

A SaaS-based tax filing platform that handles filing workflows during peak season. The process involves document collection, user authentication, tax calculation, fraud detection, filing submission, and confirmation.

Solution with orchestration

The following steps display the solution:

1. **User initiates filing** | Orchestrator starts workflow.
2. **Task 1:** Collect documents from user | invokes **`DocumentService`**.
3. **Task 2:** Authenticate user | invokes **`IdentityService`**.
4. **Task 3:** Calculate taxes | invokes **`TaxEngineService`**.
5. **Parallel tasks:**
    a. Validate documents | **`DocValidatorService`**
    b. Check for fraud | **`FraudDetectorService`**

6. **Decision point:**
    a. If fraud detected | **`NotifyComplianceTeam`**
    b. Else | Proceed to file
7. **Task 4:** Submit to government portal | **`SubmissionService`**.
8. **Task 5:** Send confirmation email | **`EmailService`**.
9. **On failure of any task** | Trigger compensation or notify support.

This orchestration:

- Provides **end-to-end visibility** into every user's filing journey.
- Allows **parallel processing** to reduce latency.
- Automatically handles retries and failures.
- Ensures **compliance and auditability**.

Let us take a look at the pictorial difference among choreography vs orchestration in *Figure 9.3* to understand them in a nutshell:

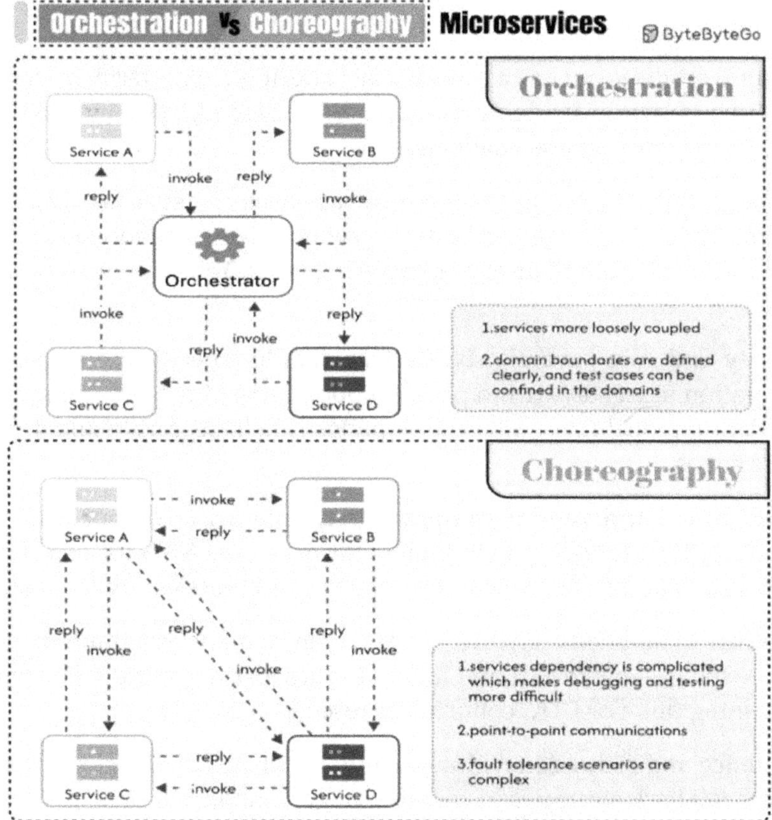

Figure 9.3: *Choreography vs Orchestration*

Source: *https://bytebytego.com/guides/orchestration-vs-choreography-microservices/*

Hybrid cloud integration patterns

In a world where digital transformation is no longer optional but inevitable, organizations are rapidly adopting the cloud. However, the journey to the cloud is rarely a **lift-and-shift** moment. Legacy systems, regulatory constraints, latency requirements, and investment realities often compel companies to retain parts of their infrastructure on-premise or across multiple clouds. This builds the case for advent of: **Hybrid cloud integration patterns**.

Hybrid cloud refers to a deployment architecture where enterprises use a combination of **public cloud**, **private cloud**, and **on-premises infrastructure**, seamlessly connected and orchestrated to function as one ecosystem. But this hybridization creates complexity especially around communication, data synchronization, and service interoperability. That is where hybrid cloud integration patterns come in. These are architectural strategies that ensure secure, reliable, and real-time communication between disparate systems across environments.

Think of hybrid cloud as a well-rehearsed orchestra of instruments scattered across different cities. Hybrid integration is the sheet music, the conductor, and the transport system, all rolled into one, to ensure every note is in sync.

The hybrid cloud model is not just a transitional state, it is a long-term operating model for many enterprises. However, bridging the gap between legacy systems and modern cloud-native applications poses several challenges:

- **Legacy gravity:** Older mission-critical applications such as ERP, supply chain systems, and mainframe applications, cannot always be moved to the cloud due to performance, compliance, or refactoring costs. Yet, new services need to talk to them.

- **Security and data sovereignty:** Certain data like healthcare records or financial information must stay within physical boundaries due to regulations like HIPAA, GDPR, or regional laws. Integration patterns help segregate and sync data across secure zones.

- **Cloud sprawl and vendor strategy:** Many enterprises do not want vendor lock-in and opt for multi-cloud strategies (for example, AWS for compute, Azure for analytics). Patterns ensure seamless operations across cloud vendors.

- **Real-time sync needs:** Hybrid setups often demand real-time or near-real-time data exchange—batch jobs and manual syncs just will not do. Patterns like event-based integration or CDC come to the rescue.

- **Resilience and redundancy:** Integrating workloads across cloud and on-premise ensures fall back strategies in case of outages, enhancing business continuity.

Without well-defined hybrid integration patterns, organizations risk creating brittle, unmanageable systems prone to failures, latency, and security breaches.

Methods of hybrid cloud integration patterns

Let us now go over some common methods of hybrid cloud integrations, weighed on use cases, tools and benefits they serve.

API-led connectivity

Expose internal systems and services through well-documented, versioned, and secure APIs.

Use case

An on-premises billing system can expose REST APIs for invoice generation, which cloud-native order management services consume.

Tools

The following are some associated tools:

- API gateways (Apigee, AWS API Gateway, MuleSoft)
- Authentication via OAuth2, JWT, or SAML

Benefits

The following are some benefits of API-led connectivity:

- Loose coupling
- Version control
- Reusability and scalability

Event-driven integration

Services communicate asynchronously using event brokers. On-prem systems publish or consume events via cloud-based message brokers.

Use case

A warehouse management system publishes **`InventoryUpdated`** events that cloud-based e-commerce platforms consume.

Tools

The following are some tools associated with event-driven integration:

- Kafka with MirrorMaker
- AWS EventBridge
- Azure Event Grid
- Confluent Cloud

Benefits

The following are the benefits of event-driven integration:

- Low latency
- Resilience
- Decoupled communication

Data virtualization and federation

Abstract multiple data sources into a single virtual data layer without physically moving data.

Use case

BI dashboards in the cloud can query both on-prem SQL Server and cloud-based Snowflake using a unified schema.

Tools

The following are some tools associated with data virtualization and federation:

- Denodo
- Dremio
- IBM Cloud Pak for Data

Benefits

The following are some benefits of data virtualization and federation:

- Real-time querying
- No data duplication
- Reduced storage cost

Service mesh across boundaries

Extend service mesh (like *Istio*) beyond Kubernetes clusters into hybrid networks for secure service-to-service communication.

Use case

Authenticate and encrypt communication between cloud-based microservices and legacy services running on VMs.

Tools

The following are some tools associated with service mesh:

- Istio
- Linkerd
- Consul

Benefits

The following are some benefits of service mesh across boundaries:

- Zero-trust security
- Observability
- Fine-grained traffic control

Integration Platforms as a Service (iPaaS)

Use low-code cloud platforms to connect and manage workflows between SaaS, on-prem, and cloud-native systems.

Use case

Sync Salesforce CRM with an on-prem Oracle DB to update leads and customer records.

Tools

The following are some tools associated with iPaaS:

- MuleSoft
- Dell Boomi
- Workato
- Informatica Cloud

Benefits

The following are the benefits of iPaaS:

- Rapid integration
- Visual workflows
- Built-in connectors

Hybrid message brokers

Use message brokers that support hybrid deployment (for example, bridging on-prem and cloud clusters).

Use case

An IoT device network in a factory (on-prem) sends telemetry data via MQTT to a cloud Kafka or Pulsar cluster.

Tools

The following are some tools associated with hybrid message brokers:

- Kafka + Confluent Hybrid
- RabbitMQ Federation
- MQTT over WebSocket

Benefits

The following are the benefits of hybrid message brokers:

- Real-time streaming
- Secure and lightweight
- Reliable delivery

Let us understand these patterns in the form of a comparison on various parameters applicable, as shown in *Table 9.8:*

Pattern	Latency	Complexity	Reliability	Security	Data consistency	Best use cases
API-led connectivity	Medium	Moderate	High (with retries)	Strong (OAuth, TLS)	Strong (request-response)	Exposing legacy or on-prem services to cloud apps; mobile and web frontends
Event-driven integration	Low	High (async + schema mgmt)	Very High (decoupled, fault tolerant)	Strong (encryption, auth on brokers)	Eventual (asynchronous model)	Real-time inventory updates, telemetry pipelines, reactive architectures
Data virtualization/ Federation	High (query time overhead)	Low to Moderate	Moderate (depends on network)	Strong (access control, masking)	Strong (live query views)	Unified BI dashboards, federated queries from multiple databases
Service mesh across boundaries	Low	Very High (operationally heavy)	Very High (self-healing, retries)	Very Strong (mTLS, zero-trust)	N/A (used for service-to-service)	Secure microservice communication across clusters or cloud/on-prem
iPaaS	Medium	Low (low-code interface)	Moderate (depends on vendor SLA)	High (platform managed)	Strong (workflow-controlled)	CRM ↔ ERP sync, marketing automation, connecting SaaS tools with on-prem apps
Hybrid message brokers	Very Low (near real-time)	High (broker federation, routing logic)	Very High (acknowledgements, retries)	High (TLS, IAM, network layers)	Eventual (streaming model)	IoT data ingestion, global telemetry systems, log ingestion across environments

Table 9.8: *Hybrid integration patterns comparison*

Hybrid cloud integration is not just a connectivity concern, it is a strategic enabler of enterprise agility, resilience, and innovation. By mastering these integration patterns, architects can future-proof their systems against shifting business models, regulatory landscapes, and technology trends. The key lies in choosing the right patterns, leveraging the right tools, and designing with a forward-thinking mindset.

Conclusion

Messaging and integration patterns are the silent contributors to cloud architecture. They are what allow us to build systems that are greater than the sum of their parts, enabling communication and coordination across distributed services.

As you design and build your own cloud applications, it is encouraged that you think carefully about how your services will communicate. The patterns we have discussed in this chapter, like message queues, pub/sub systems, API gateways, data pipelines, choreography, and orchestration, are powerful tools that can help you create extendable, fault-tolerant, and manageable cloud architectures.

Remember, the goal is not just to build a system that works today, but one that can evolve and grow with your needs. By implementing these messaging and integration patterns, you are laying the foundation for a flexible, future-proof architecture.

In our next chapter, we will explore how to keep all these moving parts under control with monitoring and observability patterns.

Chapter 10
Monitoring and Observability Patterns

Introduction

In the world of modern cloud-native systems, where microservices span across regions, containers spin up and down like mayflies, and user traffic flows like unpredictable weather, reliability is not a feature, it is a requirement. Amidst all this complexity, one critical truth stands tall: *you cannot fix what you cannot see.*

That is where monitoring and observability come into action. While these terms are often tossed around interchangeably, they serve different, complementary purposes. **Monitoring** is about looking for known problems. It answers the question, *Is something broken*? It is your system's pulse check, a dashboard full of charts, dials, and alerts that light up when something goes off-script. **Observability**, on the other hand, is about building systems that can explain themselves. It helps you ask new questions you did not think of during design like a detective piecing together how and why something broke, not just that it did.

As organizations shift from monoliths to distributed architectures, the traditional approaches to monitoring fall short. A simple CPU graph or a memory alert cannot capture a timeout caused by a downstream service five hops away. Distributed systems demand distributed visibility, spanning logs, metrics, and traces and the ability to correlate all three in real time.

This chapter unpacks the patterns that make such visibility possible. We will explore how centralized logging acts as your historical record, how instrumentation and metrics give you real-time feedback, and how distributed tracing reveals the story across services. We will also discuss the contrasting philosophies of black-box and white-box monitoring, and wrap up with a look at visualization patterns that empower teams to interpret data at a glance before their users ever notice something is wrong.

The end goal is not to collect more data. It is to reduce the time between **detection**, **diagnosis**, and **resolution**.

Structure

In this chapter, we will go over the following topics:

- Centralized logging
- Metrics and instrumentation
- Distributed tracings
- Black-box monitoring
- White-box monitoring
- Dashboards and visualization

Objectives

By the end of this chapter, you will not just walk away with a glossary of observability tools or trendy terms, but you will also gain a deep understanding of the *why* and *how* behind each pillar of observability. You will be equipped to make thoughtful, scalable architectural decisions that thrive amid complexity, rather than crumble under it. Along the way, we will explore what truly makes a logging system actionable instead of merely verbose, and how to extract meaningful metrics without getting buried in telemetry noise. We will unpack the moments when distributed tracing becomes the irreplaceable source of truth in debugging tangled systems, and examine how black-box and white-box monitoring approaches, often treated in isolation, actually work better together. Moreover, we will even get into what separates a genuinely insightful dashboard from a pretty but pointless one. This chapter is written for architects, engineers, and DevOps professionals alike, aiming to shift the mindset from reactive firefighting to proactive design, where observability is not bolted on at the end, but baked in from day one.

Centralized logging

Imagine trying to debug a production incident in a distributed system, and you are remotely login in (SSH) into five different nodes, tailing log files, and trying to piece together what happened. It is like finding a needle in five haystacks blindfolded. This is precisely the chaos centralized logging aims to eliminate.

At its core, **centralized logging** is about gathering logs from all your services across nodes, regions, containers, and functions and consolidating them into a single, searchable, and easily queried manner, and often in a visual interface. Whether it is an unexpected 500 error in your API gateway or an edge-case exception in a downstream billing service, centralized logging ensures that every log entry, from every corner of your system, is captured and can be correlated with others.

In the context of cloud-native systems, particularly those deployed on container orchestration platforms like Kubernetes or ECS, centralized logging is not just a nice-to-have. It is essentially a set of survival tactics. It turns chaos into clarity and transforms logs from post-mortem artefacts into real-time operational intelligence.

Need of centralized logging

Logs were once simple. You had an app, it ran on a box, and it wrote logs to a local file. But then came containers, microservices, serverless functions, and hybrid clouds. Now, applications are often spread across hundreds of services, with ephemeral containers that may vanish the moment something crashes. Good luck logging into a terminated pod.

The need for centralized logging arises from this very **ephemerality** and **scale**. Centralized logging enables the following:

- **Single-pane-of-glass visibility** across the entire ecosystem.
- **Historical context** for issues that span across deployments or services.
- **Faster incident response** by allowing correlated searches across services.
- **Security and auditability**, especially in regulated environments.
- **Compliance and retention** by keeping logs for a defined period, securely.

It is not just about collecting logs; it is about using them to **understand, act,** and **improve** your system.

With the preceding thoughts, centralized logging offers the following benefits:

- **Faster troubleshooting:** When an issue arises, you do not have to log into multiple servers or services. All the information is at your fingertips.
- **Correlation of events:** You can easily connect the dots between seemingly unrelated events across different parts of your system.
- **Historical analysis:** With logs stored centrally, you can look back in time to identify patterns or the root cause of recurring issues.

Types of centralized logging

Let us look at and understand various types and techniques of centralized logging, along with their use cases, to have a better grasp.

Agent-based logging

In this type of logging mechanism, logs are collected via agents installed on nodes or containers. These agents forward logs to a central system.

Use cases

Kubernetes clusters, EC2-based applications, edge nodes.

Benefits

The following are some benefits of agent-based logging:

- Real-time ingestion.
- Custom parsing and filtering.
- Support for multiple destinations.

Drawbacks

The following are some drawbacks of agent-based logging:

- Resource overhead on nodes.
- Complexity in agent lifecycle management.

Examples are:

- Fluentd, Logstash

Sidecar or DaemonSet pattern

In this type of logging mechanism, used heavily in Kubernetes, a logging container runs alongside your app and handles log shipping.

Use case

Microservices running in Kubernetes/EKS.

Benefits

The following are some benefits of Sidecar/DaemonSet:

- Clean separation of concerns.
- Language-agnostic.

Drawbacks

The following are some drawbacks of Sidecar/DaemonSet:

- Increased deployment complexity.
- Higher resource footprint.

Application-level log forwarding

In this type of logging mechanism, applications directly push logs to an API or stream.

Use case

Highly specialized applications or edge services.

Benefits

The following are some benefits of application-level log forwarding:

- Real-time delivery.
- No intermediary dependencies.

Drawbacks

The following are some drawbacks of application-level log forwarding:

- Requires dev effort.
- Risk of log loss if destination unavailable.

Example:

- Kafka, HTTP, gRPC.

Tools for centralized logging

Modern centralized logging stacks have evolved to not only store logs but make them actionable. *Table 10.1* gives a snapshot of some popular tools for centralized logging:

Tool	Core functionality	Strengths	Weaknesses
Elasticsearch, Logstash, Kibana (**ELK**) Stack	Ingest, index, visualize	Rich ecosystem, open source	High memory usage, scaling complexity
Loki + Grafana	Log aggregation and visualization	Lightweight, integrates with Prometheus	Limited search vs ELK
Fluentd / Fluent Bit	Log collectors	Versatile, efficient	Configuration complexity at scale
Amazon CloudWatch Logs	AWS-native log management	Seamless AWS integration	Expensive at scale, limited retention
Sumo Logic / Datadog Logs / New Relic	SaaS-based logging and analytics	Easy setup, great UI	Cost and vendor lock-in.

***Table 10.1**: Centralized logging tools*

When choosing a tool, trade-offs around cost, latency, retention, and compliance should guide your decision, not just features.

With the preceding concepts in mind, let us look at implementing the aforementioned components into action implementation for a business problem.

Scenario: A SaaS company runs a shipping platform with dozens of microservices deployed on AWS EKS. The platform handles millions of transactions daily, and customer support depends heavily on identifying and resolving issues quickly.

The architecture can consist of the following recommendations:

- **Log generation:** Microservices emit JSON-structured logs with trace IDs, customer IDs, and service-specific tags.
- **Collection layer:** Fluent Bit as a lightweight agent runs as a DaemonSet on every EKS node, tailing container logs from `stdout/stderr`.
- **Processing layer:** Logs are enriched and filtered via Fluentd and shipped to two destinations:
- **Loki** for real-time developer queries.
- **Amazon S3** for long-term archival and compliance.
- **Visualization layer:** Grafana dashboards allow querying by customer, trace ID, and error patterns.
- **Alerting:** Custom queries detect repeated error signatures or latency spikes and trigger alerts via PagerDuty.

This architecture enables teams to correlate a user-reported delay with backend service latencies and pinpoint the problematic service in seconds. It also ensures logs are preserved securely for regulatory audits. *Figure 10.1* is a pictorial representation of the preceding sample architecture for easy reference:

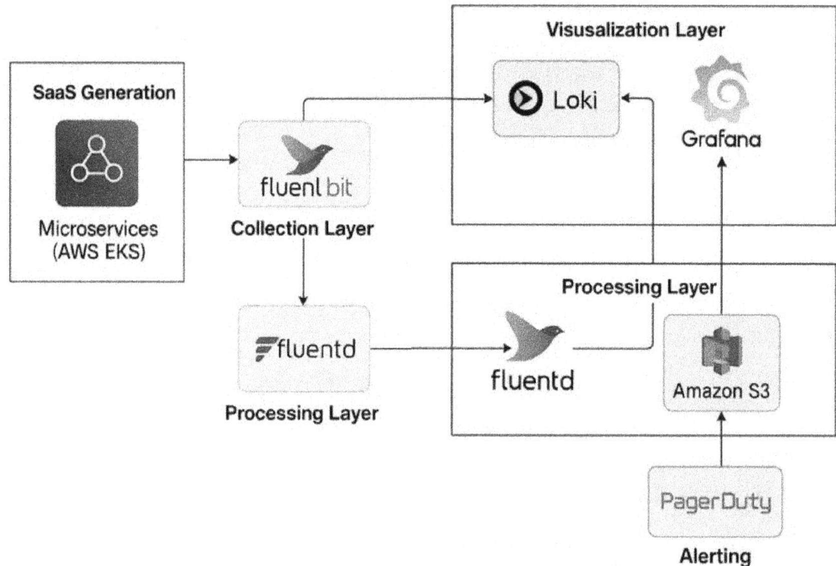

Figure 10.1: Centralized logging architecture

Best practices for effective logging

The following are some best practices associated with effective logging:

- **Use structured logging:** Instead of free-form text, log in a structured format like JSON. This makes it easier to parse and analyse logs programmatically.
- **Include context:** Always include relevant context in your logs. For a user-related event, include the user ID. For an API call, include the request ID.
- **Use log levels appropriately:** Not all log messages are created equal. Use different log levels (`DEBUG`, `INFO`, `WARN`, `ERROR`) to categorize your logs.
- **Be careful with sensitive data:** Never log sensitive information like passwords or API keys. Be mindful of privacy regulations when logging personal data.
- **Implement log rotation:** In production environments, implement log rotation to manage log file sizes and prevent disk space issues.

Code implementation of centralized logging

The following subsection consists of a practical implementation of centralized logging using the popular Fluent Bit + Fluentd + Loki + Grafana stack for an application running in Kubernetes (EKS). We will simulate a Golang microservice logging JSON-formatted logs and show how logs are ingested and visualized.

Setup overview

The following is the premise of tools and framework that we will use to delineate the example:

- Microservice in Golang generates logs.
- Fluent Bit as a lightweight log collector (DaemonSet).
- Fluentd for log enrichment and forwarding.
- Loki for log aggregation.
- Grafana for visualization.

Golang microservice (log in on JSON)

The following code generates the `INFO` level log with a timestamp and a message:

```
package main

import (
  "log"
  "time"
)
```

```

func main() {
 for {
  log.Println(`{"level":"INFO","timestamp":"` + time.Now().
 Format(time.RFC3339) + `","message":"Package shipped","order_
 id":12345}`)
  time.Sleep(5 * time.Second)
 }
}
```

Build and push the container to ECR or Docker Hub and deploy it to your EKS cluster.

Fluent bit (DaemonSet)

The following configuration, in the file Fluent-bit-configmap.yaml, defines the FluentBit config map that collects log from Kubernetes container, enriching them with Kubernetes metadata and forwards them to Fluentd service:

```
apiVersion: v1
kind: ConfigMap
metadata:
  name: fluent-bit-config
  namespace: logging
data:
  fluent-bit.conf: |
    [SERVICE]
        Flush         1
        Daemon        Off
        Log_Level     info
    [INPUT]
        Name              tail
        Path              /var/log/containers/*.log
        Parser            docker
        Tag               kube.*
        Refresh_Interval  5
    [FILTER]
        Name                kubernetes
        Match               kube.*
        Kube_URL            https://kubernetes.default.svc:443
        Merge_Log           On
        Keep_Log            Off
    [OUTPUT]
```

```
    Name  forward
    Match *
    Host  fluentd.logging.svc.cluster.local
    Port  24224
```

Deploy Fluent Bit as a **DaemonSet** so each node has a collector.

Fluentd config

The following Fluentd config defines a Fluentd configuration that acts as a log aggregator, receiving logs from sources like Fluent Bit, and forwarding them to a Loki backend for storage and querying:

```
apiVersion: v1
kind: ConfigMap
metadata:
  name: fluentd-config
  namespace: logging
data:
  fluent.conf: |
    <source>
      @type forward
      port 24224
      bind 0.0.0.0
    </source>
    <match **>
      @type loki
      url "http://loki.logging.svc.cluster.local:3100/loki/api/v1/push"
      extract_kubernetes_labels true
      tenant_id "shipping"
    </match>
```

Deploy Fluentd as a **deployment** and make sure it has network access to Loki.

Loki and Grafana setup

You can install Loki + Grafana using Helm charts:

```
helm repo add grafana https://grafana.github.io/helm-charts
helm install loki grafana/loki-stack --namespace=logging --create-namespace
```

Once Grafana is up, configure **Loki as a data source**, and query logs like:

```
{job="fluent-bit", level="INFO"}
```

The preceding code example gives a hands-on experience on implementing the centralized logging.

Centralized logging is not just a checkbox in your observability stack, it is your narrative engine. It tells the story of your system, one timestamped line at a time. But like any good story, it is only valuable if it is clear, searchable, and complete. When implemented thoughtfully, centralized logging can accelerate **mean time to resolution** (**MTTR**), aid in root cause analysis, support proactive security measures, and most importantly, free up developers from chasing ghosts in the logs.

But remember, *collecting logs is easy. Making them useful is an art.*

Metrics and instrumentation

As software systems scale to support millions of users and complex workflows, the need to make informed, real-time decisions about performance, health, and usage grows exponentially. This is where metrics and instrumentation become the heartbeat of observability in modern cloud-native architectures. Metrics provide numerical data points about system behavior, while instrumentation refers to the code and mechanisms embedded within applications to collect these metrics. Together, they empower engineers to move from reactive firefighting to proactive insight and optimization.

Unlike logs, which offer granular insights post-event, metrics offer continuous aggregation and trend data. Think of them as the vital signs of your infrastructure. Whether you are managing throughput, latency, error rates, or memory consumption, a well-instrumented application provides the pulse of your ecosystem. Metrics, when collected and visualized effectively, act as the early warning system for operational issues, allowing teams to detect and resolve problems before customers even notice.

Need for metrics and instrumentation

Monitoring without metrics is like flying a plane without an altimeter; you can guess you are flying straight, but you would not rather know for sure. Metrics are foundational for **Service Level Indicators (SLIs), Service Level Objectives (SLOs),** and ultimately for maintaining **Service Level Agreements (SLAs)**. They help determine baseline performance, detect anomalies, and support capacity planning and auto scaling decisions.

Instrumentation is essential for this process. It must be thoughtfully designed, not just sprinkled across the codebase, so that it provides actionable, meaningful data. Properly implemented, it can uncover slow database queries, inefficient API endpoints, memory leaks, or subtle regressions in performance. It also plays a critical role in distributed tracing and event correlation across microservices.

Type of metrics

There are primarily three categories of metrics:

- **System metrics:** CPU, memory, disk, and network utilization, typically collected from the OS or container runtime.

- **Application metrics:** Business-specific or custom metrics like order processing rate, API request durations, or cart abandonment rate.
- **Service metrics:** Availability, request count, error rates, and latency metrics that indicate the health of services.

Use cases

The use cases are as follows:

- **Autoscaling:** Using CPU or request rate metrics to trigger horizontal scaling in Kubernetes.
- **Alerting:** Notifying SREs when 95th percentile latency breaches thresholds.
- **Performance tuning:** Identifying slow endpoints or resource-heavy microservices.
- **Business insights:** Tracking key business events like payment failures or login trends.

Tools for metrics and instrumentation

A well-rounded metrics stack often includes the following:

- **Prometheus:** The de facto standard for Kubernetes-native metrics scraping and alerting.
- **OpenTelemetry:** A vendor-agnostic framework for generating, collecting, and exporting telemetry data.
- **Grafana:** A powerful visualization tool to query, analyze, and display metrics data.
- **StatsD / Telegraf:** Lightweight daemons for metrics collection.
- **AWS CloudWatch / Azure Monitor / Google Cloud Monitoring:** Native cloud provider monitoring services.

These tools allow developers to define custom metrics, monitor system-level statistics, and build alerting pipelines that surface critical issues in real-time.

Let us have look at a practical implementation of collecting metrics of a microservice in the upcoming subsection.

Use case

A SaaS ecommerce platform wants to track the real-time performance of its payment service and ensure that latency remains under 200ms for 99% of requests.

Let us look into the implementation:

- Use **OpenTelemetry SDK** in the Golang microservice to instrument custom metrics, request count, success rate, and latency.

- Export metrics to **Prometheus** via **`/metrics`** endpoint.
- Visualize the data in **Grafana** using dashboards and heatmaps.
- Set up SLO-based alerting for latency spikes or request failures.

Let us look into the architecture flow:

- Service emits metrics via embedded OpenTelemetry exporter.
- Prometheus scrapes metrics from exposed endpoints.
- Grafana queries Prometheus to visualize trends.
- Alertmanager (Prometheus) sends alerts to Slack/Email when thresholds are breached.

The following is an example code snippet implementation:

```
import (
    "go.opentelemetry.io/otel"
    "go.opentelemetry.io/otel/metric"
    "time"
)

var meter = otel.Meter("ecomm/payment-service")
var requestLatency, _ = meter.Float64Histogram("payment_request_latency_ms")

func handlePaymentRequest() {
    start := time.Now()
    // business logic
    duration := float64(time.Since(start).Milliseconds())
    requestLatency.Record(context.Background(), duration)
}
```

Best practices for metrics and instrumentation

The following are some best practices associated with metrics and instrumentation:

- **Start with business and SLO-driven metrics:**
  - Define what success looks like before you start measuring.
  - Tie metrics to SLOs, SLIs (Indicators), and SLAs (Agreements).
  - Include both **technical** (latency, error rate, CPU) and business metrics (cart conversion, payment success rate).
  - **Example**: Tracking API latency is good. Tracking *95th percentile latency vs. SLO* is great.

- **Choose the right cardinality and labels:**
  - Limit the number of unique label combinations (aka cardinality).
  - High cardinality metrics (for example, **`user_id`**, **`session_id`**) can blow up your Prometheus server or cost you $$$ in hosted tools.
  - Use meaningful but bounded labels like region, **`status_code`**, **`api_endpoint`**, etc.
- **Prioritize latency histograms over averages:**
  - Never trust averages in distributed systems—they lie. Use **percentiles** (P50, P90, P99).
  - Use **histograms** or **summaries** to capture true performance.
  - Capture end-to-end latencies, not just internal service timings.
  - **Example**: Instead of average latency: Track **`http_request_duration_seconds_bucket`**
- **Instrument code with context:**
  - Use OpenTelemetry or vendor-neutral libraries (not tightly coupled SDKs).
  - Attach relevant context like **`trace_id`**, **`span_id`**, and business-relevant tags.
  - Encapsulate instrumentation logic using middleware or interceptors where possible (for example, HTTP, gRPC, DB queries).

The preceding examples are a few best practices for metrics and instrumentation. However, as you keep working, you will develop your own practices with the experience.

Metrics and instrumentation are not just operational necessities, they are strategic assets. They allow engineering leaders to make data-driven decisions, support teams in building resilient services, and offer visibility that aligns with both technical and business KPIs. In a world where uptime and performance define customer satisfaction, mastering metrics is mastering the health of your platform. When implemented holistically, metrics transform chaos into clarity, making systems observable, tune-able, and trustworthy.

Distributed tracing

Distributed tracing is like a detective sniffing their way through a maze of services to find out who can solve the case. With the complexity of cloud-native architectures, legacy logging and metrics fail to provide the ability to identify how and where the problems are taking place throughout the tangled web of services. Distributed tracing provides a magnifying glass into how individual requests move through these pieces, exposing vital information about where your performance may be bottlenecked, where latency is hurting you, and how the interplay of microservices is affecting your system.

In the early days of the monolithic world, when investigating a function call or debugging a slow response, it used to be easy to look into a few logs on a single server. Today, in our microservices world, that user request might be flowing through a dozen different APIs, databases, queues and caches, every one of them deployed in separate containers, perhaps stretching across several regions. Here comes distributed tracing, the glue that binds together the journey of an incoming request from start to finish.

Distributed tracing allows you to follow a request as it moves through your system, giving you visibility into the entire request lifecycle. It is like leaving breadcrumbs throughout your application, allowing you to retrace the path of any request.

Need for distributed tracing

Without tracing, diagnosing issues in modern architectures is like trying to solve a maze while blindfolded. Distributed systems introduce unpredictable latencies, network retries, dependency failures, and hidden service chains. Traditional logs can only tell us *what happened*, not necessarily *why* or *where* it happened.

Some use cases that necessitate tracing are as follows:

- **Latency analysis:** Where does most of the request time get consumed?
- **Dependency mapping:** What other services does Service A depend on?
- **Bottleneck identification:** Which component is the slowest or failing?
- **User impact analysis:** How many users are impacted by a slow DB call?

Core concepts of distributed tracing

The following are some core concepts of distributed tracing:

- **Trace:** A record of a single request as it flows through a system.
- **Span:** A single operation within the trace. Every span has:
    - A start time
    - Duration
    - Metadata (tags, logs)
    - Parent-child relationships
- **Context propagation:** Carrying the **trace ID** and **span ID** across process boundaries (via HTTP headers or message queues).
- **Trace visualization:** Often shown as Gantt-style waterfall diagrams to visualize bottlenecks.

Methods and use cases

Let us look at and understand some of the prominent methods and use cases for distributed tracing to have a detailed understanding along with their benefits and drawbacks.

Synchronous HTTP tracing

Synchronous HTTP tracing is the most straightforward and common approach to distributed tracing, especially in REST-based microservice architectures. In this method, trace context (typically a **`traceparent`** header) is injected into HTTP requests and passed along from service to service. This allows each service in the chain to generate a span while maintaining a shared context. This method is ideal for real-time user transactions such as login, search, and checkout flows.

Use case

Tracing a user request from the frontend through the API gateway, authentication, product catalog, and payment services.

Benefits

The following are some benefits of synchronous HTTP tracing:

- Easy to implement using middleware libraries.
- Seamless trace propagation.
- Minimal setup.

Drawbacks

The following are a few drawbacks of synchronous HTTP tracing:

- Limited to synchronous HTTP flows.
- Does not support asynchronous or event-based patterns.

Asynchronous messaging tracing

Modern systems rely heavily on message queues like Kafka, RabbitMQ, or AWS SQS for decoupled communication. In these cases, asynchronous tracing is required. Trace context must be embedded in the message headers or payload and explicitly extracted by the consumer services. Proper instrumentation ensures that the producer's trace ID and span context are preserved and linked in the consumer spans.

Use case

Tracing a background job triggered by an event, such as processing an order placed via the checkout service, or analyzing user activity in batch jobs.

Benefits

The following are some benefits of asynchronous messaging tracing:

- Enables visibility across asynchronous.
- Decoupled systems.
- Helpful in debugging event flow failures.

Drawbacks

The following are a few drawbacks of asynchronous messaging tracing:

- Requires custom context propagation mechanisms.
- Increased complexity in message parsing and trace stitching.

Full-stack end-to-end tracing

This method aims to stitch together the user's journey across frontend and backend services. It typically involves instrumenting frontend applications (**JavaScript in web browsers, mobile SDKs**) with trace IDs that are passed into backend API calls. This provides visibility into client-side performance and how it correlates with backend latencies.

Use case

Tracing a user clicking a **Place Order** button on a web page all the way to the backend order confirmation logic and email dispatch.

Benefits

The following is a benefit of full stack end-to-end tracing:

- Offers complete visibility into user experience and backend performance.

Drawbacks

The following is a drawback of full stack end-to-end tracing:

- Requires consistent instrumentation across heterogeneous tech stacks and adherence to common standards like W3C trace context.

Service mesh tracing

Service meshes like Istio, Linkerd, and Consul provide tracing out-of-the-box by intercepting service-to-service traffic via sidecars. These proxies automatically collect spans and forward them to tracing backends. This approach minimizes developer overhead while maximizing consistency.

Use case

Observability in Kubernetes environments where microservices communicate through a mesh.

Benefits

The following are some benefits of service mesh tracing:

- Low effort instrumentation
- highly scalable
- Resilient

Drawbacks

The following are a few drawbacks of service mesh tracing:

- Traces only network calls.
- Does not capture in-app logic or internal function spans.

Trace sampling strategies

Capturing every trace in a high-throughput system can be costly and unnecessary. Trace sampling strategies allow organizations to balance visibility and cost. Head-based sampling (deciding at the beginning of a request) and tail-based sampling (deciding after spans are collected) are common techniques.

Use case

Sampling 1% of traffic for performance analysis in a high-volume payment gateway.

Benefits

The following is a benefit of trace sampling strategies:

- Reduces storage and processing overhead.

Drawbacks

The following is a drawback of trace sampling strategies:

- Might miss rare or intermittent issues if not tuned correctly.

Tools for distributed tracing

Let us look at *Table 10.2*. It provides a snapshot of various tools that can be used in corresponding scenarios listed:

Tool	Language support	Cloud-native	Notes
Jaeger	Go, Java, Node	Yes	CNCF project, built on OpenTracing
Zipkin	Java, Python	Partial	Lightweight, good for quick setup
OpenTelemetry	All major	Yes	Standard vendor-neutral observability APIs
AWS X-Ray	.NET, Java, etc	AWS-native	Good AWS integration, limited cross-cloud
Datadog APM	All	Yes	Hosted, rich visualization and analytics

***Table 10.2**: Tools for distributed tracing*

Recommendation: Use **OpenTelemetry** for vendor-neutral instrumentation, and plug it into any back-end collector (Jaeger, Datadog, etc.).

Best practices for distributed tracing

The following are a few best practices associated with distributed tracing:

- Use baggage **sparingly**: Avoid injecting large values into trace context.
- Instrument every **critical** path, not just one or two services.
- Adopt **trace correlation** with logs and metrics.
- Implement **trace sampling** and **retention policies.**
- Educate teams to read and act on **trace data.**

Distributed tracing bridges the observability gap in today's cloud-native systems. It does not replace logs or metrics; it completes them. While the initial setup may seem like overhead, the payoff is immediate during outages, performance degradations, and even during feature rollouts. As systems grow, tracing becomes not just a debugging tool but a **performance governance framework**.

If metrics answer *how often* and logs answer *what happened*, then traces answer *how it happened*, and that makes all the difference when uptime and user experience are on the line and are utmost crucial for trust.

Black-box monitoring

The idea of black-box monitoring is treating a system as an opaque box and monitors its behavior from outside it. What this means in practice is either emulating user behaviors, or probing service endpoints without any kind of internal understanding. A black-box monitoring tool **unwraps metrics and inspects the end-user experience**, considering only externally visible signals. In other words, it inspects how the system works as the user would like?

This view is like the flight's **black box** on a plane, it records what happens and gives information on what broke during or after an event. Black-box monitors generally collect health metrics of high-level such as availability, response time, and error rate. By viewing the application as a black box operators verify service-level objectives (such as the web uptime, or the API responsiveness) only as the user would experience them.

Black-box monitoring using synthetic tests or active probes is a common approach. For instance, you have a synthetic test that fires a scripted HTTP request off to a web service every minute, and you want to make sure it responds the right way. Black-box monitoring is *the way a customer operates on your application or site specifically, the externally visible resources.*

In a modern-day, cloud-native world, a black box could involve pinging a database endpoint, or testing a DNS resolution or a multi-step transaction. In any case, we are concerned only about the end-to-end behavior, whether a site is reachable, a login flow is successful, or we receive data from an API in a time frame we anticipate. When black-box monitoring is done well, it provides a user-centric signal; if something breaks for users, black-box tests will catch it.

Need for black-box monitoring

Black-box monitoring is important for guaranteeing customer experience and service availability. If teams are constantly checking that systems are up and performing from the outside, then every time there is a problem in reaching some part of the service, they will notice the outage or degradation, right when it is happening to users. For instance, an internal server metric would not tell you that a downstream API is returning **Connection Refused**, or that a network partition has isolated clients, only an external check could catch that.

This translates to the following, **no matter how all internal metrics look good on graphs, if a synthetic user transaction fails or slows down, the system is actually down for customers**.

Therefore, black-box monitoring is an essential safeguard against such cases. It offers early warning for user-facing problems (for example, a third-party service is failing or a DNS failure) that is not observable in internal telemetry. In regulated industries such as finance, black-box tests also help meet compliance requirements by proving end-to-end uptime and performance guarantees. If a black-box probe fails, it raises alerts that things are wrong at the user-facing layer.

In practice, many organizations employ black-box monitoring to maintain 99.9% uptime, catching site-wide failures before users do, (for example, running HTTP checks or synthetic login tests on critical paths every hour). Without these outside checks, an overlooked bug or an external network outage could go unnoticed until the customer complaints start to appear.

Use cases of black box monitoring

Typical scenarios of black-box monitoring are based on the validation of end-to-end functionality and availability. Some key scenarios are as follows:

- **Website and API uptime monitors:** Verify if websites or APIs are accessible and giving right responses. For example, a monitoring job may execute a HTTP GET request to **https://api.example.com/health** every minute and notify if it is down. That is the classic **uptime monitoring** use case.
- **Performance and load testing:** Monitor response times or delays under typical operating conditions. Black-box tests have the capability to measure the time to load a page, or round-trip time of an API call. If the average response time at an endpoint goes over a threshold, a performance problem that affects users becomes apparent. For instance, measuring it on a webpage can help identify CDN or network problems before they impact customers.
- **Synthetic transaction tests:** Model the complete end-user workflows. This is much more than a single HTTP ping, but a multi-step flow/control (ie: **user**

login, **search**, **addToCart**, **checkout**) automation. These tests ensure that complicated business flows are still working. If any one thing in the transaction script goes wrong or slows down, the monitoring goes off. E-commerce websites typically run synthetic tests to verify that the purchasing flow, payment gateways or checkout pages work after every deployment.

- **End user experience monitoring:** Evaluate real-user metrics or simulations of real users, such as page load time, error rates, and availability, at several locations. For instance, you can track the average page load time from both Europe and Asia, helping you identify regional issues. There are so-legit black-box solutions (from modern **Real User Monitoring** (**RUM**) to browsing-based synthetic tests) that measure how long it takes a user action to complete. Providing good user experience (low latency, low errors) is a primary objective of black-box monitoring.
- **Third-party service being checked:** Monitor your dependencies' dependencies. Although harder, you can achieve this when your system depends on a third-party API, DNS provider or an external OAuth service through black-box probing. For instance, a service may monitor a payment gateway API with polling and raise an alarm when it starts returning 5xx errors. This works well with white-box alerts, even if your code is performing fine, a black box check may identify an external outage.
- **Security and compliance monitoring:** Although addressed by dedicated tools, some security problems can be picked up by dumb black-box bits. For example, you can use simulated login attempts to verify that rate limiting is working correctly or that unexpected 403/401 responses are not being issued. You may also find black-box scans can uncover certificate expiration, or SSL/TLS configuration issues as part of regular uptime checks or the like.

In reality, most organizations use a combination of the two. For example, an e-commerce website may use black-box monitoring to detect whether a **DDoS** attack or slowdown is affecting end users but use white-box metrics when performing in-depth diagnostics.

For these types of external threats (such as DDoS attacks or hacking attempts) and monitoring the user experience, black-box monitoring makes sense. In all sectors, when the real health is a function of the end-user performance, black-box monitoring is needed.

Techniques of black-box monitoring

To realize black-box monitoring, active probing and synthetic testing are the standard technologies used. The following are some key methods:

- **Uptime/Heartbeat checks from the outside:** These are the most basic ways to monitor the availability of an endpoints, in the form of a periodic ping or HTTP request to a specific endpoint within a microservice. Tools such as Nagios,

Pingdom, or Datadog can run checks (TCP, ICMP (ping), DNS, HTTP(s)) on a regular basis from external nodes. These checks will raise an alert if the endpoint is not available or if it is responding with an error. For instance, a Pingdom's uptime check could visit a site every minute and create an alert for 5xx HTTP status code. This guarantees liveness of the most basic service.

- **Synthetic transaction monitoring:** As described earlier, scripted workflows can mimic the actual user. These scripts may be as simple as a login and account page load or as complex as clicking through and checking out a cart. They typically run in actual browsers or through API calls. The monitoring tool tags any step if it fails or if response times are above certain thresholds. Examples are browser-based synthetic tests in Datadog or Azure Application Insights, or Selenium scripts run by a cron job. Checkpoint-based validation can be utilized with synthetic monitoring tools to verify that each stage returns the desired content.

- **Prometheus blackbox exporter:** In cloud native architecture, the black box checks are frequently integrated into the group's metrics stack. The Prometheus Blackbox Exporter is a popular tool for the same.

  This allows you to integrate uptime and response time metrics into your already defined Prometheus/Grafana dashboards and alerting. For example, an operator may periodically scrape a web URL using the Blackbox Exporter with an http_2xx module, triggering an alert via Prometheus Alertmanager if the probe fails or gives a code not in the 2xx range.

- **Uptime status pages:** Most platforms now offer built-in support for public uptime monitoring. For example, among cloud providers, AWS Route53 has health checks and Cloudflare has uptime monitoring and services like Uptime.com or StatusCake can send warnings and display status pages. These are DNS, HTTP, TCP checks with alert hooks. For some teams these services are a first offense.

- **Real User Monitoring (RUM):** RUM is more concerned with passively capturing real user data but is frequently classified with black-box methods. RUM tools measure real users' load times and errors by injecting JavaScript into websites. In essence, RUM offers a perpetual **black-box** perspective into actual traffic. This is complementary to synthetic tests, as it captures problems that people actually experience, but it only works if there is user traffic. Plenty of SaaS monitoring platforms (New Relic Browser, Dynatrace RUM, etc.) conflate synthetic and RUM.

- **Network path tracing:** Traceroute or other dedicated network monitors can detect problems in this route selection. Some black-box solutions periodically do a traceroute or TCP handshake to catch network partitioning, or higher latency between data centers. For instance, following an issue, the status page of Pingdom could support a traceroute to troubleshoot the connectivity.

- **Cloud-native probes:** In a cloud environment, like containerized or serverless, teams may run small pods or functions that periodically attack service endpoints. For example, putting a Kubernetes CronJob that curls an API and logs anomalies, or simulating user traffic with an AWS Lambda function and CloudWatch Events. These home-brewed black-box checks could be customized for the environment or even emulate user agent strings or geographic dispersion.
- **Scraping third-party APIs:** As these systems or apps often depend on remote APIs (think payment processors, auth providers, SaaS services), passive probes monitor whether those endpoints respond correctly. You could potentially use Postman monitors or Datadog to periodically hit a 3rd-party REST API that your app depends on and be alerted to vendor outages before your users are impacted.

The following tools in the ecosystem illustrate these methods:

- **Pingdom** is a popular service (now SolarWinds Pingdom) for external uptime and synthetic transaction tests.
- Similar is the offering from Site24x7 and Datadog Synthetics which enables multi-location probes and visual flow recording.
- **Graphite or InfluxDB** users might rely on the Prometheus Blackbox Exporter for flexibility.
- Monitoring suites (like Datadog or New Relic) will have **Synthetics** or **Browser** monitoring as part of the product. Black-box options are also commonly available from cloud vendors: for example, AWS has CloudWatch Synthetics (canary tests), and Google Cloud Monitoring can do uptime checks.

In all these scenarios, the point is to force the application from the outside and observe its behavior in terms of external, not internal, to the system.

White-box monitoring

White-box monitoring, by contrast, looks inside the system to harvest data that only someone with internal visibility can glimpse. This is treating the system as a **white box**, since the internals of the system are visible. Applications, servers and infrastructure are instrumented by teams so they can emit metrics, logs and traces. To put it another way, it asks, **how comfortable is the system within its own skin?**

White-box monitoring gives you the ability to measure low-level things, from CPU and memory usage, disk I/O, to thread pools, database query times, and app-specific counters. For instance, instrumenting an HTTP server with Prometheus client libraries may result in getting request rates and latencies per endpoint. Similarly, in a Java application you may run an agent to measure heap usage and GCs. In cloud-native scenarios, white-box monitoring usually uses the open standards as we have them: **OpenTelemetry** for traces and metrics, **cAdvisor/Prometheus** for container stats.

With full control over your own code and environment, you can collect granular data. This depth is the feature of white-box monitoring, seeing into the **guts** of your infrastructure in order to anticipate issues and make your systems run smooth and fast.

Such practices might include placing Prometheus exporters on servers or instrumenting the code with **StatsD** or **OpenTelemetry** spans or excessive logging. A service mesh such as Istio also gives you white-box telemetry for all Kubernetes microservices, including egress and ingress traffic. Application logs are also streamed into logging pipelines (for example, **Elastic Stack**, **Splunk**) for analysis. White-box monitoring, in short, is what most people mean when they say observability as it is about collecting logs/metric/traces from inside your system and not just at the border.

Need for white-box monitoring

White-box monitoring is essential for root cause analysis, performance tuning and proactive problem avoidance. Black-box testing tells you that something is wrong for users, white-box metrics and traces explain why and where. For instance, a counterfeit test would draw attention to a slow web page. Without white-box data, at best you now know that it is slow. With white-box data (CPU %s, DB query times, trace spans), you can identify the bottleneck and resolve it. In the age of microservices where you need white box visibility, there are generally dozens of moving parts (databases, caches, message queues, k8s nodes, etc.) and without an instrument in such a black-box, you cannot really get a picture of the system healthy. In practice, white-box monitoring allows you to know about problems before they reach the users.

For example, your alerts may be fired ahead of any outages due to an unexpected memory consumption peak or an increasing number of threads. White-box data can also be used for capacity planning (for example, calculate the CPU to saturation), automated auto-scaling, and AI/ML-based anomaly detection. In regulated fields, such a level of detail in audit logs and metrics capture is necessary for compliance. Even for security, looking inside can catch brute-force logins or data exfiltration patterns that a black-box test might never uncover. And teams shifting to a DevOps model and cloud-native methodologies frequently adopt **shift-left** monitoring, developers instrument their code directly (for example, creating their own app metrics, adding custom tracing spans), so that problems can be identified earlier in the CI/CD pipeline. This means that when code from the dev environment arrives in production, engineers already know what to expect. For instance, in the context of a Kubernetes rollout, these white-box types of measurement, containers restarting, or threadpool saturation might immediately signal misconfigurations. Without that transparency, teams would be operating in the dark and would be forced to diagnose purely based on post failure symptoms. In other words, white-box monitoring is a prerequisite for in-depth observability and resiliency at scale. It is complementary to black-box monitoring in that it allows a proactive and forensic approach. By analogy black box alerts might say **the elevator is not coming**, whereas white box data tells you, **the motor on the elevator overheats after 100 uses so it is stuck**. Both are crucial because one recognizes the symptom, the other reveals the cause.

Use cases of white-box monitoring

White-box monitoring excels when deep visibility into system internals and fine granularity of diagnostics are required. The following are some typical use cases:

- **Host and infrastructure metrics:** This monitors fundamental parameters like CPU, memory, disk I/O, network traffic, and hardware performance. For example, on Kubernetes nodes or cloud VMs, you have tools like Prometheus Node Exporter or cloud provider metrics that collect kernel-level stats. If you have a spike in CPU or disk latency, it could be a sign that you need to scale out resources or an indication that you have some misbehaving processes.

- **Application Performance Monitoring (APM):** This involves instructing the code to record things like how many requests it is making, how many errors it is encountering, the latency of methods, the duration of calls to the database, etc. Requests can be traced automatically through your microservices by agents (**Datadog**, **New Relic**, **Dynatrace**) or libraries (**OpenTelemetry**). Some use cases for DD include tracking the number of requests the API method is processing per second, tail latency measurements, and slow database queries. For example, if you suddenly notice a 50% increase in latency for a login endpoint in APM, you can see that engineers know how to look into the authentication service or database.

- **Distributed tracing:** This involves tracing across different services in a large service mesh to find out where a single user request was going. **OpenTelemetry** based traces (collected by Jaeger, Zipkin or commercial solutions) provide insight into which downstream service or database call is taking longer than it should. This would send a signal back up to the microservice team that 80% of their request time was spent in an external HTTP call and they may decide to add a cache. Distributed tracing is a foundational white-box approach for cloud native apps.

- **Database and cache monitoring:** It involves metrics specific to data stores and similar systems such as **queries per second** (**qps**), cache hit rates, or replication lag. You can obtain this information from tools such as AWS RDS Performance Insights, Prometheus exporters or the metrics available in the dashboards of MongoDB or Redis. Both detecting runaway queries (longer than 100 times typical) or cache thrashing (extremely high cache miss rate) only make themselves known from the inside out at the hardware layer.

- **Log analysis:** It involves aggregating, analyzing application and system logs to identify errors, exceptions and unusual activity. From such white-box logs, it is possible to tell when certain patterns appear (**NPE inside payment processor** or **extremely 500 errors**). For instance, an increase in the error logs for authentication could indicate a bug in the login service. These logs are frequently combined with metrics in an observability solution that allows searches and dashboards (for example, **Elasticsearch, Splunk, cloud logging**).

- **Container and orchestration metrics:** Container restart counts, pod CPU/ memory consumption and custom Kubernetes events are all part of the white box data set in Kubernetes. These can be gathered by the Kubernetes Metrics Server and Prometheus. Examples: finding out about a **CrashLoopBackOff** pod as soon as it crashes, or a particular microservice's pods are always close to running out of memory.
- **Service-level indicators and business metrics:** Many teams focuses on custom business logic bound metrics (for example, orders processed per minute, new users, payment transaction error rate). By tracking these internal metrics, IT organizations can better correlate monitoring with overall business results. For example, you might notice that the **orders/minute** is decreasing, indicating a checkout bug that is affecting revenue, then low-level health checks would have passed.
- **Security and compliance monitoring:** Within vantage, white-box logs and metrics can fuel security dashboards. Anomaly detection, for instance, could be set off by abnormally large numbers of failed login attempts. Audit trails (who asked for what data) are also a white-box issue. For cloud, AWS CloudTrail or GCP Audit Logs are used as access and permission event white-box monitoring log sources.
- **Profiling and debugging:** So fine-grained white-box instrumentation can be used to analyze memory profiles, thread dumps, or custom debug events. They are not operational 24/7 because they are helpful for a root-cause analysis after an incident.

In Kubernetes clusters, for example, Prometheus scrapes a bunch of internal metrics **(application, node, kube-state etc.**) to check the health of each part.

Example: Datadog customers often use custom application metrics and distributed traces to debug latency spikes, while also employing Datadog's RUM to correlate real-user load times. More broadly, white-box monitoring is encapsulated by platforms such as New Relic and Datadog, which both provide APM, infrastructure metrics and distributed tracing. The recent push into observability space has meant the rise of white-box monitoring: OpenTelemetry has become **a universal standard for collecting and exporting metrics** from applications.

That means that regardless of what language or framework you are using, you can emit telemetry to centralized dashboards. In other words, when you want to know what is going on under the hood in your code and infrastructure, you use white-box concepts. They are giving insights with the depth of information that is necessary for capacity planning, performance tuning and pro-active incident prevention.

Techniques of white-box monitoring

Practicing white-box monitoring is the collection and processing of internal telemetry via a variety of tools and techniques, such as the following:

- **Instrumentation:** It means metric export using agents and libraries. For example, Prometheus client libraries (for Go, Java, Python, etc.) enable developers to instrument code with counters and gauges (for example, the duration of an HTTP request). These are the metrics that Prometheus servers scrape. Additionally, you can use tools such as **StatsD** or **Telegraf** to gather and forward metrics. In reality, teams are creating dashboards and alerts on these internal metrics. A reasonably standard real-world scenario: instrument every service to provide Prometheus with an HTTP endpoint to scrape, exposing standard-process metrics as well as custom app metrics.
- **Log aggregation and analysis:** Aggregate and analyze application and system logs with **Fluentd**, **Logstash**, **Vector**, etc. Logs are goldmine of knowledge (stack traces, error messages, user id, and so on). Log storage/search systems (Elasticsearch, Splunk, cloud log services) receive the LOGS. Teams create logging based on alerts (for example, if **OutOfMemoryError** appears on a page, alert), they troubleshoot using queries. For example, in Kubernetes, the console (**stdout**) logs of containers are typically fed by Fluentd / FluentBit into a cluster logging pipeline.
- **Tracing:** Services can do their distributed tracing. These traces are exported to backends such as Jaeger, Zipkin, or proprietary products. Every incoming request gets traced by a unique trace ID; end-to-end latency profiling is possible. Tools such as SigNoz or Lightstep have rendered trace spans. In practice, you could imagine a team creating an HTTP client and server middleware which magically records trace spans for you, with limited intrusions in your code. Tracing is particularly useful for cloud-native microservices: it allows you to see, for any given request, where time went in both your services and in calls to external systems.
- **Monitoring infrastructure:** It means utilizing exporters and agents to collect host/container statistics. Examples are the Prometheus Node Exporter for Linux servers, cAdvisor for Docker metrics, kube-state-metrics for Kubernetes object status. These feed in time-series databases and dashboards (Grafana is a common one). In cloud environments, you might also grab metrics from cloud provider APIs (e.g., AWS CloudWatch metrics using the CloudWatch exporter). Real workflows, for example, contain dashboards showing pod CPU utilization, memory saturation, and disk IOPS, which help to manage capacity more easily.
- **Application Performance Management (APM) tools:** Proprietary APM applications (New Relic APM, Datadog APM, Dynatrace) offer white-box observability out of the box. They install agents or SDKs, automatically capturing metrics and traces without the need for manual metric configuration. For

example, you will be able to Auto-Instrument a Java or Node. js app to monitor services' response time and percentage of error. Such tools frequently offer end-to-end views (from infrastructure to code). APM allows companies to gain fast visibility into how their applications are performing without having to start from scratch when building their own instrumentation.

- **Service mesh metrics:** If you are using a service mesh such as Istio and Linkerd, its sidecars are injected to collect metrics for all inter-service communication. The mesh reports request counts, success rates and latencies for every service-to-service call. This is a white-box technique, being an internal traffic interception attack. For instance, Istio emits Prometheus metrics from Envoy proxies. Teams can identify troublesome service interactions using mesh dashboards (such as Kiali).
- **Alerting and dashboards:** The endgame of white-box monitoring is actionable alerting. Teams configure alerts on internal metrics such as high error rates in their code, slow db queries and create dashboards for SREs and developers. For instance, an alert could be sent if a Java garbage collection pause crosses a threshold, or if average response time in a service goes above an SLO. The richer white-box data makes it possible to write better fine-grained alert conditions than black-box data alone.
- **Machine learning and anomaly detection:** AI/ML to detect anomalies on metric patterns is increasingly built into modern whitebox solutions. Datadog, Dynatrace, and the like, based on historical internal metrics, auto-detect abnormal CPU spikes or latency outliers. This is a white-box approach as it works on internal telemetry. For cloud-native behemoths like Netflix or Google, these AIOps techniques are crucial given the scale of the data involved.

In conclusion, whitebox monitoring approaches require instrumentation (client libs, agents) scraping/collecting (Prometheus, DataDog Agent, cloud APIs) and analysis (logging platforms, tracing backends, dashboards). Real-world practitioners will tend to be bandying around open-source stacks certainly, a Kubernetes team might ship with Prometheus + Grafana + Loki (for logs) with alertmanager, for example, whilst a SaaS team could prefer to lean on Datadog or New Relic for an integrated view. The point is that no metric, or even log, is collected from outside the system.

Black-box vs white-box monitoring

Let us take a summarized view of black-box and white box monitoring comparison on various applicable parameters with the help of the following *Table 10.3:*

Aspect	Black-box monitoring	White-box monitoring
Perspective	External / end-user viewpoint, treats system as an opaque "box"	Internal viewpoint, system is transparent and instrumented

Aspect	Black-box monitoring	White-box monitoring
Focus	High-level system behavior (uptime, latency, functionality)	Detailed component behavior (CPU, memory, application metrics, logs, traces)
Data sources	Synthetic tests, external probes (HTTP/TCP pings, DNS checks, etc.)	Instrumented metrics, logs, traces collected from inside applications, hosts, containers
Typical tools	Pingdom, Site24x7, Datadog Synthetics, StatusCake, Prometheus Blackbox Exporter	Prometheus, Grafana, Datadog (APM), New Relic, OpenTelemetry, ELK/EFK stack, Grafana Loki, Jaeger/Zipkin
Common use cases	Website/API uptime, external service health, end-to-end transaction testing, real-user experience metrics	Host/container monitoring, application performance (APM), database health, logging analysis, tracing requests
Strengths	Validates real user experience; detects external/network outages; simple high-level health checks	Provides deep diagnostic data; proactive detection (for example, resource saturation); identifies root causes
Limitations	Cannot see internal details; often reactive (detects issue after symptoms appear at edge)	May miss pure external issues (for example, DNS outages); requires instrumentation effort; generates large data volume

Table 10.3: *Black box vs white box monitoring*

Black-box and White-box monitoring are both essential in a cloud world. By contrast, black-box testing keeps services working for the users by only checking the end-to-end functionality, with white-box instrumentation giving the fine-grained visibility required to prevent and diagnose issues within. And in a nontrivial, distributed system, relying on one perspective is dangerous, and there is no shortage of industry experts who recommend a combination approach, beginning with user-centric black-box checks for fundamental health checks and availability, while adding white-box metrics, logs, and traces for more in depth looks.

Nowadays, most observability tools (*Datadog, New Relic, Dynatrace, Site24x7, etc.*) can operate in either mode. For instance, Site24x7 sells centralized black-box website monitors along white-box APM and infrastructure agents, explaining that ultimately, *by using black box monitoring, you can ensure a positive user experience, and with white box monitoring, you can proactively identify the root cause of underlying issues*.

In practice, an architect could ping a customer-facing API with Pingdom, while using Prometheus to scrape internal metrics from the API's containers. With time, most mature groups settle on a blending of the two- black-box alerts that trigger on symptoms at boundaries, while white-box dashboards and logs are used to drive investigation and optimization. To sum up, black-box monitoring informs you *what's going on with our service from the outside?* Whereas white-box monitoring shows you, *what's happening inside our system, and why?* Adopting both are essential for reliability in a cloud-native world. A more widespread monitoring strategy between external probes and internal details means that we have a more healthy system, faster potential troubleshooting, and in the end a better user experience.

Dashboards and visualization

Imagine driving a car with no speedometer, fuel gauge, or GPS. That is what leading a business or managing a digital product feels like without dashboards and data visualizations. In today's data-driven world, where decisions are made at the speed of thought, dashboards offer a crucial control panel—bringing together a wide array of metrics into a cohesive and digestible view.

Dashboards are not just static displays of numbers or graphs; they are dynamic interfaces designed to tell the story behind the data. They help stakeholders at every level from executives to product managers and engineers, monitor performance, spot trends, and act quickly when things veer off course. When built thoughtfully, dashboards eliminate the guesswork from strategic and operational decisions.

Visualizations, on the other hand, translate complex datasets into clear, intuitive graphical representations; charts, heatmaps, histograms, and more. They provide context, spotlight anomalies, and surface hidden patterns that raw tables or spreadsheets simply cannot convey.

Combined, dashboards and visualizations turn data into a narrative—a real-time pulse of what is working, what is not, and what needs urgent attention. Whether it is tracking NPS scores, system uptime, churn rate, or deployment velocity, these tools are essential for fostering clarity and accountability in high-performing SaaS environments.

Need for dashboards and visualization

SaaS platforms, particularly those serving both SMB and Enterprise clients, operate in a complex, high-velocity environment. Engineering leaders, product managers, SREs, and business stakeholders are often flooded with raw data but lack the time to sift through it. Dashboards and visualizations become the single source of truth that bridges this gap. Here is why they are indispensable:

- **Real-time decision making:** Dashboards make it possible to detect anomalies (for example, sudden spike in error rates, server load, or customer drop-offs) and respond proactively rather than reactively. This supports SLAs, SLOs, and high availability goals.

- **Cross-functional alignment:** Whether it is sales watching MRR growth or engineering tracking MTTR, dashboards create a shared understanding of progress, bottlenecks, and business health.
- **Performance monitoring:** From code deployment frequency to QA pass rates, dashboards help engineering leaders identify delivery gaps and improve time-to-market.
- **Accountability and transparency:** Teams can be more data-driven and accountable when KPIs are openly tracked. It is hard to argue with a red flag on a burn-down chart.
- **Customer-centric view:** Dashboards that show user adoption, feature usage, or CSAT/NPS trends allow teams to prioritize customer needs and inform roadmap decisions.

In essence, dashboards create a rhythm of operational excellence. They drive focus by continuously answering two core questions: *How are we doing?* and *What should we do next?*

Tools for dashboards and visualization

A well-designed dashboard is not about flashy visuals; it is about choosing the right tools and configuring them thoughtfully to serve the right audience. Let us discuss some commonly used tools in the industry, especially for SaaS environments, along with techniques to get the most out of them.

Grafana + Prometheus

Combination of Grafana and Prometheus helps in creating dashboards providing deep insight into metrics, which are very critical from an engineering and infrastructure perspective, and also take meaningful actions.

Use case

Observability of infrastructure, service health, and real-time alerting.

Best practices

The following are some best practices:

- Use Prometheus to scrape metrics from microservices, and Grafana to visualize time-series data like CPU usage, API latency, and memory leaks.
- Build layered dashboards: one for execs (for example, SLA, Uptime %), another for engineering (for example, pod restart count, queue lag).
- Apply threshold coloring to highlight deviations, and panel links for drill-down capabilities.

Example: Display a dashboard showing 99.98% service uptime with latency breakdown by endpoint across services, with drill-down into failed API calls sorted by error code.

Datadog or Dynatrace

Datadog and Dynatrace collectively helps us in complete full stack monitoring providing unified view across all the tools and services playing along.

Use case

Unified view across infra, application, logs, and APM.

Best practices

The following are some best practices associated with Datadog or Dynatrace:

- Use pre-built templates for cloud-native environments and customize with application-specific metrics (for example, login success rate).
- Enable **synthetic monitoring** dashboards to visualize frontend journey failures.
- Integrate with incident alerting tools (like PagerDuty) for real-time action from dashboard triggers.

Example: Dashboard tracking P95 latency of the shipping rate calculator microservice with linked traces from problematic customer sessions.

Tableau or Power BI

Tools like Tableau or Power BI offer rich capabilities and offerings centered towards insights useful for executive dashboarding and even for product stakeholders to make key critical business decisions.

Use case

Customer trends, feature adoption, revenue analytics, and cohort performance.

Best practices

The following are some best practices associated with Tableau or Power BI:

- Set up auto-refresh intervals and role-based access (for example, Execs get topline metrics, PMs see feature usage funnels).
- Blend data sources like Snowflake, Salesforce, and usage logs to offer 360° dashboards.
- Use **storyboards** in Tableau to walk stakeholders through a narrative (for example, **Why is churn increasing in Q2**?).

Example: Cohort dashboard showing first 90-day retention curves across customer segments by plan type and onboarding channel.

Dashboards and visualizations are not just reporting tools, but the nervous system of a modern SaaS organization. From real-time firefighting to quarterly planning, they drive awareness, enable agility, and enforce accountability. When designed with care and used thoughtfully, they not only save time, but shape better decisions, faster.

Observability ecosystem

While we have discussed logging, metrics, tracing, and alerting separately, in practice, these components work together to form an inclusive observability ecosystem. Here is how they typically interact:

- **Logs provide context:** When investigating an issue highlighted by metrics or tracing, logs often provide the detailed context needed to understand what went wrong.
- **Metrics trigger alerts:** Threshold-based alerts are typically based on metrics, notifying you when key indicators deviate from normal ranges.
- **Traces help diagnose:** When an alert is triggered or a performance issue is noticed in metrics, distributed tracing can help pinpoint where in the request lifecycle the problem occurred.
- **Correlation is key:** By correlating data across logs, metrics, and traces (often using shared identifiers like request IDs), you can get a complete picture of system behavior.

Let us walk through a scenario to see how this might work in practice:

- Your alerting system notifies you that the error rate for a particular service has spiked.
- You check your metrics dashboard and confirm that there is indeed an increase in HTTP 500 errors.
- You use distributed tracing to identify which specific operation in the service is failing.
- Armed with this information, you dive into the logs for that service, filtering for the relevant time and operation.
- In the logs, you find exception stack traces that point to the root cause of the issue.

This holistic approach to observability allows you to quickly identify, diagnose, and resolve issues in complex distributed systems.

Challenges and considerations

While the benefits of ample monitoring and observability are clear, implementing these patterns comes with its own set of challenges, such as the following:

- **Data volume:** With detailed logging, frequent metrics collection, and complete tracing, you can quickly accumulate large volumes of data. This can lead to storage and processing challenges.

- **Cost:** Many cloud providers charge for ingesting and storing monitoring data. Without careful management, costs can escalate quickly.
- **Privacy and compliance:** With the increase in data protection regulations, you need to be careful about what data you are collecting and how you are storing it.
- **Complexity:** Setting up a all-inclusive observability stack can be complex, especially in large, distributed systems.
- **Tool sprawl:** With the multitude of tools available for different aspects of observability, it's easy to end up with a fragmented toolset that is difficult to manage.

To address these challenges, do the following:

- **Implement data retention policies:** Not all data needs to be kept forever. Implement policies to age out older, less critical data.
- **Use sampling:** For high-volume systems, consider sampling your traces and logs to reduce data volume while still maintaining visibility.
- **Centralize your observability stack:** Where possible, use integrated solutions that cover multiple aspects of observability to reduce complexity and tool sprawl.
- **Automate:** Automate as much of your observability setup as possible, using infrastructure-as-code principles.
- **Educate your team:** Ensure your team understands the importance of observability and knows how to use the tools effectively.

Conclusion

As we transition into cloud-native architectures, our approach to monitoring and observability must also mature. The landscape is rapidly evolving, shaped by several powerful trends that are redefining how we understand and manage systems at scale. One major shift is the rise of AI-fed analysis, where machine learning algorithms are being leveraged to detect anomalies and predict potential failures, essentially allowing teams to get ahead of issues before they impact users. Another important movement is the emergence of **observability as code**, a practice that mirrors the principles of infrastructure and security as code, enabling monitoring configurations to be versioned, automated, and tightly integrated into deployment pipelines. At the same time, we are seeing a consolidation of tooling through integrated observability platforms that unify logs, metrics, and traces under one umbrella, reducing silos and improving operational coherence. With the explosion of telemetry data, real-time streaming analytics is gaining traction, offering engineers the ability to act on insights as events unfold rather than relying on post-mortem analysis. Adding to this, advancements in technologies like eBPF have opened new doors into kernel-level observability, providing highly efficient, low-overhead visibility directly from the operating system. As you continue to architect cloud-native systems, remember that observability is not just about tools; it is about building a culture that prioritizes transparency, resilience, and continuous improvement. With the strategies and insights shared in this chapter, you are equipped not only to react to incidents but to proactively shape healthy, high-performance platforms from the ground up.

In the next chapter, we will see the future of cloud architecture, speculating about upcoming trends and technologies, and their impact on how we build and design cloud systems. We will discuss serverless architectures to edge computing and how these developments are redefining the limits of what is doable on the cloud.

Join our Discord space

Join our Discord workspace for latest updates, offers, tech happenings around the world, new releases, and sessions with the authors:

https://discord.bpbonline.com

CHAPTER 11
Future Trends

Introduction

As we stand on the precipice of technological evolution, the cloud computing landscape continues to transform at a breath-taking pace. In this final chapter, we will explore the emerging trends that are set to reshape the future of cloud architecture. Cloud architecture has never been a static discipline, it is an ever-morphing canvas that reflects the speed and scale at which technology, business models, and user expectations evolve. What started as a quest to virtualize infrastructure has transformed into a mission to reimagine how businesses operate and innovate. Today's cloud-native systems are no longer just extensible, they are intelligent, decentralized, and increasingly autonomous.

The industry stands at the intersection of massive technological shift. Serverless models are removing infrastructure boundaries, edge computing is shrinking latency to the speed of thought, AI is no longer an enhancement, it is the brain of digital experiences. And as concerns such as sustainability and cybersecurity move from afterthoughts to boardroom priorities, cloud architecture is being tasked with solving not just technical challenges, but existential ones as well.

This chapter also explores the trends shaping the **next decade** of cloud design, not as buzzwords, but as **architectural imperatives**. Each section will take up a modern trend, discuss how it is being used in production environments, and identify the skills, patterns, and decisions that architects must embrace to stay relevant and build for the future.

Structure

In this chapter, we will go over the following topics:

- Serverless architecture
- Edge computing architecture
- ML and AI integration
- Sustainable cloud architecture
- Zero trust and secure-by-design architecture
- Integrated vision of how these trends converge
- Strategic considerations for leaders

Objectives

The goal of this chapter is to empower cloud architects, engineering leaders, and strategic decision-makers with a deep, well-rounded understanding of the most impactful architectural trends shaping the future of distributed systems. Rather than skimming the surface, we will dive into each trend with purpose; exploring not just what is happening, but why it matters, how it works in practice, and where it fits within real-world enterprise ecosystems. Readers will learn to identify and interpret emerging architectural models that are actively redefining how modern cloud platforms are designed and operated. With this understanding, they will be better equipped to determine when and how to embrace these innovations within their own systems, taking into account the readiness of their organization, the implications on tooling and processes, and the evolving skill sets required for successful adoption. Ultimately, this chapter is designed to help decision-makers not only follow trends but also anticipate change, enabling them to make thoughtful, future-proof choices rooted in resilience, adaptability, and long-term value.

Serverless architecture

Serverless architecture represents a mindset shift in cloud computing, where developers can build and run applications without managing the underlying infrastructure. In this model, cloud providers automatically handle the provisioning, scaling, and maintenance of servers. Developers focus solely on writing code, which is executed in response to events. Even though these patterns are now widely used, and may not be completely futuristic, discussing and understanding their benefits and trade-offs is necessary from a cloud architecture perspective.

Benefits

The following are the benefits of serverless architecture:

- **Cost efficiency:** With serverless, you pay only for the compute time you consume. There is no charge when your code is not running, leading to significant cost savings, especially for applications with intermittent workloads.
- **Scalability:** Serverless platforms automatically scale your applications in response to incoming traffic. This elasticity ensures optimal performance during peak times without manual intervention.
- **Reduced operational overhead:** By reducing the complexity of server management, developers can deploy applications faster and focus on core business logic, enhancing productivity and time-to-market.

Trade-offs

The following are the trade-offs of serverless architecture:

- **Cold start latency:** Functions may experience latency during their initial invocation, which can impact performance-sensitive applications.
- **Limited execution time:** Serverless functions often have execution time limits, making them unsuitable for long-running processes.
- **Vendor lock-in:** Utilizing provider-specific services can lead to dependencies, making it challenging to switch providers or adopt multi-cloud strategies.

Enterprise use case

Coca-Cola implemented serverless architecture to manage its vending machine operations. By leveraging AWS Lambda and other serverless services, they achieved real-time data processing, reduced operational costs, and enhanced scalability to handle varying workloads across different locations.

Design patterns

Here are a few example patterns that serve as best practices for the preceding use case:

- **Function-as-a-Service (FaaS):** Deploying individual functions that respond to specific events, enabling modular and scalable application design.
- **Backend for Frontend (BFF):** Creating specifically focused backend services for different frontend interfaces, optimizing performance and user experience.
- **Event-driven architecture:** Building applications that react to events, facilitating decoupled and scalable systems.

Edge computing architecture

Edge computing brings computation and data storage closer to the data source, reducing latency and bandwidth usage. This approach is crucial for applications requiring real-time processing, such as IoT devices, autonomous vehicles, and industrial automation systems.

Benefits

The following are the benefits of edge computing architecture:

- **Reduced latency:** Processing data at the edge minimizes the time taken to send data to centralized servers, enabling faster decision-making.
- **Bandwidth optimization:** By filtering and processing data locally, only relevant information is transmitted to the cloud, conserving bandwidth.
- **Enhanced reliability:** Edge computing allows systems to function autonomously during network disruptions, ensuring continuous operation.

Trade-offs

The following are the trade-offs of edge computing architecture:

- **Management complexity:** Deploying and maintaining numerous edge devices can be challenging, requiring robust management solutions.
- **Security concerns:** Edge devices may be more vulnerable to physical tampering and cyber threats, necessitating stringent security measures.
- **Resource constraints:** Edge devices often have limited processing power and storage, which can restrict the complexity of applications.

Enterprise use case

Netflix utilizes edge computing through its Open Connect program, deploying servers within ISPs to cache content closer to users. This strategy reduces latency, improves streaming quality, and decreases bandwidth costs.

Design patterns

Here are a few example patterns that serve as best practices for the preceding use case:

- **Fog computing:** Extending cloud capabilities to the edge, enabling data processing between the cloud and end devices.
- **Micro data centers:** Deploying compact data centers at the edge to handle localized processing needs.
- **Edge AI:** Implementing machine learning models on edge devices for real-time analytics and decision-making.

ML and AI integration

Integrating **machine learning (ML)** and **artificial intelligence (AI)** into cloud architecture enables intelligent applications capable of learning from data, making predictions, and automating decision-making processes. This integration is transforming industries by enhancing personalization, optimizing operations, and driving innovation.

Benefits

The following are the benefits of ML and AI integration:

- **Enhanced customer experience:** AI-powered applications can provide personalized recommendations, improving user engagement and satisfaction.
- **Operational efficiency:** Automating routine tasks and predictive maintenance reduces downtime and operational costs.
- **Data-driven insights:** ML algorithms analyze vast datasets to uncover patterns and trends, informing strategic decisions.

Trade-offs

The following are the trade-offs of ML and AI integration:

- **Data privacy concerns:** Handling sensitive data requires compliance with regulations and robust security measures.
- **Model interpretability:** Complex models may act as *black boxes*, making it difficult to understand decision-making processes.
- **Resource intensive:** Training and deploying ML models demand significant computational resources and expertise.

Enterprise use case

Spotify employs ML algorithms to curate personalized playlists for users. By analysing listening habits and preferences, Spotify enhances user engagement and retention through personalized music recommendations.

Design patterns

Here are a few example patterns that serve as best practices for the preceding use case:

- **Model-as-a-Service (MaaS):** Deploying ML models as APIs, allowing applications to access predictive capabilities without embedding models directly.
- **Continuous learning systems:** Implementing feedback loops where models are regularly retrained with new data to maintain accuracy.
- **Federated learning:** Training models across decentralized devices while keeping data localized, enhancing privacy, and reducing latency.

Sustainable cloud architecture

GreenOps focuses on optimizing cloud operations for environmental sustainability. By implementing energy-efficient practices and monitoring resource usage, organizations can reduce their carbon footprint while maintaining performance and cost-effectiveness.

Benefits

The following are the benefits of GreenOps:

- **Environmental responsibility:** Reducing energy consumption and emissions aligns with corporate social responsibility goals.
- **Cost savings:** Efficient resource utilization lowers operational expenses.
- **Regulatory compliance:** Adhering to environmental regulations and standards avoids potential penalties and enhances brand reputation.

Trade-offs

The following are the trade-offs of GreenOps:

- **Initial investment:** Implementing sustainable practices may require upfront costs for new tools and training.
- **Performance considerations:** Aggressive resource optimization could impact application performance if not carefully managed.
- **Complexity in measurement:** Accurately tracking and attributing energy usage across services can be challenging.

Enterprise use case

Microsoft has committed to becoming carbon negative by 2030. Through initiatives like using renewable energy in data centers and implementing sustainable software development practices, Microsoft aims to lead in environmental stewardship within the tech industry.

Design patterns

Here are a few example patterns that serve as best practices for the preceding use case:

- **Auto-scaling:** Dynamically adjusting resources based on demand to prevent over-provisioning.
- **Serverless computing:** Leveraging serverless architectures to run code only when needed, reducing idle resource consumption.
- **Energy-aware scheduling:** Deploying workloads during periods of lower energy costs or higher renewable energy availability.

Zero trust and secure-by-design architecture

Zero Trust Architecture (**ZTA**) is a security model that operates on the principle of **never trust, always verify**. It assumes that threats can exist both inside and outside the network, and thus, no user or system is inherently trusted. Secure-by-design complements this by integrating security considerations into every phase of the software development lifecycle.

Benefits

The following are the benefits of ZTA:

- **Enhanced security posture:** By continuously verifying identities and enforcing strict access controls, organizations can better protect against breaches.
- **Regulatory compliance:** Implementing ZTA helps meet stringent data protection regulations by ensuring controlled access to sensitive information.
- **Reduced attack surface:** Limiting user and system privileges minimizes potential exploitation points.

Trade-offs

The following are the trade-offs of ZTA:

- **Implementation complexity:** Transitioning to a ZTA model requires significant changes to existing infrastructure and processes.
- **User-experience impact:** Frequent authentication prompts may affect usability if not balanced properly.
- **Resource intensive:** Continuous monitoring and verification demand robust systems and potentially increased operational costs.

Enterprise use case

Google implemented its BeyondCorp initiative, adopting a Zero Trust model that allows employees to work securely from any location without the need for traditional VPNs. This approach enhances security while supporting a flexible work environment.

Design patterns

Here are a few example patterns that serve as best practices for the preceding use case:

- **Micro-segmentation:** Dividing networks into isolated segments to contain breaches and limit lateral movement.
- **Identity and Access Management (IAM):** Implementing robust authentication and authorization mechanisms to control user access.

Integrated vision of how these trends converge

In isolation, each cloud trend, be it serverless, edge computing, AI/ML, sustainability, or zero-trust security, offers transformative potential. But when orchestrated together, they create something far more profound, a cloud-native operating model that is adaptive, intelligent, and inherently secure. The **integrated vision** is a composable, data-driven, and boundary-less architecture where the lines between infrastructure, application, and intelligence are blurred to meet real-time, user-centric demands.

Consider this scenario: A smart logistics platform processes real-time shipment tracking at the edge (near IoT devices), predicts delays using embedded ML models deployed serverlessly, and ensures secure transactions with zero-trust authentication, all while optimizing for carbon impact through GreenOps observability hooks. This is not a sci-fi narrative, it is already unfolding in modern supply chain architectures at companies like *Amazon* and *Maersk*.

The convergence happens across **three critical planes**:

- **Execution plane:** Serverless at the edge pushes compute to where latency matters. Combined with AI, services can **think and act** near the user without round-trips to a centralized cloud.
- **Data plane:** Edge computing generates real-time signals. AI/ML models consume and act on this data and observability tools log carbon impact alongside performance telemetry.
- **Security plane:** Zero-trust is not a bolt-on, it is baked into APIs, service mesh, and identity enforcement, especially vital when workloads are fragmented across clouds, edges, and CDNs.

Key insight

The future of cloud is not about **choosing** between trends but about composing them into adaptive, intelligent ecosystems. These patterns reinforce each other. AI at the edge thrives on serverless for scalability. GreenOps relies on telemetry from serverless workloads. Secure-by-design thrives when policies are enforced from build-time to run-time.

In practice, building such systems requires a shift from **platform thinking** to **ecosystem orchestration**, designing not just for efficiency, but for cohesion across distributed and autonomous components.

Strategic considerations for leaders

As cloud architecture evolves, so must leadership strategy. The future is not just built by engineers; it is shaped by product, finance, and executive decision-makers who must navigate trade-offs in technology, cost, and capability. The following are some top-level considerations:

Vendor lock-in vs. velocity

Serverless and AI platforms (like *AWS Lambda + Bedrock* or *Azure OpenAI*) promises speed but can force organizations into proprietary and vendor-specific ecosystems. Leaders must weigh immediate innovation benefits against long-term portability.

Strategy: Adopt **portable abstractions** (for example, Knative, OpenTelemetry, or LangChain with open models) where feasible.

Skill gaps and culture shift

Trends like AI/ML at the edge or GreenOps demand hybrid skills—engineers who understand model pipelines and infrastructure carbon telemetry. Organizations must shift from T-shaped to **comb-shaped** skill models, broadly aware across domains, with multiple deep verticals.

Strategy: Invest in **cross-functional pods** that blend DevOps, data science, security, and cloud FinOps. Encourage job shadowing, knowledge bridges, and collaborative architecture reviews.

Managing technical debt in a pattern-heavy world

Modern architecture is pattern-rich—serverless, event-driven AI pipelines and mesh networks. The risk is accidental complexity or inconsistent governance.

Strategy: Institutionalize **pattern portfolio management**. Maintain a library of vetted architecture blueprints. Use scorecards for sustainability, performance, and cost before approving a new service architecture.

Sustainability as a strategic KPI

GreenOps is not a feel-good initiative but a board-level KPI. Energy-efficient code, renewable-region deployments, and carbon-aware scaling are now part of enterprise OKRs.

Strategy: Establish **Cloud Sustainability Offices (CSOs)** that govern infrastructure decisions from procurement to decommissioning. Integrate carbon cost into architecture reviews.

From resilience to anti-fragility

It is no longer enough to bounce back from failure as architecture should **improve** under stress. Trends like AI and observability enable predictive failure remediation and intelligent scaling.

Strategy: Evolve SRE from operational guards to **Resilience Engineering Architects** who use ML insights, chaos experiments, and zero-trust triggers to preempt disruptions.

Conclusion

Cloud architecture is no longer just a technical discipline. It is a strategic capability that defines how fast a company can respond, how intelligently it can operate, and how responsibly it can grow. As the past decade was about migrating to the cloud, the next is about mastering the meta-cloud, where architectures span edges, cores, public clouds, and AI meshes seamlessly.

This new era is about composability over control, intelligence over infrastructure, and ethics over just efficiency. Architects of tomorrow must become translators between technology and business, between innovation and compliance, between local action and global impact. They must design not only for throughput and latency, but for privacy, fairness, sustainability, and trust. The blueprint for the future is clear, be serverless where speed matters, edge-native where presence matters, and AI-driven where insights matter. Architect for resilience but operate for evolution. Make security and sustainability defaults, not afterthoughts.

As we have explored in this chapter, the future of cloud architecture is not just promising, it is thrilling too. From serverless innovations to edge computing and sustainable data centers, tomorrow's cloud is becoming more powerful, adaptable, and eco-conscious. However, with every leap forward comes new complexity. Architects and leaders will need to navigate the tangled terrain of multi-cloud ecosystems, responsibly harness the disruptive force of AI, and ensure security in a landscape constantly under threat. The key is not to chase every trend; it is to stay curious, keep learning, and thoughtfully integrate what truly fits your organization's goals. The architecture you build today will evolve dramatically in the next five to ten years, so start small, stay agile, and grow with intent. The cloud has already transformed our digital world, and this is only the beginning. The real question now is whether you will be one of the builders shaping what comes next.

Join our Discord space

Join our Discord workspace for latest updates, offers, tech happenings around the world, new releases, and sessions with the authors:

https://discord.bpbonline.com

Index

A

B

C

D

E

F

G

H

Q

R

S

T

www.ingramcontent.com/pod-product-compliance
Lightning Source LLC
Chambersburg PA
CBHW070150240326
41599CB00057BA/6885

* 9 7 8 9 3 6 5 8 9 5 1 3 1 *